W9-CSI-334

GRAY AREAS

ALSO BY ADIA HARVEY WINGFIELD

Flatlining: Race, Work, and Health Care in the New Economy

Doing Business with Beauty: Black Women, Hair Salons, and the Racial Enclave Economy

No More Invisible Man: Race and Gender in Men's Work

GRAY AREAS

HOW THE WAY WE WORK
PERPETUATES RACISM AND WHAT
WE CAN DO TO FIX IT

ADIA HARVEY WINGFIELD

AMISTAD
An Imprint of HarperCollins*Publishers*

DISCARD
CARLSBAD CITY LIBRARY
CARLSBAD CA 92011

The names and identifying characteristics of some individuals in this book have been changed to protect their privacy.

GRAY AREAS. Copyright © 2023 by Adia Harvey Wingfield. All rights reserved. Printed in the United States of America. No part of this book may be used or reproduced in any manner whatsoever without written permission except in the case of brief quotations embodied in critical articles and reviews. For information, address HarperCollins Publishers, 195 Broadway, New York, NY 10007.

HarperCollins books may be purchased for educational, business, or sales promotional use. For information, please email the Special Markets Department at SPsales@harpercollins.com.

FIRST EDITION

Title art © Social Media Hub / Shutterstock

Library of Congress Cataloging-in-Publication Data has been applied for.

ISBN 978-0-06-307981-6

23 24 25 26 27 LBC 5 4 3 2 1

NOV 2 9 2023

TO THE MEMORY OF LOVED ONES WHO WENT ON AHEAD—
SHERIDA, LEE, ELIJAH, BERNADINE, ERIC, AND JOHN

CONTENTS

CONTENTS

x CONTENTS

PART III: RELATIONAL
Who's Got Your Back?   *181*

Getting into the Gray Areas

On March 6, 2016, I opened my work email to find a message with the subject line "Go to Africa if You Don't [Like] America You Retarded Ape." The sender was anonymous, a stranger who felt compelled to inform me in the body of the email that "white lives matter way more than you stupid monkeys do." For variety, he tossed in an additional racist slur, then closed with several lines chanting "USA USA USA" followed by streams of text laughter. I was surprised to see the email—it wasn't at all what I was expecting when I opened my inbox—but I also felt curiously detached from the sender's jeering taunts.

I had a feeling I knew why I was being targeted that day. I'd recently written an op-ed piece for *Fortune* magazine considering how the Black Lives Matter movement would impact workplaces going forward and guessed that perhaps this sender was, rather inarticulately, expressing disagreement with my conclusions. This wasn't the first email I'd gotten from an irate stranger contacting me out of the blue to offer their unsolicited opinion of me, my research, and Black people in general. I usually see an uptick in these kinds of messages if I've recently appeared on a podcast, spoken on public radio, or written an op-ed. Usually the messages are lengthy, riddled with typos, and brimming with visceral rage and hostility. Usually they also go right into my Trash and are not given a second thought. But this one came on the heels of several others with similar content and tone, so I passed them on to my university's public safety office in case this was the beginning of a more sustained and threatening harassment campaign. After that, I deleted the messages. It wasn't like I planned to reply and open a dialogue with racist strangers, so that was that.

Getting the email was not ideal—obviously I'd prefer not to receive racist hate mail—but at the time, I was more focused on whether it was possible to report it to campus security in a way that would establish a record in case the sender escalated things but that wouldn't create additional problems for me as an employee. I didn't say anything about this to most of my colleagues when it happened. I was new to the university, and at the time I was the only faculty member in my department who was not a white man. And although I liked all my co-workers very much and trusted that they wouldn't take the side of the emailer, quite simply, I did not feel like having a conversation with them about this. I knew they would be sympathetic, but I also knew that opening this line of discussion with my colleagues would mean managing *their* emotions: assuring them that I was perfectly fine, commiserating about the lack of civility today, and sympathizing with their sadness and frustration about an event I'd already moved past. What I wanted most was to get back to being about my business, and having a conversation with my co-workers about this would just mean spending more time and energy on an anonymous racist who did not deserve my attention. I had better things to do.

Eventually, though, I did briefly discuss the situation with a few colleagues. When I sent the messages to campus safety, they contacted our head of IT, who reached out to me to offer his apologies and let me know they had a record of what had happened. He also told my department chair, who notified the dean to ensure this was

on her radar as well. But I didn't really expect anything to l
and they all confirmed that there wasn't much anyone could
track down the offender. We didn't discuss whether receiving
hate email compromised my ability to do my job, or whether
university had any resources available to assist faculty affected
incidents like these.

Despite my initial reluctance to share, many years later when
knew my colleagues better, I showed a white male co-worker one
of the crasser messages I'd received. This colleague also writes
about racial matters occasionally for public outlets and sometimes gets unsolicited responses from strangers telling him why,
in their view, he's got it all wrong. He was shocked and surprised
at the contents of the message I shared with him, which opened
with the subject line "You're a Massive Hypocrite and That's Why
White People Hate You." In the body of the email, the sender
advised that I "try teaching these gimme gimme niggers in your
class responsibility and accountability," questioned "where the
FUCK are all of their FATHERS????," and concluded with the
opinion that "Black culture is fucking PATHETIC." After seeing
this, my colleague told me that the most offensive emails he'd
gotten were from strangers calling him stupid. "Yours are on a
whole other level," he said. Indeed.

Luckily, these messages never escalated to the point of outright
threats. I never felt in any physical danger, and the senders did not
follow up. I presume they stewed in their own fury for a while and
then eventually directed their energy elsewhere—maybe toward
finding the next Unite the Right rally or brushing up on Great
Replacement theories. But my experience is illustrative of a couple of things. One is that for many Black workers today, racism is
not a relic of the past. It is not tangential. It is a core part of the
Black experience, front and center in ways that elude even the most
well-meaning white co-workers. Even sitting at home minding my
own business, on the faculty of a university that explicitly states

commitment to justice and racial equity, racism still became art of my work life when it popped up in my inbox in response to me doing my job. My qualifications, experience, and skill set don't matter to these anonymous senders. What bothers them is a Black woman professor who studies racial and gender inequality in the workplace. It feels like an affront to them.

The second point is that because racial issues are also entrenched, dealing with them is difficult. It requires copious amounts of time, energy, and effort. But much of that labor falls solely on Black employees, in ways that are overlooked and ignored, because most companies aren't fully prepared to address these dynamics. Instead, Black workers figure out on their own how to manage everything from overt harassment to cumulative microaggressions. Even in my own case, it might seem surprising that I had such a dispassionate response to getting racist hate mail and that my primary reaction was to dismiss it. This isn't because my meditation game is just that strong. It's definitely not because I tend to be a calm person by nature. It's because I've learned from experience that the most effective response is no response. At bottom, racist hate emailers want to upset me, and I'm too competitive and stubborn to allow them to win. But that itself is a sad commentary—that facing and managing racist harassment for doing my job is normalized to the point where being unaffected by it has become the best reaction.

The times that I've recounted this story to other Black professional friends, they immediately understand my initial reluctance to discuss this with my white colleagues. And I was in a relatively fortunate position in that I knew my colleagues would have been sympathetic, which many Black workers can't say. No one in my department would have sided with the emailer ("Well, just to play devil's advocate, from a sociological standpoint, white lives really *do* matter more!"), relied on exhausting and clichéd tropes ("Heard about the messages—just wanted to make sure you know *I* don't hate you. In fact, some of my best friends are Black!"), or clumsily tried to shift the focus to more comfortable territory ("Speaking of emails, you haven't replied to my message about the spring course schedule yet."). Their concern would have been immediate and genuine. But it still would have created more work for me, by requiring more emotional management than I was interested in providing. Even if I had needed any resources or support services, the university was unprepared to offer them to help me deal with this. I was on my own.

Racist hate mail is just one example of the denigration Black workers face every day, and its likelihood and extent probably vary depending on the field of employment. But racism at work is pervasive and endemic, arriving in many forms. It's baked into the experiences of Black teachers who find themselves punished for developing strategies that help Black children excel academically. It's embedded in the daily reality of Black nurses who find themselves segregated onto the night shift while their white counterparts are concentrated on the more desirable day shifts.[1] And it's the norm for Black attorneys whose efforts to make partner mean socializing with white partners at country clubs with a long history of excluding Black members.[2]

Which factors lead to these unjust scenarios, and what this book will explore, is *why* work remains a site where race is central and where Black workers bear the brunt of that reality. Because despite efforts to construct it as such, work isn't a neutral, unbiased sphere driven solely by economic production. Rather, work has always been a mechanism for maintaining racial inequality, as we'll discuss later in this Introduction. Key aspects of work—from getting a job and establishing workplace norms to advancement and mobility—were not built with Black people in mind. This means that in a modern era, when many organizations experiment with diversity programming and profess a commitment to principles of inclusion, these efforts in their current iterations are destined to fail.

For me, studying work and race is both a personal and professional endeavor. Many of the topics that I research are also things I experience in my own life. I've been the first Black hire or tenured Black professor in every department I've worked in and have usually been the only or one of few Black women in most professional settings. This means I've had firsthand experience with many of the issues that are present for Black workers today—having to compose myself for work minutes after seeing yet another news account of an unarmed Black man, woman, or child killed by police or armed vigilantes; having my professional qualifications doubted or downplayed; or challenging colleagues' openly stated beliefs that hiring Black workers would "just bring down [the department's] quality," to name a few. And my research has shown that I'm one of the (relatively) lucky ones—Black workers in other professional settings, like law, business, and engineering, often confront these issues in even more inhospitable climates. What I've found in my research is that efforts toward diversity and inclusion will never succeed until they address the ways that work does what it has been designed to do—perpetuate and maintain racial divides.

Gray Areas: How Work Drives Racial Inequality

There was once a time when it was perfectly unremarkable for employers to hang signs declaring "Whites Only Need Apply" when advertising for open positions. The Civil Rights Act of 1964 made that illegal, but that doesn't mean work has since become an equitable space. Today, work drives racial inequality through its cultural, social, and relational aspects—what I refer to in this book as the *gray areas*. Gray areas exist apart from the specific expectations and duties that are required for a given job, and because of this, they are much more amorphous, ambiguous, and difficult (though absolutely possible) to change. They can inform how we gain employment, how those jobs are done, what norms and values are given priority in a workplace, or how we advance or leave a company.

Take for example an airline pilot, whose job is to fly passengers safely from one location to another. Pilots are expected to have the technical skills and know-how to do this job effectively, but no one simply lands in the cockpit out of nowhere. How do pilots learn that a particular airline is hiring? How do they gain information that helps them succeed in the job interview? How do they navigate an environment where they must fit in with copilots, flight attendants, and other crew members? How do they know when there are opportunities for advancement? How can they get the necessary support to move into supervisory roles?

These processes all exist apart from the basics of flying passengers from one location to another. Many commercial pilots, for instance, move into these jobs after stints in the armed services, meaning they can rely on the connections and networks they build in those spaces to learn about position openings and generate referrals. Cultural norms in the airline industry promote strict hierarchies that both reflect military structure and define clear relationships between pilots, copilots, and flight attendants. Additionally, the relationships that pilots build with others in the field can determine their opportunities for certain positions and with specific airlines.[3] These aspects of work are distinct from the requirements of the job, yet they matter significantly because they constitute a core component of how we work today.

To some degree, gray areas have always been a part of how we work. Humans are social creatures, and our jobs entail more than just our basic responsibilities and assigned duties. During the Industrial Revolution of the 1800s, personal ties likely gave some workers leverage over other job candidates when looking for factory work. In the post-Fordist workplace of the 1950s, managers created an environment that prized efficiency, speed, and productivity, and this surely benefited employees who could adhere to these ideals.

Work has always been about more than just the job, and gray areas have long functioned to shape and determine how work gets done, and to maintain some inequities.

In our modern workplace, however, gray areas take on greater significance. For one thing, in the service-driven, highly specialized, tech-based economy in which we now live, relationships and networks matter more than ever. They determine how we learn about potential jobs, who gets serious consideration for them, how performance in those jobs is evaluated, and who has access to and information about other positions when it's time to move on.[4] Cultural dynamics matter more too, as organizations often prioritize teamwork and collaborative initiatives as key parts of how work is designed. No matter how technically skilled, the product engineer who doesn't have connections to anyone in Silicon Valley and doesn't work well with others will have a hard time landing a job at Facebook. Today, gray areas are nearly—or sometimes equally—as important as one's capacity to perform the technical requirements of a job.

What Qualifies as a Gray Area?

As the cultural, social, and relational parts of work, gray areas help to contextualize many of the slights and offenses that Black workers encounter in these spaces. Derald Wing Sue has popularized the concept of microaggressions, those seemingly small, minor offenses that accumulate over time and that Black employees regularly confront.[5] A Black man may arrive at work at the same time as a white colleague who mistakes him for a stranger and attempts to bar him from the premises—an incident that happened to William, a Dallas-based lawyer I interviewed. Or Black employees may face "glass cliffs" or "glass ceilings"—invisible pitfalls or barriers that curtail or stymie advancement. This was the case for Shaundra, an executive in Philadelphia, who, despite qualifications, experience, and interest, watched several colleagues who lacked one or all of those criteria get promoted past her. Tokenism, when employees are hired because of their underrepresented status but only marginally included in workspaces, is also a common issue for Black workers. Dennis, an engineer in Atlanta, encountered a form of this firsthand when he was asked to represent his company when it needed to show its commitment to diversity but was otherwise excluded from important projects that would have aided his advancement.

These processes are not the gray areas themselves: the gray areas are the contexts, the cultural, social, and relational norms in contemporary workplaces, that allow microaggressions, glass ceilings and cliffs, and tokenism to thrive. In other words, when company culture discourages attention to racial matters, microaggressions and tokenism transpire more easily and with little recourse. When advancement is based on relationships with managers and supervisors rather than on transparent, specific barometers, glass ceilings and cliffs may be widespread. Looking at the gray areas in a workplace helps to explain why such issues are so prevalent and commonplace, and why companies often fail to take them seriously.

A Brief History of Race and Work

It may seem unorthodox to think that work drives racial inequalities, but a look back through American history reveals this has always been the case. Beginning in 1619, America's reliance on race-based slavery meant that Black labor served many fundamental purposes. It powered the nation's economy, but it also crystallized racial lines around work, labor, and citizenship. Black slave labor was critical for building white wealth, but it also functioned as a means of denying Blacks the rights and privileges associated with US citizenship. The legal foundations of slavery meant that white owners were entitled to Blacks' labor. But the institution also created a dynamic in which work in the form of hard labor and production of goods and services was something done by Blacks and some lower income whites—even if the economic, social, and psychological value of that work went directly to whites.

When the Civil War brought slavery to a close, the relationship between race and labor changed. With slavery no longer legally permissible in its earlier iterations, the US economy had to shift and readjust. In some states, this meant that Black labor could still be appropriated by state institutions. Consequently, Black citizens remained enmeshed in a form of legal slavery as a result of state codes that disproportionately targeted poor Blacks for vagrancy laws and then forced them to work for free for the state as part of the terms of their incarceration. In some states, these work arrangements were foundational to industrialization.[6] Blacks continued to be the people who did the most difficult, degrading work, while being denied compensation for their efforts.

For nearly a century after the Civil War, from the end of Reconstruction in 1877 to the passage of the Civil Rights Act in 1964, Blacks were relegated to underfunded schools and dilapidated neighborhoods and were consigned to the lowest paying and least desirable jobs. The most common occupation for Black men during this period was sharecropping, while Black women were most likely to find employment doing domestic work. Extensive barriers and rigidly segregated social institutions (neighborhoods, schools, hospitals, public spaces) prevented Blacks from accessing jobs in the emerging manufacturing industries and professional spheres. (The exceptions to the latter were those who attended historically Black colleges and universities [HBCUs] and went into jobs catering primarily to Black communities—attorneys like Thurgood Marshall, teachers like Nannie Helen Burroughs, or doctors like Charles Drew.)

In a system of rigid segregation, work remained a way of maintaining racial differences. Whites—men in particular—had greater access to a wider array of jobs and occupations simply because legal and political strictures ensured that there was much less competition from other groups. Women of all races also encountered widespread discrimination that excluded them from high-paying, influential work. And as long as Blacks were restricted to the worst jobs that left them largely impoverished, it became easy to use circular reasoning to justify their treatment. In other words, Blacks' concentration in low-wage jobs and poor neighborhoods was often touted as evidence of their weak moral fiber, proclivity toward crime and disease, and inability to integrate, rather than being a consequence of long-term, institutionalized racial segregation.[7] Blacks were denied access to the kinds of jobs that offered influence, power, economic stability, and wealth. Consequently, work differentiated the emerging, predominantly white middle class from its poorer Black counterparts.

From the Black Codes in the South to redlining in the urban North, laws and policies ensured that Blacks would not have access to work that could potentially create economic stability and perhaps lead to racial equality. Today these laws are no longer in place. The Civil Rights Act of 1964 specifically forbids any discrimination based on race. Employers can no longer openly state that they will not hire Black candidates. Those "Whites Only Need Apply" signs are relegated to vintage photographs and museums, as markers of an ugly history that is no longer acceptable in the present.

In the wake of these changes, the mechanisms of racial division in our workplaces have become more covert than they once were. When I talk with Black employees about work, they rarely describe explicit rules specifically singling them out for differential treatment. They don't encounter openly discriminatory policies requiring them to enter through different doors or use separate facilities. In fact, those forms of discrimination would be easier to identify and change. But because overt, explicit racism is no longer (for the most part) legally or socially sanctioned, it has become common to think of work as a neutral, objective space where people get jobs on the basis of skills and qualifications, operate in a competitive but fairly structured labor market, are paid what they deserve, and get ahead because of their talents and ability to outwork others. As a society, we've constructed this narrative that work is an equitable space, a meritocratic environment where workers compete on a level playing field.

This perception of work, however, is as inaccurate today as it ever was. Although discrimination no longer occurs through explicit mechanisms, work continues to confer legitimacy and maintain racial hierarchies by enshrining barriers for Black employees that are not present for their white counterparts. Employers still discriminate against applicants whose names seem to signal a Black identity, with such candidates less likely to receive callbacks than whites with identical résumés. Black workers are subject to different rules and harsher sanctions than their white colleagues, even for the same infractions. Seemingly race-neutral policies that ban dreadlocks, cornrows, and braids disproportionately disadvantage Black employees. These barriers create patterns of employment segregation that have persisted well past the end of the civil rights era and continue even amidst widespread moves toward corporate diversity, equity, and inclusion policies.[8]

At the same time, we live in an era where work has become increasingly uncertain and insecure. In the modern economy, growing numbers of Americans toil in "bad jobs"—those that offer low pay, unpredictable schedules, few benefits, and little prestige.[9] These are not the middle-class jobs of the mid-twentieth century that allowed many white men to support families and move to comfortable houses in (racially segregated) suburbs. These are jobs in the service sectors of the economy where employees are subject to unpredictable schedules, few to no benefits, and a minimum wage that falls well below the cost of living in many areas. Even the emerging gig economy, which purports to offer more autonomy and control for workers, comes with heightened surveillance and minimal or nonexistent antidiscrimination, labor, or safety protections.[10] And with the fallout from the coronavirus pandemic continuing to upend much of our economy, many of these jobs, particularly in the retail sector, may be gone for good.

With this mix of occupational uncertainty, increasingly covert manifestations of racism, and the widening economic inequality, the flash points around race and work have become even more incendiary. Immigrants—particularly those of color—are pilloried for "taking jobs" from "real Americans" or are stereotyped as "illegals" who risk inviting unwelcome attention from authorities.[11] Programs promoting affirmative action and diversity frequently elicit backlash and anger from whites who believe that, with existing prohibitions on racial discrimination, Blacks are now being unfairly advantaged at their expense. Work, particularly in the form of "good jobs" that offer stability, benefits, and security, remains implicitly—and sometimes explicitly—characterized as the province of white Americans, with people of color perceived as usurpers moving into territory in which they do not belong.

When work isn't just about paying bills but takes on outsize importance as something that confers legitimacy, belonging, and citizenship, then it becomes easier for it to take on racial connotations. And in a society where work itself has now become more insecure, elusive, and precarious, the stakes attached to it become even higher. For much of US history, work has been a way of maintaining racial hierarchies and dividing those deemed "deserving" from those who were not.

Today, the gray areas of work—the relationships, networks, and cultural norms that are increasingly salient in the modern workplace—allow this to continue. They are present in traditional models where hourly or salaried workers are directly employed by a company and in nontraditional platform-based arrangements where independent contractors are paid for their services. They affect men and women alike, in jobs that involve work as varied as making movies to using nanotechnology to delivering food. What is the result of these gray areas? Black employees are less likely to be hired, more likely to stall out at middle levels, and ultimately rarely progress to senior leadership roles. We can do better.

Why Gray Areas Matter Now

Right now, the United States is entering a period of unprecedented demographic change. Most projections suggest that there will be no clear racial majority group within a few decades, a prospect that leaves many whites with a great deal of angst and unease.[12] At the same time, the country is in the midst of extreme levels of income inequality, driven in no small part by shifts in our economy, reconfigurations in work over the past half century, and public policies that exacerbate difficulties for working families.[13] Though workers continue to increase productivity, a combination of factors including antiunion legislation, technological shifts, the gutting of the public sector, and minimal limits on executive compensation means that economic gains aren't going to workers—they are going to those at the very top.

As work perpetuates racial inequality, Black workers are largely locked out of the most influential, high-status jobs and are disproportionately represented among low-wage workers or those seeking regular employment. This presents a serious problem for a society that is rapidly becoming more and more racially diverse. At the time of this writing, Americans who identify as Latinx and/or Black are nearly a third of the US population, Asian Americans are the fastest growing racial group, and the numbers of those who identify as multiracial increased by 35 percent between 2010 and 2018.[14] These numbers are poised to increase in upcoming years, meaning that earlier depictions of the United States as a mostly white country are simply becoming less accurate and applicable.

As the US population becomes more racially diverse, it is incumbent upon companies to rise to the occasion by reflecting these changes among employees and leadership. Not only that, upcoming generations of workers of color are forcefully and loudly demanding organizational change. Millennial and Gen Z workers are no longer content to play by the old rules that necessitated working long hours with little to no work–life balance. They want workplaces that allow them to live life more fully; but critically, many of them also want to work in environments that offer a real commitment to racial diversity and equity.[15] Organizations are going to have to adapt to meet the needs of a shifting employer and consumer base, and workers deserve to labor in companies where they are welcomed, can thrive, and have a path to leadership positions should they want to pursue them.

If work continues to remain a source of racial inequality, then not only will we continue to waste human capital, but we will establish a culture where, by design, a growing majority of the population is blocked from fully contributing to the society at large. As a society, we're at an inflection point: we can continue marginalizing and disadvantaging a rapidly growing segment of our population, or we can finally begin to confront how work is one of the major mechanisms that perpetuates racial inequality and start fixing it.

The Research

How is it possible to understand and identify how and where gray areas exist and the ways they make work fundamentally unequal? By going straight to the source—the workers themselves. Since I was a graduate student, I've been interested in understanding how Black workers navigate the complexities and challenges of the labor market, jobs, and organizations. Given the inordinate amount of time Americans spend working, their places of employment are prime sites for studying racial dynamics, perceptions, and inequalities. Hearing about these firsthand from Black workers who can narrate their experiences is a fascinating way to shed light on how the way we work maintains racial inequality.

Over the course of my career as a sociologist examining how and why racial and gender inequality persists in professional occupations, I've interviewed hundreds of Black workers about their lives, experiences, challenges, and opportunities at work. I've spoken with doctors, lawyers, entrepreneurs, EMTs, teachers, and countless other workers in places as varied as my university office, public parks, coffee shops, and in one memorable case, when no other quiet location was available, in a restricted stairwell for maintenance workers at Union Station in Washington, DC, that was accidentally left unlocked. These interviews, which form the basis for the analysis in this book, provide a unique and illuminating view into the landscape Black workers face in the United States today.

I usually find respondents through "snowball sampling," a methodology in which respondents refer others who might be interested in participating in a research project. It's particularly useful when seeking out hard-to-find or underrepresented populations like Black male nurses or Black female physicians. Using this methodological approach, I've researched Black men working in male-dominated professions to understand how being in the racial minority and gender majority affects how they experience tokenism. A different project focused on Black health-care workers to understand how they navigate increasing privatization, staffing shortages, and efforts to diversify their industry. Yet another study examined how Black professionals manage and control their emotions while at work and considered how being in the minority shapes their emotional expression.

These interviews usually follow a similar process. I spend an hour, sometimes more, talking in detail with respondents about multiple aspects of their professional lives—how they got interested in the work that they do, what they see as their biggest challenges, whether and how they think race has an impact on their work. Sometimes I also spend time with respondents at their jobs to try to understand how they experience work on a daily basis. I usually start with scripted questions, but over time the interviews can come to feel more like conversations about what work is like for Black employees today. In many cases, the issues respondents discuss with me are things that have been nagging at them for some time but that they only now have the opportunity to put into words and articulate to someone who's genuinely interested.

With this book, I took a similar approach. *Gray Areas* draws from more than a decade's worth of research to show how these nebulous aspects of the modern work world facilitate ongoing racial inequality. I relied on multiple interviews with most of my sources to get a clear understanding of their lives. The book follows seven Black workers from a range of backgrounds to highlight how, via gray areas, the way we work maintains racial inequality. I have altered their names and identifying details (as well as for others in this book) and lightly edited their words for clarity but not content. Alex works in the gig economy, Max is an emergency medicine doctor, Constance is a chemical engineer, Brian is a filmmaker, Amalia is a journalist, Darren is a corporate vice president, and Kevin works for a nonprofit.

These seven workers provide a view of how larger structural issues beyond their control—the growth of gig and contract work, the expansion of the service industry, intersections of race and gender—affect Black employees trying to navigate workplaces that often do not "work" for them. Their narratives highlight how gray areas are present in three core aspects of work: hiring, navigating the job, and promotion. Together, these workers' accounts show the scope and breadth of gray areas, and the urgency of attending to them if we genuinely want to see workplaces that are equipped for a more racially diverse future.

A Different Future

As we meet and learn about these seven workers, I make suggestions for how we can shift aspects of the hiring process to include rather than exclude Black workers, rethink organizational cultures so that Black employees' experiences are central rather than peripheral, and establish pathways that move capable Black candidates into leadership roles. I'll also overcome the sociologist's tendency toward fatalism by providing actionable items that can help address the gray areas of work. At the close of each section, I provide key takeaways, along with a checklist for everyday workers, DEI practitioners, HR leaders, and executives and senior managers. These checklists offer solutions that different categories of workers can consider implementing so that the gray areas of work offer more equitable opportunities instead of restricting them along racial lines. These will be major changes, but ones that could bring major benefits: the most significant being that for the first time, American workplaces might actually look like America.

PART I

CULTURAL

Doing Diversity Badly

It may seem odd to focus on company culture as an example of a gray area that perpetuates racial inequality. After all, diversity in the workplace is no longer a marginal issue, and many if not most organizations would say that they prioritize diversity as a core value. In 2003, companies spent about $8 billion per year on diversity initiatives, and the field has only grown since then. A 2019 survey of 234 companies found that nearly two-thirds had hired diversity managers in the previous three years.[1] Diversity has become big business, and this might seem to suggest that companies are now committed to advancing this cause in ways that they weren't even a few years ago.

Despite the stated focus on diversity, however, Black workers continue to face racial slights, indignities, and worse. In summer 2020 during the Black Lives Matter movement, news stories revealed systemic racism in a wide array of industries. In real estate, Black developers noted the racial biases and assumptions that made it difficult for them to secure financing to build properties and provide housing, especially outside of predominantly Black areas.[2] Accounts of racism in policing and the impact it has, not just on citizens, but on Black officers, became commonplace.[3] And even as journalists were reporting these stories, newsrooms began to wrestle with their lack of racial diversity and the impact that has for adequately covering breaking news about racial matters.[4]

These stories surfaced relatively recently, but the sentiments underlying them weren't new. For decades, Black workers have been calling attention to the adverse assumptions and expectations they face at work. And during much of that time, companies have responded by restating their commitment to diversity, spending money to bring in consultants, and assuring employees, shareholders, and the public that this is an issue of utmost importance to them. Yet the problems persist. This is because focusing on diversity alone accomplishes absolutely nothing. Unless companies are also committed to changing their cultures, the barriers that Black workers identify will persist.

When we refer to a company's culture, what are we talking about? Organizational culture refers to the norms, expectations, and values that are collectively held among members of an organization. Leadership in an organization usually develops the culture and then inculcates it in employees and patrons through various processes. When launching Facebook, creator and owner Mark Zuckerberg created a culture encouraging informality, creativity, and thinking outside the box. In contrast, former employees of the now-defunct company Theranos alleged that disgraced founder Elizabeth Holmes developed an organizational culture built on paranoia, mistrust, and secrecy.[5] While the outcomes were different, in both cases, leadership set the tone and then established the culture through personnel decisions, workplace expectations, and other aspects of the work routine.

Four Types of Culture

Management scholars Kim Cameron and Robert Quinn argue that most corporate cultures fall into one of four typologies. *Clan culture* encourages workers to see one another as family and to prioritize interpersonal relationships. *Adhocracy culture* is encapsulated in Mark Zuckerberg's motto "move fast and break things," prizing innovation, unorthodoxy, and risk-taking. *Market culture* is highly results driven, with a heavy focus on outputs. And *hierarchy cultures* emphasize interactions and norms driven by existing rules, regulations, guidelines, and procedures.[6] These varied cultures can have a critical impact on how workers interact with others in a company as well as the extent to which an organization feels like a comfortable place for them.

As we'll see here in Part I, these cultures can create various challenges that make it hard for Black workers to fit in and find their footing. The emphasis in clan cultures on "being part of a family," for instance, can be off-putting for Black employees who experience hostility or alienation from white colleagues. Adhocracy cultures prize unorthodox thinking and risk-taking, but Black workers have less leeway to bounce back from risks that go wrong.[7] Market culture focuses on numbers and bottom lines but ignores how persistent discrimination can impede Black workers' ability to meet targets and goals. Finally, hierarchy culture's rigid focus on extant norms and regulations overlooks how rules themselves can be structured in ways that neglect and ignore Black employees' realities.

Over time, the beliefs and assumptions that are part of an organization's culture typically become unspoken and frequently taken for granted. When this happens, leaders do not necessarily need to remind workers or customers of the expectations at their company. The norms become embedded into the ways workers interact, the options they have, and the decisions they make. Critics of policing, for instance, often argue that part of the reason why police violence persists is because the organizational culture of many police forces is one that tolerates or even encourages it.[8] Thus new employees do not have to be told the culture in explicit terms but observe the behaviors and interactions that are normalized and then act accordingly.

As a result, organizational culture can become most visible when it is violated (whether intentionally or unwittingly). In the US Congress—a governing body but still a workplace for the legislators who assemble there—the organizational culture mandates that representatives dress conservatively and follow precise rules and formalities for interacting. Yet as elected congressional representatives Cori Bush and Alexandria Ocasio-Cortez pointed out, an organizational culture that requires formality in the form of demure dress and business clothes can be costly for those who are unaccustomed to this work and do not come from backgrounds where such clothes are already in their wardrobe. As Bush tweeted after winning her election, "The reality of being a regular person going to Congress is that it's really expensive to get the business clothes I need for the Hill."[9] For Bush, and presumably for other new representatives from comparable backgrounds, the organizational culture in this space may not be a perfect match with their previous experiences.[10]

Colorblind Ideology

What goes unspoken in many workplaces is that organizational culture is rarely created with Black workers' realities, lives, and experiences in mind. Often this takes the form of a colorblind organizational culture, where the workplace norm is that attention to racial issues is impolite at best and racist at worst. If the everyday norms in a workplace demand that employees keep silent about racial matters, or if no policies are in place to protect workers who speak up about racial issues, then an organization communicates pretty clearly that it intends to be colorblind rather than color conscious.

The concept of colorblind ideology, developed by sociologist Eduardo Bonilla-Silva, refers to a belief system that downplays and ignores race and racial differences.[11] On its face, such an ideological bent might seem benign or even admirable, particularly given the long struggles for racial equity and efforts to make racial differences irrelevant in social, economic, and political outcomes. But by dismissing race, colorblind ideology also overlooks the mechanisms that allow racial disparities to persist. In other words, if we don't "see" race, then it becomes impossible to "see"—and eradicate—the ongoing processes that perpetuate racial inequalities.

Colorblind ideology did not emerge in a vacuum. Rather, it is the result of political, economic, cultural, and social shifts over centuries. In America's earliest days, explicitly racist ideologies and practices were normative, commonplace, and unremarkable. As discussed in the Introduction, slavery was a core part of the engine of the US economy. The corresponding, dominant racial ideology that developed to justify this practice argued that because Black Americans were racially inferior, if not subhuman, slavery was for the good of all (including Blacks, who, according to this extremely faulty logic, would not have to trouble their weak minds with the responsibilities freedom demanded). As such, it simply maintained the natural racial order.

In the aftermath of the slavery era, the racial ideology had to shift to accommodate new social, economic, and political realities. Slavery was illegal, but after Reconstruction, states enacted increasingly restrictive laws that largely mandated segregation and entrenched racial inequality. As Jim Crow–era policies became increasingly common, a cultural shift also had to accompany this new reality and explain why Blacks, who under slavery could live and work in close proximity to whites, now needed to be rigidly separated. This is where we see ideology move from one explaining that slavery is a "peculiar institution" that benefits Blacks and whites alike, to the "separate but equal" ideology asserting that Blacks are violent, dangerous threats to the social order who must be controlled through strict separation and lynching if necessary.

The Civil Rights Act of 1964 put an end to legal, overt, race-based discrimination. Correspondingly, survey data show a change in American attitudes about racial matters. Respondents are less likely to identify as racist, to say they oppose integration, and to support banning interracial marriage. But the mechanisms that perpetuate racial inequality still exist. Voting districts remain gerrymandered, schools that serve mostly Black students are disproportionately underfunded, and most neighborhoods and cities remain highly segregated.[12] How do we explain persistent race-based inequalities in an era when being racist is no longer socially acceptable?

Colorblind ideology offers a way to do just that. By drawing from a belief system which maintains that race doesn't matter anymore, those who use this ideology downplay the very real ways that systemic racism operates to shape multiple aspects of social life, from where we live to who our friends are to what we learn in school. Being colorblind means that there's no need to pay attention to or talk about racism, and that even doing so is gauche and impolite. After all, if the civil rights movement put an end to racism, then there is no need to continue discussing or attempting to address it. But more perniciously, avoiding the subject means that the more covert mechanisms that allow racial inequalities to thrive—the gerrymandering, racial disparities in school funding, and housing discrimination—continue to do so unabated.

Drawing from interviews and survey data of Black and white Americans' racial attitudes, Bonilla-Silva found four key frames that comprise and justify colorblind ideology. *Abstract liberalism* refers to the broad practice of opposing policies designed to create more racial equity because of a commitment to individual liberty. Here, respondents argued that they opposed reparations, affirmative action, and other policies designed to address racial inequalities because they believed these impinged on individual freedoms—especially their own. This broad approach allowed people to focus on personal autonomy while ignoring how group-based processes like redlining, intergenerational wealth transfers, and neighborhood segregation maintain discrimination. The *minimization of racism* frame labels racism and racial inequality as rare and elusive, categorizing "real" racism as the stuff of Klan rallies, thus pushing people to justify many existing racist practices as acceptable and excusable. The *biologization of culture* frame presents certain behaviors as endemic among Black communities, thus suggesting that deficient cultural values explain racial disadvantage better than systemic processes. This frame lets users excuse racial inequality by attributing it to the "fact" that Black culture devalues education and work, thus overlooking the documented existence of extensive labor market discrimination or the effects of persistent school segregation. Finally, the *naturalization* frame explains racial inequalities as inevitable, suggesting that it's just "normal" for people to want to live around, marry, or go to school with similar others—even if that leads to racially discriminatory behaviors to achieve these goals. Ultimately, the real utility of these colorblind frames is that they allow people to remain blind to the ongoing, persistent realities of contemporary racial inequality.

Abstract Liberalism: Opposing Racism with Inaction

When it comes to organizational culture, abstract liberalism may mean that companies put forth carefully crafted statements that support their commitment to diversity and profess their belief in inclusion and equity. These statements can hit all the right notes about the importance of having a diverse and inclusive workspace and reiterate the message that the organization will not stand for or tolerate racism within its ranks. Some organizations may even hire high-ranking managers and vice presidents whose purview focuses on diversity and inclusion. In times of racial unrest, companies may release public statements affirming their opposition to racism, as many organizations did during the summer of 2020 when Black Lives Matter protests rocked the country.

Statements sound good, but they are not policies. Without concerted action, words alone don't create internal change. And when it comes to policies, organizations that have a culture of abstract liberalism fall far short because they do not develop practices or inculcate norms that consider how organizations can actively work to create more racial equity. Companies steeped in the culture of abstract liberalism may state their commitment to diversity but shy away from enacting policies that protect Black workers from customers' (or colleagues') racist harassment. They may do so because the default focus is on (white) individuals' right to express their views, rather than on Black employees' right to work without racial animus.[13] Or they might hire a vice president for diversity and inclusion while discouraging concrete policies that would increase the number of workers of color in management roles.[14] If an organization's colorblind culture is driven by abstract liberalism, it may say the right things but will likely not have measures in place that would create a truly racially inclusive workplace.

This mismatch between words and action may not be an accident. Legal scholar Lauren Edelman has shown that changes in enforcement mean that many organizations are more focused on ensuring compliance with regulations than on implementing policies that actually move the needle.[15] In other words, organizations know that they must take proactive measures not to run afoul of regulators or leave themselves open to legal liability. No one wants to be sued for racial discrimination, and companies do not want to be sanctioned. So they establish measures that ensure that they are protected from any legal action, but regulators and legal standards do not mandate that these protocols actually have to work. And without that requirement, many companies don't take that extra step to ensure their policies really succeed.

Diversity training provides an excellent example of how this occurs in many workplaces. Such training has become nearly ubiquitous in corporate spaces; as sociologists Frank Dobbin and Alexandra Kalev report in a 2016 *Harvard Business Review* article, "nearly half of midsize companies use it, as do nearly all the *Fortune* 500."[16] Workers are often required to attend diversity training as part of onboarding or routine compliance. Yet despite being widespread, little evidence suggests that it actually improves either the numbers or the general experiences of Black workers in areas where they are underrepresented.

In a landmark study of more than seven hundred private-sector companies, Dobbin and Kalev, along with sociologist Erin Kelley, found that mandated diversity workshops accomplished virtually nothing when it came to getting more women of all races and men of color into managerial roles.[17] In fact, these programs actually had the potential to backfire, as they often induced resistance and resentment from white workers required to attend them.[18] And it's not just white workers who chafe at these trainings. Many Black workers also find such initiatives unhelpful when they are decoupled from specific measures to address the underlying factors that leave them underrepresented in high-status jobs.[19]

Diversity training, and the responses it elicits, is not helpful. Rather than creating more racial diversity, especially among the top ranks, such programs instead often generate exasperation, annoyance, and backlash.[20] By using programming that is widespread yet ineffective, companies remain in compliance with government regulators who monitor workplace discrimination, but nothing changes. And when organizations continue to double down on this approach despite a consistent lack of results, it contributes to the ennui many workers feel about the possibility of creating actual change.

Biologization of Culture: The Art of Fitting In

Organizations that focus heavily on the idea of "fit" may also find that they employ the biologization of culture frame as part of their organizational culture. In other words, the culture of some organizations may glorify certain traits, attributes, and ideals. On the face of it, these characteristics are likely to appear race-neutral. Companies may adopt a culture of outdoorsiness, for example, where they offer team-building activities in spaces that encourage hiking, camping, or rafting. Or the culture may encourage collaborative teamwork, where employees must work closely in small groups and thus could conceivably benefit from sharing common interests, personalities, and outlooks. Yet still other organizations may cultivate a culture that is socially and politically conservative, where workers are expected to follow a formal dress code or express fealty to certain ideologies.

None of these cultures mentions race specifically, or even indirectly, but they may still pose particular challenges for workers of color. Research shows that Black Americans are less likely to engage in certain outdoor activities than whites, possibly because of the ways that peers in these spaces can be unwelcoming and inhospitable, and perhaps because Blacks are more likely to live in cities and away from spaces that easily lend themselves to hiking, rafting, or camping.[21] Thus, a company that cultivates an organizational culture which emphasizes outdoorsiness doesn't need to state explicitly that Black colleagues are not welcome. The company leadership may in fact genuinely want to attract more workers of color, but the culture will mitigate against this.

The Meritocracy Myth

In conjunction with a colorblind organizational culture, many organizations also develop a culture that values and idealizes the concept of meritocracy. Indeed, it seems self-evident that companies should be built on the idea that the most talented person and the best candidate wins out, whether that means getting a job in the first place, meeting various goals and targets, or advancing to another position in the company. These ideas of meritocracy are tightly wedded to broader ideas about American society and reflect larger cultural ideas that the United States is a level playing field where achievements result primarily from hard work, equal opportunity, and objective standards.

In a workplace, a company that promotes a culture of meritocracy might employ seemingly objective metrics as a basis for determining who is selected for important, key groups or use "pay-for-play" performance metrics, where salary is tied directly to output. As Jim Whitehurst, former CEO of the software company Red Hat, puts it: "What is a meritocracy in the workplace? In a meritocracy, everyone has the right to express their opinions and are encouraged to share them openly and often. Those opinions are listened to and decisions are then made based on those that are deemed the best." Whitehurst continues, "In many technology companies that employ a meritocracy—Red Hat being one example—people forge their own path to leadership, not simply by working hard and smart, but also by expressing unique ideas that have the ability to positively impact their team and their company."[22]

In many ways this approach may seem ideal. It suggests that all workers have equal chances to contribute and advance, that the value of their ideas and performance is what matters most, and that employees are constrained only by their own limitations. Plus, the idea of meritocracy appeals to our innate sense of fairness—it doesn't seem right for someone to benefit from or achieve gains that they did not earn but that were given to them on the basis of more subjective criteria. What better way to develop an organizational culture than by norms that promote ideas of fairness, equity, and merit?

The problem with this approach isn't in its underlying sentiments. It's in the fact that meritocratic cultures in organizations, perhaps counterintuitively, actually work to entrench racial and gendered inequalities. In a classic study, sociologists Emilio Castilla and Stephen Benard looked at a wide variety of companies that proudly touted their meritocratic ideals. Many of these corporations developed merit-based compensation systems designed to reward high performers. But Castillo and Benard found that white women and people of color consistently received smaller wage increases than their white male colleagues, even after the researchers controlled for job type, division of the company, and perhaps most important, workers' performance scores. In other words, even when everything else was equal, workers of color and white women were still paid less than their white male counterparts—in a system that emphasized merit only.[23]

How could racial and gender pay disparities persist under these circumstances? Castillo and Benard attribute these ongoing inequities to what they refer to as "the paradox of meritocracy." When organizations, and the workers within, are suffused in a culture that is supposed to be equitable and fair, it is more difficult for employees to see their own biases. After all, if the company is a meritocracy where only performance matters, managers do not need to check themselves to see whether they are awarding a larger bonus to a white man than to a Black woman with the same performance scores. If a culture encourages managers to believe that the system is ultimately fair and unbiased, there is no reason for them to consider whether racial stereotypes come into play when they are evaluating employees of color. Ironically, an organizational culture steeped in ideals of meritocracy can ultimately perpetuate the very inequalities it seeks to reduce. Embracing this concept isn't enough unless companies are also devoted to identifying and rooting out the ways systemic biases can still persist—and many companies that are driven by the meritocratic ethos don't take this additional step.

The fact that meritocracy is not only a myth but perpetuates inequality may not shock Black workers who are rightfully suspicious of companies that flaunt this ideology. It helps explain what many Black employees observe as they see others get second chances and opportunities that they themselves are denied. And this is part of the problem with the erroneous belief that companies operate as meritocracies—it elides the ways inequalities persist and makes it more difficult for anyone to see and change the processes that allow the inequalities to continue.

Black Workers and Organizational Culture

The particulars of an organization's culture vary widely and are shaped by a multitude of factors—how long the company has been in business, its leadership, and its mission and goals. Universities, for instance, are often perceived to be places with very liberal organizational cultures (though this varies widely both between and within universities), while firms in the financial industry have a reputation for nurturing a more socially and politically conservative culture. Alex, Darren, Constance, Max, Amalia, Brian, and Kevin are employed in a range of different industries, with organizations that have notably different cultures. Part I highlights how, even among organizations with cultures that vary from those that focus explicitly on diversity to those that are studiously colorblind, a common thread is the fact that many workplaces still build organizational cultures that are uncomfortable for Black workers or oblivious to the challenges they face.

CHAPTER 1

Race Blindness and the Liberal Paradox

"THEY JUST DON'T WANT TO"

Colleges and universities are complicated places to consider organizational culture. While most adults do not hold college degrees, those degrees can be important credentials in an increasingly tight job market. Yet the numbers of Americans who view higher education adversely are on the rise. In 2019, the Pew Research Center reported that nearly 40 percent of Americans felt that colleges and universities contributed negatively to society. Gallup polling found similar results, showing that between 2015 and 2018, the percentage of respondents who had a great deal of confidence in higher education dropped nine points, to 48 percent.[1]

This decline is driven not just by a rising mistrust of institutions, but also by a growing number of Americans who believe that colleges and universities have become too liberal. Polling indicates that many respondents think professors use the classroom as a space to inculcate students with their own left-leaning perspectives. These respondents also believe that this practice precludes colleges from adequately preparing students for the workforce. The mere existence of programs and departments focusing on race, ethnicity, and gender likely contributes to these views that colleges and universities are bastions of liberal thinking that fail to train students effectively for the "real world." Furthermore, attempts to criminalize educators for teaching philosophies such as critical race theory, a legal perspective which argues that racism in the United States is systemic and institutionalized rather than individually driven, coexist neatly with the idea that universities are places of liberal indoctrination, particularly on racial matters.

Perception isn't always reality, but whether or not colleges and universities truly are organizations that lean left, their reputation as such is well established. Thus, it might seem that these would be places where the organizational culture would be particularly favorable to Black workers. Certainly many universities have highly paid vice presidents for diversity and equity; student- and faculty-led affinity groups are not uncommon; and in 2020 and 2021, after widespread protests for racial equity, schools such as Stanford, the University of Virginia, and Columbia launched high-profile cluster hires designed to attract faculty focusing on issues related to race and ethnicity. These kinds of actions would seem to be exactly the practices that suggest a welcoming, hospitable organizational culture for Black workers.

In reality, however, universities present what we might call a "left-leaning paradox." Their reputation as liberal institutions is firmly cemented, but the reality is more complicated. Universities mostly are not-for-profit enterprises, but they still need money to function. Historically, they could count on state and federal dollars to constitute a sizable chunk of their budgets, but over the past few decades, as student bodies began to diversify, many state legislatures began to devote smaller budget amounts to funding public services, including education. Consequently, many universities started making up the difference by turning to wealthy private donors for gifts and large financial awards.[2] Though ostensibly such donations should not affect the university's academic mission, questions and doubts about that possibility still arise, especially if those donors are less likely to espouse and support progressive values. Florida State University wrestled with the consequences of this when billionaires David and Charles Koch offered a million-dollar gift to support faculty and courses focused on free enterprise, raising questions of whether new hires would be able to pursue independent inquiries that challenged the donors' known conservative beliefs.[3]

Additionally, university leadership ultimately answers to a board of trustees that typically is composed of elites from the business and/or political world. That dynamic can set up clashes when faculty want to move in more progressive or left-leaning directions than board members would like. One notable recent example of this is the case of Professor James Thomas, a sociologist at the University of Mississippi whose scholarship on race and racism, coupled with critical tweets about members of the Trump Administration, led to an unusual closed-door meeting that ended with his being granted tenure "with dissent" from members of the board.[4] Ultimately, the close interconnection between academic and corporate worlds means that the picture of universities as paragons of liberal bias is not quite that straightforward.

Colorblindness and Clan Culture in "Liberal" Institutions

Constance's work experiences in academia reflect these contradictions. Petite and caramel-skinned, with neatly braided hair and a quiet, serious demeanor, she has a bit of a protective shell to her that I suspect comes from many years as the lone Black woman in professional spaces. She works as a professor of chemical engineering at one of the top research universities in the country.

Chemical engineers have access to enormous labs and complicated-looking stainless steel equipment that I find both confusing and intimidating. Given that the extent of my own knowledge of chemistry peaked in an eleventh-grade high school course, I was not at all clear about the particulars of what went on in her lab and realized (to my former chemistry teacher's disappointment, I'm sure) that all I remember from that class is what a Bunsen burner is and does. But these are far more comfortable spaces for Constance, who told me about some of her current projects in terms simple enough that I almost understood what she was talking about. For my part, I resisted the urge to reference the television show *Breaking Bad* and its main character, a high school chemistry teacher who builds a crystal meth empire, as I suspected that this might not be the time or place to crack Heisenberg jokes.

As a chemical engineer, Constance is not housed in one of the units where her colleagues are likely to engage in researching or teaching issues related to race. Most of her departmental colleagues are, like her, scientists who focus on the natural world of metals, particles, and chemicals. Yet departmental norms and politics encourage teamwork and collaboration, particularly between faculty and graduate student researchers and between faculty who can work together to produce results. In Cameron and Quinn's typology, the department could be construed as a clan culture where employees are encouraged to foster ties and connections, make decisions by general consensus, and communicate effectively.

Despite this clan culture, Constance's department does not engage in much discussion of matters of race or pay attention to the kind of challenges that Black students or faculty might encounter. This is not to say that departments in the natural sciences are necessarily able to develop a culture free from bias. Black students are disproportionately underrepresented in the natural sciences, and those who do enter this field report exclusion, stereotyping, and being "pushed out" by faculty and student peers who do not believe they belong in or are suited to a rigorous environment characterized by advanced math and science skills.[5] In other cases, perceptions of the field as being very "white and male" discourage students from pursuing careers.[6] The data-driven, technical world of the sciences is still one in which the culture can be alienating for Black students.[7]

In that context, Constance's departmental culture is largely race-blind. Colleagues prefer to focus on their scientific endeavors, publications, and attempts to secure external funding, and the culture valorizes efforts to achieve these metrics and conduct top-quality research. But Constance still encounters difficulties that seem directly related to her position as a Black woman in this setting. She has had undergraduate students openly speculate that she doesn't understand her own research, colleagues who ignore her when she sees them off campus, and proposal reviews that reflect clear racial and gender bias. She told me about one of her most memorable cases of egregious behavior from a white male colleague: "I've had a man call me out of nowhere and tell me my stuff wouldn't work and then publish a paper on the same thing. We hadn't met—we've still never met. But yeah, he basically called me to tell me what I was doing would never work. And then he put out a paper doing the exact same thing!"

In a department where the norm is to avoid talking about race or racism, however, these issues go unnoticed. Constance remarked that most of her departmental colleagues refused even to acknowledge openly racist teaching evaluations she received or casual stereotyping from peers. They were oblivious to the stonewalling and general uninterest she faced when trying to establish the collaborative relationships that are necessary for scientists in her field. She noted with frustration: "You can't go and complain about racism every time something happens that's bad, because nobody's going to believe you. They want proof. And then when you tell people what happens to you, they want to tell you how it wasn't racist. They're not going to experience your perspective, so there's no point in going down that road."

For Constance, this dynamic—knowing full well that racism impedes her while colleagues implacably refuse to recognize this fact—is disorienting and unsettling. She is positive that her department's culture overlooks the racial biases that make it harder for her to thrive and succeed in her job. But having this experience doubted and ignored is infuriating. As a result, Constance often second-guesses herself. Other times, she struggles to identify when and where her own personality quirks—being somewhat shy, introverted, at times uncomfortable speaking up—are an issue, and when racial (and gender) bias is at fault. She doesn't doubt her grasp of the science and the legitimacy of her ideas, but she does face an ongoing challenge of trying to fit into a workplace that, because of its gray areas, isn't so hospitable to Black women. And by being mired in colorblind discourse, the organizational culture at her university only aids in perpetuating this.

The Masquerade

During one of our conversations, I asked Constance what she thought her department or her university could do to address the issues she faced. Clearly she did not find the approaches her department chair and dean were using to be effective. "They could acknowledge that racism is real and affects our job," she replied emphatically. For instance, she continued, "They could acknowledge that people look up profiles online when they [evaluate research proposals], and as soon as they see you're Black, they have made some biased assumption about your proposal. [The process] is *not* reviewer blind. If administrators wanted to acknowledge that [racism is] real and affects our performance and it's a real challenge, they ought to be taking into consideration, that would help. But nobody's going to do that."

Constance's department appears to be espousing a culture of meritocracy, based in the belief that the environment is a fair and equitable one where hard work can be adequately measured and objectively rewarded. However, the assumptions underlying this belief in meritocracy mean that the department leadership has no way to recognize and assess the racial challenges Constance encounters. Without an organizational culture that attends to, or at least acknowledges, the racial dynamics that are part of her reality, it becomes nearly impossible for Constance to fit in at work. The department's commitment to colorblindness, coupled with a meritocratic ideal that employees will succeed or fail solely on the basis of their own merits, pushes Constance to a place where she doesn't feel comfortable sharing how she is affected by her experiences with racism at the university and in her discipline. As a result, it becomes harder for her to be herself at work.

In this environment, Constance took pains to present a façade that allowed her to make the best of a difficult situation. She did this by "masquerading." "When I started working here at the university," she told me, "I would say absolutely no, I did not fit in. I would say I was masquerading." This masquerade allowed her to put forth the genial face she needed to accommodate colleagues' expectations of pleasantness and courtesy, while concealing how she really felt about the racial dynamics in her department.

Describing what would today be called "code switching," back in 1895 poet Paul Laurence Dunbar wrote in "We Wear the Mask" that in order to fit into predominantly white spaces, Black Americans "wear the mask that grins and lies, / It hides our cheeks and shades our eyes." I expected that Constance's "masquerade" would be consistent with the many ways Black workers "wear the mask": hiding preferences for foods, music, or entertainment commonly associated with Black culture; taking pains to present a consistently pleasant demeanor; and most important, always concealing frustration with and irritation at racist comments.[8] This mask can help Black workers acclimate to colorblind organizational cultures where discussion of or attention to racial issues is unwelcome or discouraged.

Constance's masquerade did in fact evoke Dunbar's metaphorical mask. She told me that when she first started working at her university, "the women in my department would go to lunch together. I'm already an introvert, but I went to all of these lunches. They were very—it was all white women, talking about the things that they talk about, so I was quiet most of the time. They were talking about personal things, but I'm not going to talk about getting my hair done, what types of music I like, what shows I'm watching. I made an assumption on my part that I would be the only one doing those things, but it wasn't a stretch based on what they were talking about. So I was not completely being myself."

Like Dunbar's mask that "hides," many Black workers report concealing parts of their personality, identity, and preferences in workspaces, particularly when they are in the minority. To some degree, this is true for workers of all races—young white associates at an investment or law firm might feel the need to cover tattoos or remove facial piercings before coming into the office. However, research indicates that bringing a sense of authenticity to work is far more difficult and time-consuming for Black employees than white ones. A 2019 report from the Center for Talent Innovation (now Coqual) found that although Black professional workers did say that eventually they could "be themselves" at their workplaces, the process required the expenditure of enormous amounts of energy. This is largely because the parts of themselves that Black workers are concealing aren't just tattoos or tongue rings but involve what legal scholars Devon Carbado and Mitu Gulati refer to as the "identity work" of anticipating and pre-empting racial stereotypes—a process that can be exhausting.[9]

Given that Black workers often do this "identity work" of concealing their authentic selves to avoid evoking whites' racial stereotypes, Constance's desire to avoid being a curiosity or a standout because of her hair, music interests, or entertainment preferences was to be expected. She reflected that at another social event with colleagues, an old rock song from the 1980s came on, "and they were all like, 'Wow, remember this song?' And I was like, 'I don't know this song, I've never heard it.' But they were like, 'You don't know it?' All surprised. And I was like, 'Don't you realize that when we came up it was Black radio or white radio and you listened to one or the other? No, I've never heard this song!' But I didn't say that. Because again, masquerade."

I laughed a little bit as Constance recounted this story because I found it relatable. I recalled my own white fifth-grade classmates' condescension in the cafeteria one day when the topic of our parents' musical preferences came up and I told them that we did not own any Beatles records because my parents' tastes ran more toward Anita Baker, Luther Vandross, and Billy Ocean—none of whom were artists they recognized. (My mother did once share that she appreciated that the Rolling Stones were at least honest about copying Black musicians like Little Richard and Chuck Berry, but at the time it did not seem helpful for me to introduce this into the lunchroom discussion.) Feeling like a racial oddity isn't fun at any age, so I could appreciate Constance's annoyance at a similar event in her adulthood.

But her story also underscores how, for many Black workers, these cultural divides are deep and long-standing. It's not just that Constance had different musical tastes in childhood and presumably now in the present day from many of her white co-workers; it's that these tastes and preferences are built out of and reinforced by entertainment media, peer groups, sports, and other institutions such that activities, hobbies, and even music that are associated with whites are normalized and unremarkable, while cultural products and work by people of color are depicted as niche and unrepresentative. When the organizational culture of a company purports to be a race-blind meritocracy, Black workers like Constance wear the mask as a result.

How Diversity Fails

But what about university-level initiatives meant to highlight and promote issues related to diversity? After all, Constance's department is one unit housed in a much larger university community—one that, according to its website, takes these issues quite seriously and is committed to equity. Her university has several senior leaders who focus on diversity, along with multiple research centers that study various aspects of race and racism in society—key components that contribute to academia's reputation as a liberal bastion and a culturally progressive space. Even if the department's culture was race-blind, why wouldn't the university's focus on diversity help create a more welcoming environment?

Constance's offhand comment about having lunch with groups of women provides some clues. When we spoke, I found it particularly interesting that she mentioned that some of the discussions where she engaged in the masquerade occurred with a *group* of women from the engineering department. This struck me because of the well-documented gender disparities in STEM fields (science, technology, engineering, and mathematics). In processes that parallel those of men of color, women of all races in STEM fields face a multitude of challenges: repeated pressure to prove their competence; the difficulty of combating gendered stereotypes of incompetence without appearing aggressive, cold, or unfriendly; dealing with sexual harassment; and coping with exclusion and isolation.[10] Thus, I was very curious about how her department got to a point where it included more than one woman (a total of seven) but she remained the only Black faculty member.

She explained that at one point, "My dean decided they wanted to hire women, so guess what? They hired five women in one year. It was that simple. So you can make these kinds of changes—*if* you want to. They just don't want to when it comes to getting Black people. People will say, 'Oh, we need to hire women.' That's okay, maybe even admirable. But not one person will say, 'Oh, we need to hire Black people.' Ever."

Constance noted that in a previous year she was assigned to the provost's diversity committee. When I asked how that went, she described it as "a *complete* waste of time. Look, the way you solve this is not rocket science. You just invest money and hire people, but they want people to come up with it organically. It's a thing they can do to check a box so they can say they did it. If they really cared about it, they would just do it!" Her reaction wasn't because she felt these issues were unimportant, but because she lacked any faith that the university took these problems seriously. Having seen that the university continually failed to devote its ample resources to hiring more Black faculty, and pinpointing her own resulting feelings of isolation, she harbored serious doubts that these symbolic gestures would yield concrete change.

Is It Just a Numbers Game?

Constance's point here reflects something I heard from many Black workers I've interviewed. Often, there is a push to bring in more Black employees, particularly in industries and occupations where they are underrepresented. Ryan, a doctor from New Jersey who was openly critical of his hospital's diversity and inclusion policies, lamented that "doing the hard work, really changing the profession to get more Black and brown people in here—that's not sexy." The hope for many Black employees is that hiring enough other Black workers changes the nature of work.

But just hiring more people isn't enough unless the cultural, social, and relational aspects of work—the gray areas—change as well. Oftentimes bringing in more underrepresented workers leads to that outcome, but it's important to stress that changing workplaces requires more than that. Take for example the point Constance made about her dean's desire to bring in more women. Increasing the number of women faculty by five in a single year certainly is noteworthy. But unless those five women are also able to compel institutional change to eradicate sexual harassment, improve recognition of women's contributions to scientific research, and challenge a gendered culture of overwork where women are seen as less serious and committed, then just having more of a presence doesn't do much.

A similar parallel exists for Black workers. Hiring more Black chemical engineers could certainly help Constance feel less in the minority, alienated from unaware (or oblivious) colleagues, and alone. And it is worth it to try to improve the numbers for both that reason and to dismantle the systemic barriers that keep Black workers out of STEM fields. But to create real change, those scientists would also have to disrupt the pernicious networks that exclude them, alter the cultural biases against research that Black investigators may be more likely to pursue, and develop pathways to promotion.[11] In short, it's not just a question of numbers, but also of exposing and eliminating the gray areas that allow racial workplace inequalities to persist.

Race-Blind Diversity

Constance's frustrations also highlight some larger issues around the limitations of diversity and inclusion initiatives, even those that are present in organizations that have supposedly liberal, progressive cultures. When companies commit to an abstract concept of "diversity" writ large, the specific challenges facing workers of color—and facing Black workers in particular—can easily get lost. Not only that, the ease with which administrators moved to hire women (but not Black faculty) underscores the reality that white women have largely benefited from affirmative action and other programs designed to change the demographic makeup of the workforce, in many cases more so than workers of color.[12] Ironically, this has not made white women more supportive of these initiatives—as of 2014, polling from the Cooperative Congressional Election Study found that 67 percent of white women surveyed opposed affirmative action.[13]

This move away from race-based (and gender-based) affirmative action to diversity, broadly conceptualized, is a process that has been ongoing for decades. In the immediate wake of the civil rights movement, many companies responded to the new legal landscape by attempting to comply with new directives that outlawed racial discrimination. Much like their counterparts in 2020 that offered public support for the Black Lives Matter movement and disavowed systemic racism, many of these companies in the post–civil rights era were likely responding to the current political and social mood when supporting racial equity and antiracism was popular. At that time, these organizations hired managers who instituted policies focusing explicitly on reducing racial divides and attending to the concerns of Black constituents both within and outside the company.[14]

But as political support for explicit affirmative action guidelines eroded in the neoconservative movements of the late 1980s and early 1990s, managers responded by shifting their focus from measures openly intended to close racial and gender gaps to loosely defined initiatives that encouraged diversity writ large. This expansive framing meant that achieving "diversity" could allow for including workers who had a range of religious beliefs, who came from different parts of the country, or who held contrasting political opinions. It's how, as former Apple vice president for diversity and inclusion Denise Young Smith (herself a Black woman) claimed, "There can be 12 white, blue-eyed, blonde men in a room and they're going to be diverse too because they're going to bring a different life experience and life perspective to the conversation."[15] This abstract idea of diversity as "happy talk"—as conversations that occur detached from the difficult work of assessing ongoing inequalities—leaves organizations ill-equipped to acknowledge, much less address, the issues Black workers confront.[16] The end result today is that more companies state their support for diversity and inclusion without simultaneously developing organizational cultures that explicitly acknowledge how race and racial inequality may be manifest in the workplace.

This shift away from affirmative action toward diversity writ large has adverse consequences for Black workers. It means that companies are often less attuned to the specific, particular challenges that their Black employees face. For Black women workers like Constance, this is underscored by the unique bind in which she finds herself. On one hand, the dean of her college is quite comfortable drawing attention to the issues women face in engineering and moving decisively to begin addressing this by hiring more women. But for *Black* women like Constance, that solves only part of the problem. Even in the company of a relatively large number of women faculty in her department, Constance still feels isolated and ignored. She still struggles to figure out when and where she can change and when that change needs to come from the university. When the organizational culture of a workplace is one in which dealing with the complexities around racial diversity are taboo or peripheral, even diversity efforts that garner some success on other fronts (such as gender or sexual orientation) will leave out Black workers.

Dropping the Mask

These days, however, Constance says she is more comfortable in her department and that she is less committed to the masquerade that got her through her early years. Reflecting on the time that she's spent at her university, and especially comparing it with when she started, she realized that she is much more comfortable being herself now than she was before. This is not because the department has changed, but because she has. She has lowered her expectations for what's possible for her career and future at the university and has decided that she won't let that upset her. Now, she's willing to talk more about her family life with colleagues and avoid giving the impression that all she does is work. "When I started," she told me, "I wanted people to think I was working all the time. I wanted them to see I was the first car in the garage, working all the time, on weekends, at night, but I don't care about that anymore. But that's because promotions and having a family shifted my priorities. This is my priority now, so I'm not going to be here all the time."

In some ways, this shift Constance described is a rebellion against an organizational culture that emphasizes the ubiquity of work. Seeds of this change are present in many professional occupations outside of academia as well—tech, medicine, and law are all fields that place increasing expectations and demands on employees' time. This culture of overwork is frequently stressful and harmful for workers, resulting in increased health problems, and ironically, lower productivity than that produced by more measured hours.[17] These increased demands also have a gendered component, in that managers often assume that women will prioritize family demands over onerous workplace requirements, and thus they sidetrack or derail women from leadership opportunities.[18]

But Constance's decision to acknowledge and share that she has a family and a life outside of work does not extend to a willingness to be completely open and honest with her colleagues. She is slowly becoming comfortable with her colleagues knowing she doesn't spend all day in the lab, that she is not the first to arrive at work nor the last to leave. And as she realized, some of that increased comfort comes with the security of being promoted. But the organizational culture that fosters colorblindness and an unwillingness to wrestle honestly with the complexities of being a Black professional woman in this space still leave her mostly uncomfortable sharing that aspect of her life with her colleagues.

It is important not to present this as a zero-sum situation. Constance does not define her situation as one in which she bites her tongue on all racial matters. Rather, like many other Black workers, she makes calculated decisions about whether and when it makes the most sense to speak up. In her department, she ignores her colleagues' occasional remarks about diversity because she doesn't believe they are genuine, and beating this drum seems like a waste of her time.

She recalled a recent example. Her department chair approached her and requested that she talk with her department colleagues and persuade them to become more supportive of diversity and inclusion. Constance immediately refused and countered that if university leadership was really committed to bringing in more Black workers, they would have already done so. She noted that she was unusually direct in this case, stating: "In the past I would not have been that blunt. But after this summer, after George Floyd, doing some soul searching, realizing they're never going to give me anything, I just didn't care."

When Constance told me this story, I found the chair's request egregious but unsurprising. For one thing, persuading her colleagues to support racial diversity is unequivocally not Constance's job. As the one Black woman in her department—and one who routinely copes with isolation exacerbated by a colorblind culture—expecting her to persuade her colleagues of the importance of bringing in more Black professors is at best a heavy lift and at worst a tone-deaf request that is far outside the bounds of her job description. Yet I wasn't shocked that her chair would put her in that position. It's not uncommon for Black workers to find themselves in situations where they are explicitly or implicitly tasked with the equity work of taking on additional responsibilities around diversity and making the organizations where they work more palatable to communities of color.[19] The problem with that approach, however, is that not only does it saddle Black workers with additional, unrecognized labor, but it doesn't work. We'll discuss solutions to cultural challenges at the close of Part I, but in short, asking a few isolated Black workers to fix organizational culture does not create that outcome. Instead, it engenders burnout, alienation, and dissatisfaction—all of which Constance was feeling.

Constance's reaction should not be misread as giving up on, or giving in to, the pressures that accompany her work environment. Dropping the mask does not mean she is comfortable with or happy about the limitations of her workplace. She sees it now as a place where colleagues' commitment to diversity, though openly expressed, doesn't extend to the realities Black women face in chemical engineering or other STEM fields. But whereas before that realization would have compelled her to try to explain those realities to her colleagues in hopes that they would change the culture in her field, now she doesn't bother. She finds ways to make her work palatable and satisfying to her, even if this includes reducing its overall importance in her life. And she is more honest when she suspects she's getting fed platitudes about diversity and equity. At this point, she just doesn't care enough to play the game.

CHAPTER 2

Gendered Occupations and Organizational Culture

"IT'S THE EXACT SAME THING"

Kevin, a nonprofit worker, is always dressed to the nines when I see him. He looks as though he's stepped out of a page of *GQ*'s style guide. When we meet up, he's polite enough never to comment on my typical uniform of jeans and sneakers, but I'm aware that we always look like we've come from totally different places: him from a photo shoot, me from . . . my couch.

Kevin's sharp presentation probably suited him well in the various professional spaces he's had to traverse. With experience in both corporate and nonprofit sectors—starting out at a bank and then moving on to an educational 501(c)(3) organization—his career arc has taken him on an interesting and somewhat unusual path, exposing Kevin to employment dynamics and organizational cultures that might seem wildly different—at least on the surface.

The financial sector, where Kevin started out, has a reputation for being an "alpha male" space, an environment that can be alienating to women. With its aggressive, hard-charging style and disproportionate number of male workers, finance has long had an image and a culture where women are often marginalized and sidelined.[1] It's a highly competitive space where many men work long hours and bond over drinking, sports, and the allure of making money, but for a lot of reasons, this didn't appeal to Kevin. Eventually, he transitioned out of banking into working in charter schools and other nonprofit entities designed to improve access to and the quality of children's education. Here, the culture is driven by more idealistic goals—a focus on children, their education, and ways to maximize their potential—and offers an example of a more culturally feminized space.

Sociologist Joan Acker categorizes these differences as an example of "gendered organizations." Acker has argued that far from being neutral, bureaucratic institutions, organizations are gendered in their cultures, their norms, and the expectations they set forth for their workers. A bank or financial center, then, could be considered a more culturally masculinized organization if the ethos demands that workers meet long hours (with the expectation that a partner at home could tend to caregiving responsibilities), most workers are men, and policies tend to result in men having more opportunities and paths to leadership than women. Conversely, a school could be viewed as a feminized organization if the culture elevates patience, cooperation, and caring—qualities typically associated with women.[2]

Nonprofits and banks offer an interesting contrast as feminized, clan-based and masculinized, market-driven cultures, respectively. But they also offer a way to highlight how both cultures have similarities that can be difficult, even oppressive, for Black workers. One of Kevin's primary observations from working in these spaces was that even though the organizational cultures between the two varied widely, commonalities still existed that made it difficult for Black male employees like him to flourish and succeed. In other words, the racial dynamics of both "masculine" and "feminine" organizations present hardships for Black workers. For Kevin, these organizational cultures pose challenges to figuring out who his allies are—and who's going to hold him back.

Two Types of Corporate Culture

"I did not like the culture at the bank," Kevin told me bluntly. Some of the dislike had to do with the monotony and repetition of the tasks assigned to him, but Kevin also was not thrilled with the fact that he felt his job had no real meaning or significance. Focusing on making money, expanding assets, and building wealth felt empty and hollow to him. But beyond that, the culture of the bank presented challenges as well. While the bank had its own "boys' club" culture as a male-dominated space, that was not enough to create an environment where Kevin, as a Black man, felt his particular issues and concerns were taken seriously. The extensive second-guessing he found himself subject to (but that his white peers avoided), the cold stares and chilly reception he often encountered from colleagues—the alpha male culture at the bank did not acknowledge those dynamics. Instead, he said, "The norm is for everyone to be as bland as possible because the goal is to remove any conversation that might offend or cross any line."

In a predominantly white male, market-driven culture, this approach might appear safest. Avoiding incendiary topics that can cause unrest and dissent might seem a distraction from the organization's goals and the bank's focus on maximizing profits. And certainly, discussing race at work might seem as controversial as it gets. But for Black men like Kevin, the cultural emphasis on avoiding tension meant there was no room to acknowledge or address the racial biases he encountered. An organizational culture that pushed employees to avoid the offensive and just focus on market goals left no way for Kevin to resolve racial workplace issues.

Kevin expected the nonprofit world to be different. He found a job as an operations manager for a charter school in New Orleans, where his responsibilities included coordinating the school's non-academic functions—scheduling, keeping the building in order, registration, ensuring the technology was up-to-date. Here, he believed that he would encounter a culture that was more attuned to working collaboratively and that the organization's goals would involve more than making money. Not only that, Kevin "assumed feelings and thoughts matter." By this, he meant that he was under the impression that in education, a more "feminized" space, there would be a clan-based culture that emphasized learning, focusing on children and their well-being, and providing a supportive context for them to succeed.

Kevin also anticipated that at a charter school he would have more freedom and opportunities to put into place initiatives and programming that would really speak to children and help them learn, without being hamstrung by the bureaucracies that can constrain traditional public school educators. This expectation isn't unreasonable; part of how charter schools have come to be so widespread and popular is linked to perceptions (not necessarily accurate) that public schools are more stolid, less innovative, and less capable of enabling academic excellence. Kevin certainly believed that moving into the charter school space would afford him certain freedoms and opportunities to have a positive impact on Black children specifically.

Despite these lofty expectations of the type of culture he would find in a nonprofit, Kevin actually encountered something a bit different. It wasn't so much that the culture was antithetical to these values of learning, support, and achievement; rather, Kevin noted glumly that when it came to Black children and racial issues in particular, "There's a lot of performativity in these environments. There's a lot of people saying the right things. They say, 'We hear you, we want to do these things.' They put on the smiles and the happy faces. But when it gets down to it, Black teachers were just as isolated from having input, from being able to influence the situation. To a larger scale and degree, it was the same exact thing as corporate America, just with a happy face and a happy sheen put over it."

In the nonprofit world, the culture was not a bland one that encouraged conformity and market principles. Instead, the educational nonprofit where he worked highlighted the importance of working together to ensure that all children could succeed. But this culture still did not translate into supporting Black students and their families. Kevin found this most evident when tensions emerged around how these students and their families were treated. When there were conflicts, he was often dispatched to smooth things over. But Kevin soon began to realize that while Black parents sometimes were irate, his white colleagues usually overlooked their own roles in treating those parents disrespectfully and dismissively. Yet when he pointed out that Black parents weren't angry in a vacuum or without cause, school leaders punted. Rather than directly addressing the ways school personnel sometimes interacted with Black parents in a derisive fashion, leaders instead opted to protect and support teachers who had connections to donors or other influential parties. "The idea of appeasing certain people at the expense of [those] we serve—it was rampant," Kevin said. "But what happens is the family gets more frustrated and acts out more, and I have to calm that down."

Given that he had expected more support from the nonprofit culture, Kevin found himself very disillusioned. He had hoped that in an environment that emphasized collaboration and working cooperatively, his efforts to speak up about how better to include Black families would be welcomed. Instead, they went nowhere, which hurt him on a personal level. As he put it: "You are attached to those students because they're real people with real families. The idea of utilizing a corporate, disengaging strategy chafes and rubs against doing what's right for the students. So what I see a lot in education—and I believe it's true for a lot of my friends in nonprofits too—is a level of disenchantment and disillusionment. Because you thought it was going to be one thing, and it's the exact same thing you walked away from."

Different Cultures, Same Outcomes

This similarity in both masculinized, market-driven cultures and feminized, clan-based ones—specifically, the inattentiveness to issues of race and the needs that communities of color might have—really bothered Kevin. In corporate settings, he anticipated that his voice would be dismissed. He figured that the bank would not care about issues related to race, how Black customers might be mistreated in financial institutions, and he resigned himself to those expectations. After all, he didn't intend to remain at the bank in the long term, so he just focused on biding his time and getting paid. (Although this was Kevin's view, I would counter that any modern workplace in the twenty-first century has a responsibility to be a place that encourages and allows Black workers to thrive. Having a masculinized, market-driven culture doesn't mean companies should get a pass on creating an environment in which Black employees can get support and be included. In fact, we'll see a counterexample of this with Darren later on in Part I.) But finding that the feminized, clan-based culture of the nonprofit also did not really welcome attention to racial issues and how they could potentially harm students—that stung.

Some of Kevin's frustration stems from his knowledge that Black children's educational experiences are often uniquely fraught. The inaccurate stereotype that Black families and communities don't value education or academic achievement is a persistent myth that refuses to die despite ample research disproving it. For instance, rather than achievement costing them social status, Black children who excel academically are in many cases more popular than their peers.[3] In other environments, white teachers, rather than Black youths, are often the ones who perpetuate the idea that academic achievement is associated with white kids.[4] Not only that, sociologists at the University of North Carolina and Duke University found that when stigmas around academic success are present, they aren't concentrated among Black students—white students, particularly those from low-income backgrounds, face this as well.[5] Simply put, the idea that Black kids don't succeed academically because their communities don't value education is a lie. Kevin's motivation to protect and support Black children, and his conviction that these are "real people with real families," is linked to an awareness of just how taxing their experiences in these spaces can be.

Kevin's frustration here, to some degree, echoes some of the challenges men face working in women-dominated occupations like teaching. Many men in these occupations find that, as one of few men in their workplaces, co-workers expect them to take charge when situations break out that require physical strength or potential confrontation. Men in nursing, for instance, note that female colleagues are likely to call upon them to move patients or complete other tasks that literally involve heavy lifting.[6] But it's important to note that for Black men in particular, doing this physical work doesn't extend to their colleagues' respect for or engagement with their intellectual contributions.[7]

This is precisely what happened to Kevin. He wasn't unduly bothered by the request that he step in to address issues for Black students and their families. The bigger problem was that, even in a clan-based, feminized culture that supposedly encouraged collaboration and teamwork, colleagues still focused on trying to appease and support white school personnel and donors rather than trying to address the needs of Black kids and their families. He was called in to do the "heavy lifting" of dealing with angry Black parents, but in a culture that purportedly valued promoting children and their welfare, his views about how to do just that went unheard. This inattentiveness to these families' needs made more work for Kevin, and it reinforced his perception that while the culture at the school might be a more feminized culture than the masculinized one at the bank, that did not make much difference for Black children and families who were ignored either way.

Kevin's frustrations were exacerbated by the chasm between school leaders and the Black families they served and his views that white administrators generally lacked the experience, emotional intelligence, and racial sensitivity to interact meaningfully with many Black parents. Seeing white leadership with no experience or history working with Black students or their families aggravated Kevin immensely. And those leaders added insult to injury by establishing a clan culture that stressed cooperation while sidelining him when he tried to intervene on behalf of Black kids. "They don't hear my voice," he told me. "They're only performing like they care, the mistakes I see I'm not empowered to take care of, leadership comes from the outside in, and I have no real upward mobility. It becomes very demoralizing."

For Kevin, then, both organizational cultures presented difficulties determining whom to trust and who could offer support. In the market-driven, masculinized culture of the bank, he observed few allies. But it didn't bother him much, because he expected it to be a space where individuals don't really matter, and besides, he didn't intend to stay there long anyway. In contrast, though he was genuinely motivated by wanting to be part of improving educational conditions and opportunities for Black children, the clan-based, feminized culture was equally performative when it came to issues of race and equity. And as a result, there seemed to be few people in that organizational culture whom he trusted to support Black children, or to empower him to have a positive impact.

Why the Similarities in Two Distinct Cultures?

What explains why two wholly dissimilar cultures would still prove alienating and off-putting to Black workers like Kevin? The commonality that I see is that across these gendered occupations, in both these market and clan cultures, most companies fail to grapple realistically with just how to create a culture that recognizes, speaks to, and affirms Black employees. They may have a culture where they encourage everyone to get along and paper over differences, as the bank does. Or the culture may be one where leaders express a commitment to diversity, as the school did, even as they ignored voices like Kevin's. But neither involves an approach where companies are asking—and attempting to resolve—basic questions: Do Black employees feel empowered here? Is this a space where their concerns are recognized and addressed? Does the culture here reflect the realities of being Black in America? Or do we pretend those realities don't exist? Without a culture that makes these questions central and essential, Black workers are going to be marginalized, whether they are trying to fit into the family-style clan culture or the efficient market-based one.

CHAPTER 3

When Hierarchy Doesn't Help

"NICE WHITE DOCTORS"

When I first interviewed Max, he was working as an emergency room doctor in the Atlanta exurbs. With long dreadlocks, multiple tattoos, and a wiry build, he certainly doesn't look like the pictures of doctors that come up when you search Google images. He has a welcoming presence, though, and when we met in my campus office, I noticed he had a sharp eye, correctly identifying several of my art pieces as souvenirs from a recent trip to Ghana. We chatted a little bit about our love of travel and the difficulty balancing it with our busy schedules, and then he settled into one of my office chairs and began to tell me his story.

At that point, Max had been an ER doctor for about three years. He characterized emergency medicine as the type of specialty where the culture fit his personality. Reflecting back on medical school, he recalled that his experience on rotations taught him that he wanted to avoid monotony in whatever specialty he chose. "Emergency medicine is the area where you get some of everything and you never really know what is coming up," he said. "It keeps you on your toes a lot."

As an ER physician, Max might go from treating a collapsed lung to a gunshot wound to an asthma attack all within one shift. For him, this variety was appealing and, he thought, would keep him sharp. Change was a welcome constant. Additionally, Max appreciated the challenge of emergency medicine and the opportunity to diagnose and treat a variety of different health concerns as patients rotated through the ER. Being the doctor on staff meant that he was responsible for providing care that could literally save people's lives, and he took justifiable pride in that fact.

Hospital Hierarchy

Being a doctor also means that Max holds an esteemed place in the hospital structure. Health-care facilities often have a hierarchical culture, with strict rules regarding who does what, an emphasis on following established procedures, a significant amount of organizational control, and defined expectations about coordination between workers. Doctors work in teams with nurses and technicians, but doctors are firmly established as the ones with the most status and power. This hierarchical culture gives doctors significant prestige, ensures that they take responsibility for directing the course of a patient's treatment, and requires that they follow clear protocols for providing care.

Over the past several decades, however, a profit-driven, neoliberal approach has begun to infiltrate medicine and health care. This means that in conjunction with the hierarchical culture that necessitates order, structure, and procedure, health administrators also encourage a move toward a more metrics-driven approach to care.[1] This is exemplified by an emphasis on measuring patient satisfaction, moving greater numbers of patients through the system more quickly, and catering to patients with more robust insurance plans, thus capturing greater profits. As a result, while many hospitals still maintain a hierarchical culture, that structure coexists with efforts to push providers to do their work in a more profit-driven context.

It might seem difficult to imagine how an organization with a hierarchical culture could adopt market principles, especially in health care. But the two have been merging in this industry for quite some time. Legal scholar Allison Hoffman argues that "promises of market choice now pervade all corners of health care," from patients' choice of insurance carrier to doctor to pharmacy.[2] When hospitals follow suit by, for instance, trying to attract patients with insurance plans that offer more generous reimbursements, they incorporate market dynamics into an existing hierarchical culture. Doctors remain at the top, setting treatment plans and directing nurses and technicians, but they do so in a way that maximizes market outcomes, making turning a profit more central to health care.

When the Hierarchy Won't Save You

As a doctor, Max is in an enviable position at the pinnacle of the health care hierarchy, with all the perks, responsibility, and status that brings. He stressed that his position doesn't mean he can discount the nurses or others who are under him in the status hierarchy—nurses still have to respect his ability and skill as a doctor, and that trust has to be earned through performance. But the culture means that as a doctor, colleagues are supposed to take him seriously.

It might seem that a hierarchical culture would help insulate Black workers from some of the challenges they face in many workplaces. After all, the focus on rules, structure, and process should support Black employees' authority, particularly when they are in high-ranking roles. German sociologist Max Weber conceptualized this as *rational-legal authority*, which he defined as the legitimacy that accompanies a particular role or position, and this authority is firmly reinforced in organizations with hierarchical cultures.[3] For high-status Black workers like Max, it might seem that the culture supports doctors like him because it encourages nurses, patients, and other hospital personnel to respect his position and command.

Yet hierarchical cultures can still fail Black workers. This is likely to happen when organizations do not consider how Black employees' unique experiences need to be factored into established rules, structures, and procedures. And frequently, companies with a hierarchical organizational culture fail to anticipate how Black workers encounter racism and harassment. Consequently, rules are rarely in place that address how companies should respond to these issues or how workers' colleagues can support them. Even high-status Black workers aren't immune to racism in the workplace, and this can come from many sources—customers, clients, and colleagues. Although Max occupied a rarified position in his hospital structure, the reality of being a Black doctor still meant that he found his authority and credentials challenged and his abilities undermined.

Elaborating on this point, he told me: "I myself have encountered—and I know that a couple of my other Black male colleagues have too—just blatant racism from patients. That's going to happen. I've been called 'nigger' by my patients before. Things like that. I tell them all the time, it doesn't matter who you are, I take care of you. It doesn't matter whether you're a murderer, a rapist, a racist, it doesn't matter in my job. My job is not to judge you; my job is to take care of you. But yeah, I've taken care of patients with swastikas, rebel flag ties, KKK tattoos, things like that all over them, and they made it very clear, 'I'll sue you if you don't get me a white doctor.'"

These weren't isolated experiences for Max. They didn't happen every day, but dealing with irate, racist patients was an unfortunate but commonplace part of his job. And even in a hierarchical culture, an environment that uses patient satisfaction as a tangible performance metric makes it harder and harder for Max and others to know just how to react and respond to situations like this. I felt some sympathy for Max here, as I thought about the growing emphasis in academia on student evaluations and satisfaction, despite the fact that research shows student evaluations can be heavily biased against underrepresented faculty and are not an adequate measure of student learning.[4] But in environments that are moving in this direction of focusing more on market outcomes (even when the cultures are hierarchical and lend themselves to supporting those in positions of authority), the pressure to "satisfy the customers" is always there—even when "customers" are students who are upset about not getting As or patients who are dissatisfied with wait times in the ER.

For Black workers, a company's adoption of a market-based logic can have specific effects even on those who are highly placed in the organizational hierarchy. When market logics transform patients, students, or other groups into customers who must be satisfied, it's easy for bias to creep into the evaluation process and place Black professionals in a difficult position. If, even in the hierarchical culture of a hospital, the focus becomes pleasing the patient, Black doctors may not know how to respond when the patient, as customer, expresses racist sentiments. Can doctors stand up for themselves in this context, knowing that they may then see lower rankings from that patient that can affect their annual assessments? Or are they forced to accept such mistreatment quietly on the basis of the ethos that the customer is always right?

These aren't purely hypothetical questions. In a study of Black workers in the health-care industry, I found that Black emergency medicine workers noted that patients questioned their credentials fairly often and that patients using racial slurs in their presence was not unusual. In fact, Black emergency medicine doctors and nurses cited these kinds of encounters far more frequently than Black doctors and nurses in other specialty areas such as radiology or anesthesiology, though those workers had such experiences on occasion too.[5] I suspect that some of this comes from the fraught nature of emergency room visits—no one is at their best when seeking emergency care—but it also means that even in hierarchical structures, the cultural norms that emphasize process, standards, and existing rules aren't very helpful if they gloss over the harsh reality that Black employees are going to confront racism at work.

Coping in the Hierarchical Culture

Interestingly, Max's white colleagues are not completely oblivious to all of the issues that he encounters. He told me that even if patients don't raise complaints directly to him, sometimes he will hear about it secondhand from nurses or other hospital staff. Smiling slightly with an air of resignation, wry humor, and annoyance, he shared with me: "I do hear a lot from the nurses. Sometimes patients will come right out and say they want to be seen by a white doctor. And it's funny because usually at night there's one of us there for three hours. So a lot of time I'll be like, 'You can have a white doctor if you want to wait three hours to get seen by somebody,' and I've had patients say, 'That's fine, I'll go back out in the waiting room and wait until they come in at seven in the morning.' And even if patients don't come forward—which is more common—they'll say to the nurses, 'Is that the only doctor you have? You don't have any nice white doctors around here?' And the nurses will come back and tell me, 'So-and-so said this.'"

Despite these unpleasant interactions, Max believed that he had his colleagues' respect: "I know that I have the full support of the other physicians that I work with and the nurses that I work with. I know the nurses I have worked with have turned around and told patients, 'He's as good as it gets when you're going to come here. So if you want somebody else you can have them, but you're sick.

And if I were sick I wouldn't want anybody else to take care of me.' It's nice to have that happen. So I know the people that I work with know what I can do, and as a physician, you don't get any better compliment than high praise from the nurses that you work with. It's important; they know what you do and they know how good you are and they will tell you about it, so when patients don't trust me, it doesn't really bother me that much."

Max getting support from his white co-workers mattered in this culture, but it turned out that having the empathy and backing of other Black men in medicine was even more essential. Max was fortunate enough to work in a hospital setting where there were two other Black doctors, also men, on staff. That might not seem like a lot, but when you consider that in the US, as of 2021, Black men were only 2 percent of all physicians, it matters that Max was able to land at a job where he was not the only Black male doctor in his department.[6] And being with those men in a professional capacity was critical for him. It increased camaraderie, allowed him times during the workday when he could relax and be himself, and gave him exposure to peers who understood exactly what he went through at work and how challenging it can be to train for years for a profession where patients still cavalierly dismiss your education and skills because you're Black. For Max, a first-generation college graduate and the first in his family to achieve the lofty heights of becoming a doctor, his Black male colleagues were a safe space in an environment that, despite its hierarchical structure, didn't always reaffirm his position.

I expect that many Black workers in organizations with hierarchical cultures will find this familiar, especially if they are in high-ranking positions that are supposed to yield support and deference, but don't always deliver. It might be the reason why even as a fast-rising journalist and media personality, Oprah Winfrey forged and maintained her relationship with Gayle King. As two women in the same field who may have encountered disrespect and bias despite their significant accomplishments, their shared experiences might have made it that much easier to navigate the world of journalism. Even the Queen of All Media probably needs that one bestie she can exchange sideways looks with in meetings.

Overall, support from colleagues matters enormously, and for Black doctors like Max who can and do have racist encounters at work, this support is a critical component of maintaining job satisfaction. But in a hierarchical culture that has no built-in mechanism for acknowledging and addressing the reality of workplace racism, it turns out to be a bit of a mixed blessing. Max certainly benefits from having co-workers who attest to his skill and competence as a physician, and he appreciates the fact that these co-workers back him up to patients who see his race as a disqualifier. But since the organizational culture of the hospital is not one where these issues are addressed directly and openly, the support Max has is subject to his colleagues' whims. The hospital does not have a plan for what to do when Black workers face white patients' racism. The culture is not one where this specific aspect of Max's work (and that of the other Black doctors who are his colleagues) gets attention. As a result, Max still finds himself feeling distanced from his co-workers when it comes to addressing how race affects his work and relying heavily on his Black male peers for a safe space. Within a hierarchical culture where physicians should take a leadership role and command respect, Max's colleagues thus far have had his back. But there is no room to address why they need to, and no institutional guarantee that they will.

CHAPTER 4

Colorblindness and the Market

"THOSE ASSUMPTIONS WERE PROVEN CORRECT"

Much like academia, Hollywood is another space that is widely perceived to have a liberal bent. In the 2016 election, 80 percent of campaign contributions from people involved in movies, music, and television went to Democratic candidates, while in 2018, celebrities and award show attendees at the Golden Globes and Critics Choice Awards spoke in support of progressive causes such as a free press, racial and gender equity, and human rights.[1] It is hardly unique or uncommon for visible figures in entertainment to take up specific liberal causes, such as Leonardo DiCaprio's environmental activism, Alyssa Milano's outspokenness about sexual harassment, and Don Cheadle's efforts to highlight ongoing genocide in Darfur. On the whole, these platforms and causes cement Hollywood's reputation as a generally progressive place and reinforce the idea that the entertainment industry pushes a liberal agenda.

Brian, a Black film executive at a company I'll call "Worldwide Studios," disagrees with that interpretation. Thanks to the coronavirus pandemic, we didn't meet in person but first spoke on the phone one morning when he called me from his home in California. I imagined him talking to me on a headset from a house high in the hills with sprawling views of Los Angeles, an image that was rudely disrupted when our call dropped because of spotty reception in certain areas of his home. Once we managed to course correct, however, we had several spirited conversations about race and "the industry," as he referred to it.

Based on his time working as a studio executive, Brian found clear limits to the supposed liberalism of his colleagues, supervisors, and the entertainment industry as a whole. Perhaps unsurprisingly, those limits had to do with just how progressive companies and the industry at large were willing to be when it came to matters of race and racial equity. As he put it, "Everything most people think about vis-à-vis Black filmmaking, all of their assumptions about how the system is rigged against them—and the majority of Black people think that in Hollywood—all of those assumptions were proven correct."

I was curious to know what these assumptions were. As someone who interacted with the film industry only as a consumer, I was not sure what expectations Black filmmakers had of how the industry might treat or react to them. And with figures like Ava DuVernay, Ryan Coogler, Issa Rae, and Will Packer commanding increasing clout, visibility, and power in the industry, it might seem that Hollywood was well on its way to becoming the more equitable place that lived up to its ideals. Certainly this seemed like progress from my own teen and young adult years, when the only Black filmmakers I could name were Spike Lee, John Singleton, and Julie Dash. Then again, I did have to admit to a rather cursory knowledge of the film industry at large, made more evident (and somewhat embarrassingly) when Brian asked me whether I'd seen the debut film he financed and directed and I sheepishly had to admit I had not.

When it came to the assumptions Black filmmakers had about bias in the film world, Brian quickly clarified that ideals did not yet match reality. As he saw it, Black filmmakers were right to believe that the deck was stacked against them. Sometimes this was a result of ingrained, institutionalized biases; other times, studios' general operating procedures contributed to an unequal cinematic playing field. Overall, he witnessed a general practice in which studio heads preemptively decide that films with predominantly Black casts and directors will not open to wide audiences, and on the basis of these assumptions, they assign them lower production budgets and expect them to fail.

Sociologist Maryann Erigha's study of the film industry confirms Brian's observations. Using data from IMDb, the 2017 Sony Pictures hack, and online databases, Erigha found that Hollywood studios routinely undervalue films with Black casts and directors.[2] She also noted that studio heads apply different standards to films led by Black and white directors, with white directors given opportunities to develop big-budget films even after previous flops. Brian observed that this practice even extended to attaching a market value to various actors, telling me: "Actresses are put into category A, B, or C. The As are all white women with a big tent-pole movie: Emily Blunt, Brie Larson.[3] The Bs are the same women twenty years later—Nicole Kidman, Meryl Streep. The Cs—Lupita Nyong'o, Viola Davis. The As are the films the studio will fully finance. The Bs and Cs, less so."

Compounding Brian's frustration with these racial dynamics was the fact that most of his colleagues seemed to take them for granted and to find them largely unremarkable. "This never sees the light of day. Those types of metrics aren't released to the world," he said. "Once, I brought it up. I was maybe drinking some whiskey and sent an email where I addressed the market racism of the list. No one mentioned anything about it. It was just like, the sky is blue. I wrote an email to the whole team. Everyone received it. And a bunch of people responded to me in private, like, 'Yeah man, this is really fucked up. I can't believe this sort of thing happens.' But none of those people replied 'all.' No one was like, 'We have to do something about this right now.'"

For Brian, the literal devaluing of Black actresses reinforced his view that the culture of the entertainment industry at large was only superficially committed to racial progress and advancement. It created a tension for him that resurfaced regularly in our conversations and became an ongoing theme of his work. On one hand, public statements and commitments in the film industry and the company where Brian worked unequivocally supported racial diversity and equity. But behind the scenes, entrenched practices made it much harder for this to become a reality. Thus Brian found himself constantly weighing the question: Is the commitment to change real or just for show?

The disparities in how Black actresses are paid certainly tipped the scale in the "just for show" direction. On a larger scale, too, the inequities Brian highlighted reflect the ways racial and gender biases affect Black women and contribute to lower earnings over the course of their lifetimes. On average, Black women are paid 20 percent less than their white women counterparts, and these disparities persist even when they are employed in the same occupations.[4] Even Black women with graduate degrees experience a wage gap, with the National Women's Law Center reporting that Black women with a master's degree earn, on average, less than $5,000 more than white men with associate's degrees.[5] These numbers indicate that over the course of their careers, Black women lose nearly a million dollars in earnings, contributing significantly to widespread wealth inequality and economic insecurity.

Hiding Racial Biases Behind Market Culture

The focus on metrics and outputs suggests that the studio where Brian worked employs a market-based corporate culture. When it comes to the public statements around corporate culture, he asserted that leadership touted certain ideals: "It's a company that values innovation, values loyalty, values taking initiative. So it claims. But the heads of leadership in the studio put values online that are not espoused." As evidenced by the fact that Black actresses were literally priced lower for the studio, thus limiting the types of starring vehicles to which they could be attached (and in turn suppressing their profiles and preventing them from commanding higher salaries), the studio placed a very heavy premium on market outputs and financial returns on its investments. This left Brian in a position where he believed that the studio did not practice what it preached. This gray area of corporate culture made it harder for him to assess whether the change and racial progress he sought could really happen.

Brian shared other examples of how market-based cultures could be manipulated to limit opportunities for Black workers: "There was a project that came in based on a celebrated Black political memoir by a director whose movie had just won at Sundance. This would be her next project. It had two up-and-coming movie stars attached to it already. It seems to me like there's some value in this project, some heat behind it. But I was shocked by how it was perceived internally, as being less than desirable from the moment we encountered it, let alone after we received the materials. One executive did not even want to take the meeting. She'd seen the filmmaker's movie at Sundance and found it wanting.

"The executive who ultimately took the meeting had shown a lack of interest in what I thought were particularly salient Black-centered projects by celebrated Black writers before. For example, this is the person who passed on *Moonlight* when it was a project we could have made. Anyway, he took the meeting with this film-maker with me, and then the following day suggested to our boss that we pass on the project but admitted in that email that he had not read the screenplay nor seen the Sundance-winning film! Then he used the psychology that one normally uses in Hollywood to create the 'fear of missing out' in one's boss. Usually that logic is, there are other parties that are bidding on it, so if you don't trust your taste, trust others'. He used that to sell *not* bidding: 'In a crowded biopic field, this would be a tough one to win; bidding on it would drive up the price, so it would be overvalued.' This is a logic he never uses for projects that involve white people."

Brian's experiences highlight one of the additional challenges for market-based organizational cultures. The focus on outputs in the form of financial returns, and the seemingly neutral hand of the market, can convince workers and managers that their actions simply reflect objective principles and their desire to maximize profits for the company. But as Brian's example shows, markets are hardly race-neutral. Instead, they reflect racial (and gendered) logics that devalue the labor, outputs, and productivity of Black workers.

In the entertainment industry, this can mean studios fail to invest sufficiently in films by Black directors and filmmakers that ultimately go on to exceed expectations. But more often, as Brian observed, it means that market-based cultures place lower value on products and commodities attached to Black workers and consumers, thus providing a colorblind rationale for decisions that perpetuate racial inequalities. In her study of racial dynamics in the film industry, Maryann Erigha finds much the same, arguing that Hollywood insiders "reproduce racial hierarchies but blame culture and economics for their disproportionate assignment of rewards and disadvantages along racial lines."[6] This in turn made it difficult for Brian to trust that his company was really serious about changing and increased his suspicion that it was providing just lip service to the idea of diversity.

The market-based rationale for devaluing Black content is hardly limited to entertainment. Other predominantly white industries that focus on sales and metrics often create outcomes where, under the guise of supporting "what sells," work by Black creators is underrated. In 2020, the #PublishingPaidMe viral campaign highlighted the disparity between how Black and white authors are compensated for book advances, marketing, and publicity.[7] The campaign revealed that publishing executives, who are predominantly white, routinely lowballed and devoted fewer resources to Black authors, even if they had a proven track record of success. Black author Jesmyn Ward noted that after winning her first National Book Award for Fiction (she now has two), she had to fight for a $100,000 advance for her following book. In contrast, creative writing professor Mandy Len Catron described herself as a "totally unknown white woman with one viral article" who received a $400,000 advance for a first book.[8] Because white publishing executives believe that books by, for, and about Blacks will not sell, they underpay Black authors, devote fewer resources to promoting their works, and invest less time in pushing them for awards. Without that support, these works may underperform, creating a self-fulfilling prophecy—the lack of investment results in lackluster sales, which then justifies the argument that these books won't succeed on the market.

The biggest irony is that, as with the entertainment industry, these low expectations are grounded in stereotypes that belie reality. Executives justify passing on content developed by Black creators because of the perception that these works will not sell or there is no market for them, but the data indicate otherwise. According to 2014 data from the Pew Research Center, college-educated Black women read more than any other demographic.[9] Book clubs featuring content by and about Black authors are not only thriving and becoming more widespread, but they also provide readers with resources and information for supporting Black-owned businesses.[10] Black readers, like Black filmgoers, are a wide swath of the population. They're just invisible to many white executives, who don't want or know how to create content for them, and justify this with race-neutral market dynamics.

The Diversity Officer Backfire

Interestingly, Brian noted later in our interview that he was not the only hire the studio made in an attempt to address issues of racial diversity. Around the time he was hired, Worldwide Studios also brought in a diversity officer who was tasked with addressing internal issues of diversity and inclusion and improving the studio's lackluster reputation around these issues.

As I've mentioned, diversity management is a booming business. The industry alone is a multibillion dollar one, and many companies have now moved to ensure that they have someone in these roles. The positions have evolved significantly since they first developed as affirmative action managers in the 1980s, and in many cases they now provide hefty compensation and a reporting structure directly to the CEO.[11] Yet these managers can also find that they have limited efficacy in their roles, either from personal unwillingness to address systemic racial and gender discrimination in the companies where they work or from organizational constraints on their ability to make meaningful changes.[12]

It might seem that making this hire would help reassure Brian that Worldwide Studios was serious about its commitment to racial equity. In fact, it was quite the opposite. From Brian's viewpoint, hiring a diversity officer helped the studio appear as though it was making progress but did not really do much to advance racial equity. "As #OscarsSoWhite heated up, Worldwide Studios hired a DEI person who was worthless and actually stymied my attempts to focus on Black films," he asserted. "She tried to create a culture where these issues were a constant battle instead of empowering as many Black artists and stories as possible." He went on to describe a particular case in which he wanted to produce a film based on one of the few books written by an enslaved Black woman. To his frustration, the DEI manager opposed the film on the basis of the belief that the biracial, white-presenting director who was attached to the project would open the studio up to criticism. Brian found this frustrating given that according to historical sources, the author of the book in question, like the director, was also a light-skinned Black woman with white ancestry. Yet rather than taking a chance on the movie, the DEI manager, Brian believed, took a stance that helped give the studio grounds to reject the film. "In the mind of the DEI person, this was a risk and that woman didn't have the lived experience to tell that story," Brian said. He paused for emphasis, and then continued: "*No living person* has the lived experience to tell that story! But that was seen as a legitimate complaint. And that sort of thing was common."

Brian adjusted his headset, then continued: "I think a class thing influenced that. There's a sort of PMC outlook—the professional-managerial class. So for example, she was excited to have the program Worldwide Studios has with historically Black colleges and universities. She spoke to those students. But when it came to making movies with working-class Black filmmakers, or those that have subversive or unusual themes, she was unwilling to help. So I feel like there's a class dynamic to that. It's like her work was to support her own place in the hierarchy as an arbiter of acceptable representations of Black identity or the Black elite. And in general, I think there's a lot of that kind of thinking in Hollywood, and a lot of the overlap between those two end up in the Black leadership class. Those divisions get papered over, especially in the eyes of white Hollywood that sees us as a monolith."

Class Conflict in the Black Community

The intraracial, class-based tensions Brian references here have a long history. As far back as the postslavery era, class distinctions emerged as a very small number of Blacks were able to make (curtailed) inroads into white-collar occupations, while most others toiled in the low-wage, unskilled jobs that allowed them to eke out a hardscrabble existence. As writer Lawrence Otis Graham detailed in his study of the Black elite, these class cleavages continued throughout generations, shaping choices about the "right" community organizations, fraternities and sororities, colleges, and even choice of spouses and how entry into these spaces maintained one's status among the Black upper class.[13] Concurrently, as a few

Blacks moved into positions of relative prestige and status, so too emerged the narrative of "respectability politics," which encouraged embracing behaviors and viewpoints that advocates hoped would generate a certain level of decency from white counterparts. Thus the narrative Brian described of this gatekeeping role is not without precedent; rather, it is a dynamic that has been present in Black communities for centuries.

In the creative community in which Brian is employed, however, the gatekeeping takes on a particular function. In his view, this diversity officer seemed willing to advocate for and to support only projects that presented Black people in a certain fashion. Yet there is a broader context here as well. As Brian also noted, Hollywood (and other creative fields such as literature and fashion) has a long history of offering narrowly stereotyped, one-dimensional representations of Black people as criminal, highly sexualized, violent, and/or token sidekicks.[14] Indeed, it is this very tendency that Brian wanted to challenge and disrupt in his own projects. It may be that the diversity officer's caution came from a desire to avoid taking the risk of reproducing these same stereotypes.

Regardless, the tensions Brian observed around respectability and representation had implications for his work environment. Without an organizational culture fully attuned and committed to navigating complicated racial politics, it can become all too easy for certain perspectives to slip through the cracks. Even with a diversity officer present and tasked with managing the studio's racial issues, these challenges persisted, leaving Brian feeling creatively stifled and unable to meet his goals of developing and curating diverse presentations of Black life. When these representations also have to meet the demands of the studio's market-driven culture, this difficulty becomes even more pronounced.

Brian's narrative indicates how, in a market-based, colorblind culture, some efforts to advance racial equity can actually backfire. His account also reveals an organizational culture that conforms to the ideals of abstract liberalism, where there is broad support for the idea of more diversity without the cultural shifts necessary to make this outcome a reality. As Brian noted, Worldwide Studios did attempt to make progress on issues of race and diversity by hiring a diversity officer; however, without an organizational culture that was attuned to the nuances and dynamics of racial matters, this diversity officer may have felt pressed to ensure that the studio did not perpetuate the long history of racial stereotyping in film. Additionally, depending on the organization in question, diversity managers can find themselves in the difficult position of promoting these issues, but not so much so that they make CEOs or boards uncomfortable with their advocacy.

This is not to suggest that diversity management does not work; on the contrary, having managers who can take the lead on this critical work is essential, as we will cover at the conclusion Part I.[15] But Brian's experience does suggest that when diversity officers face limitations changing the broader culture around race and racism in the workplace, that culture can remain one that constrains rather than empowers Black employees. And such constraints can make it harder for Black workers like Brian to know whether organizational commitment is real or just another performance.

CHAPTER 5

Layers and Limitations

"A LOT OF RED TAPE"

Thus far, the narratives from various workers show that clan-based and market-driven cultures can be unwelcoming spaces for Black employees, particularly if they are also suffused with colorblind norms and values. The clan culture in Constance's chemical engineering department valued collaboration and attempted to elevate diversity, but without paying explicit attention to race, her colleagues were largely oblivious to the difficulties she encountered forming the necessary relationships with and ties to others in the field. Kevin's experiences in both the clan- and market-based cultures of education and finance, respectively, showed how both "masculine" and "feminine" organizational cultures can establish barriers for Black men, making it difficult for them to determine whom to trust. The race-blind, increasingly market-driven hierarchy culture at Max's hospital meant that the organization was not equipped to address racist challenges to his authority, making support from other Black men all the more essential. Similarly, the colorblind market culture in the film studio limited the efficacy of diversity managers, leaving workers like Brian questioning the company's commitment to its values.

Amalia has had a different experience with organizational culture. COVID precautions also precluded us from talking in person, so we spoke by phone so that I could learn about her work life. But as she is a fairly prominent journalist, I already knew who she was and was familiar with some of her work for various news outlets. During our call, I resisted the strong urge to pump her for off-the-record information about some of the more well-known figures she has interviewed. ("What's Rihanna *really* like?") Instead, we settled in for conversations about the organizational culture in some of the nation's most well-known, if not universally most-trusted, news outlets. Her account gives us a window into the experience of someone who has clearly "made it" in her profession. But it also encourages us to ask—at what cost?

When Hierarchy Is a Hindrance

Like Max, Amalia also worked in an organization with a hierarchical culture. Yet her experiences in journalism provide an interesting complement to Max's work in hospital settings. As we know, hierarchical cultures are highly structured with a great deal of emphasis on process, regulations, and the need to follow existing guidelines. These strict guidelines can be beneficial to workers who appreciate the predictability, stability, and clearly defined expectations this kind of culture produces. But they can also make organizations with this culture feel inflexible and render it difficult for workers to introduce and develop new, innovative ideas.

Amalia immediately defined the media outlets where she'd worked as examples of hierarchical work cultures. She described them as "very bureaucratic" spaces with layers upon layers of hierarchy, with each level requiring approval and sign-off when she wanted to pitch new stories. This meant that if Amalia wanted to propose a story, it had to get approval from senior editors, producers, and a coterie of other colleagues in various offices before it could even get off the ground. Other journalists faced this same process, so that every story went through multiple rounds of review before getting the green light.

This approach might seem pretty straightforward. After all, if everyone goes through this process, then the rules are consistent, standard, and seemingly equitable. But as we saw with Max, rules that don't take racial differences into consideration can end up perpetuating them. In Max's case, the hierarchical culture at the hospital should have endowed him with authority, status, and prestige, but failure to account for race meant that the hospital was unprepared to deal with the consequences he faced when patients challenged and undermined his position as a doctor. Consistency doesn't always produce equal outcomes if workers are coming from unequal starting points.

Amalia experienced this phenomenon in a different way. For her, the emphasis on hierarchy and structure meant that her efforts to introduce some racial diversity into the stories, pitches, and highlights on her journalistic beat became increasingly challenging. "You go through a lot of hoops to get things done," she told me. "That's just what it is because there are a lot of different people making decisions at any step of the way. With writing, you have yourself and one, maybe two editors on one piece. But with radio or podcasters, there's producers, editors, assistant producers—all these other things to consider. So if you're trying to get things done, create something new, and not something that has an established base, there's a lot of red tape."

Concretely, this meant that if Amalia wanted to pitch a story about racial bias or adverse conditions affecting Black communities, there were more opportunities for skittish higher-ups to turn down or stymie the project. Even though she knew these stories had journalistic merit and could highlight underreported dynamics of race and inequality, the hierarchical culture of most of her newsrooms meant that producers, editors, or their deputies could easily derail these projects if they felt uncomfortable with them or doubted their merits. The hierarchical structure applied to all, but for Black journalists like Amalia, it meant her colleagues had more opportunities to marginalize and sideline narratives that dealt with issues of race.

Sometimes this was a result of a rather contradictory culture in the newsroom. On one hand, Amalia worked in an environment that embraced some aspects of color consciousness. In most of the organizations where she had worked, her colleagues at least acknowledged that race mattered and that racism was an issue plaguing society. Unlike Constance, who described an organizational culture in which her fellow scientists were largely oblivious to and unwilling to acknowledge the realities of racial bias, in Amalia's experience her colleagues understood that this bias existed and were willing to discuss it (to a degree). This was especially the case during and after the height of the Black Lives Matter movement. She noted wryly, "People are talking about racial issues, especially coming off 'the summer of our discontent' in 2020. All the bosses are talking about it."

This outcome itself is a bit anomalous. Many workplaces actively discourage explicit discussions of race and racial issues at work, and as a result, employees largely feel uncomfortable having these conversations in the office. (Recall that this was Kevin's experience when working at the bank.) According to a 2020 survey from the Society for Human Resource Management, nearly 40 percent of Black and white workers experience some discomfort discussing racial matters at work. Black employees are also more likely than their white counterparts to believe these types of conversations are frowned upon in their workplaces.[1] So Amalia feeling that her company was one where discussions of race and racism were allowed differentiates her from many other Black workers. This difference may be a function of the particular media outlet where she worked, in which staffers covered a variety of topics including race and inequality.

But competing challenges in the newsroom meant that these

conversations went only so far. Amalia also observed that although her colleagues could and did acknowledge racial differences, pressure to present a picture of "journalistic objectivity" complicated matters further. Trying to ensure that events were depicted in an unbiased fashion led to an abundance of caution from editors and producers when it came to topics that might be construed as controversial in some quarters. For instance, Amalia recounted a story of a colleague who wanted to write about how the decision to overturn *Roe v. Wade* would disproportionately impact low-income Black women. She noted: "This [story] was going to be from a critical lens. The message from [the politics desk] is that they shouldn't touch it. I've seen and experienced certain things where just because of the moment, they feel the iron is too hot, and they want to be more cautious."

In this case, management was afraid that running a story framed in this way might make the outlet appear partisan rather than objective. Yet the Supreme Court decision to overturn *Roe v. Wade* will particularly affect low-income Black women, who have less access to prenatal care and health insurance and are significantly more likely to die in childbirth. Thus the implications of the decision are staggering for Black women and have major consequences for increasing racial health disparities, worsening maternal mortality, and exacerbating economic inequality.[2] These are simply facts, but they are facts that seemed too controversial for even a relatively color-conscious news organization to acknowledge, for fear that backlash would ensue. Amalia's example reminded me of Stephen Colbert's satirical observation that "reality has a well-known liberal bias."

Amalia's descriptions underscore that for many organizations, their attempts to remain neutral or balanced all too often favor the status quo, and that status quo is one that marginalizes Black workers. Even when colleagues in the newsroom acknowledge that racial inequality is a systemic problem, and a major social movement forces them to discuss openly what this means for their profession, a hierarchical structure that fails to consider how Black workers are differently situated will ultimately reproduce these existing inequalities.

Under Assault

A hierarchical culture also left newsrooms unable to address and resolve the other major issue Amalia encountered in her profession: visibility. As a journalist, her job obviously involves gathering information and breaking the news to the public. When she's working collaboratively on podcasts, news stories, or other media that require sign-off from multiple parties in the newsroom, she is accustomed to the limitations that this red tape and bureaucracy can bring. But in other cases, her work involves commentary and critical opinion writing, which offers more independence and autonomy. For those pieces, Amalia is empowered to highlight and focus on racial issues. The newsroom where she works has not asked her to tone down her coverage of these topics—quite the opposite. As a result, Amalia has taken advantage of that position to do her job well: she interviews major figures and often writes about race in health care, culture, the economy, and politics.

But success has come at a harsh cost. In particular, Amalia noted that "being a Black woman in journalism—that impacts how outsiders, readers, listeners react to me. And being a Black woman on the internet is not fun." She was aware that part of what comes with a public-facing position is opening herself up to public response. But the vitriol, rage, and venom that accompanied that response—often with explicitly racist and sexist overtones—could and did take a toll. "There's definitely still a difference in being a Black woman compared to other colleagues," she told me. "It's different when the public can judge your work. It's not just your bosses; it's 'Grandma' in Bumblefuck, Iowa. And sometimes they'll be really vicious."

To be clear, Amalia wasn't just talking about receiving commentary that was disagreeable or insulting. She was referring here to hate mail, texts on her personal cell phone, and other messages where random strangers bombarded her with racial slurs, death threats, rape threats, and myriad forms of harassment. Not one or two messages either, but an onslaught of racist and sexist abuse simply for doing her job. I opened this book with the story of my own much smaller scale experience with this, so I sympathized with Amalia's reaction.

Sociologist Tressie McMillan Cottom has argued that for Black women in public spaces, the responses levied at them often critique their credentials and lambast their expert status. Writing in 2015, McMillan Cottom observed that she had not personally gotten rape threats but instead primarily received messages from senders whose "source of ire is overwhelmingly with the institutional legitimacy that constructs me as 'intellectual' or 'expert.'"[3] Such writers are frequently abusive as well: "Really angry commenters want to have me fired, sanctioned by the university, and my brains violently excised from my body."[4] Thus, there is some support for Amalia's belief that the types and level of vitriol that Black women receive for engaging with general audiences reflect a broader cultural perception that they are inauthentic intellectuals who have no right to offer commentary or influence public opinion.

The organization where Amalia works isn't completely unaware of these dynamics. As the political climate has grown more polarized, public figures have become subject to increasingly ugly, sometimes dangerous backlash. In some cases, this applies even to private citizens who through no fault of their own find their contact information leaked online and are doxed by internet mobs. After Joe Biden's 2020 defeat of Donald Trump, some election workers found themselves in this unenviable position, particularly if they worked in Georgia, Arizona, or other states where the results were close.[5] Thus news outlets understand that their journalists are reporting to audiences who are vocal and, unfortunately, sometimes violent.

The outlet where Amalia works has measures set up to help journalists cope with this reality. "They have set up ties to the companies that erase all your info from the internet," she told me, "so they are constantly checking for that to make sure your personal information isn't there. That's important because people *will* try and find you." This is a step toward ensuring reporters' personal safety, especially for ones like Amalia who write and talk about racial issues. And she noted that depending on the article and journalist in question, the company would step in and offer support, particularly if the author's facts were called into question or disputed.

Scrubbing personal information from the internet and asserting that reporters' facts are accurate and the newsroom stands behind them are important steps to take, and in Amalia's view, these are applied broadly to the journalists at her organization. The hierarchical culture means that everyone has this basic level of protection, because the rules dictate as such. But without acknowledgment of the fact that Black women journalists face a level of harassment that may not be quite as pronounced for other colleagues, this broad application of rules falls a bit short. This additional burden is not factored into Amalia's performance evaluation. Her benefits package is not structured to address the toll issues like this can take on mental health. Instead, successful star journalists like Amalia find themselves able to reach lofty heights, but at the cost of doing the extra work of dealing with racist hate.

CHAPTER 6

The Case of Gig Work

"I'VE BEEN TREATED FAIRLY"

Kevin, Amalia, Brian, and Constance show how various organizational cultures can be inhospitable for Black workers. As gray areas of work, these organizational cultures drive the norms, values, and everyday expectations that shape how employees interact, what they say, what they do, and how they behave. Yet whether these cultures are clan-based, hierarchical, or market-based, the common theme that spans them all is the unwillingness of organizations to confront the reality of racism overtly and directly. This shared approach makes it very difficult for Black workers in various occupations and from different backgrounds to succeed, thrive, and offer their best in these environments.

But not all workers find these cultures stifling or oppressive. In fact, some workers assert that the organizational culture has no direct impact on their ability to do their jobs effectively. This is particularly true for Black workers who operate as independent contractors rather than direct employees, an arrangement that is becoming increasingly common in the current economy.[1] Although the organization with which they contract still has a particular culture—and that culture may well be one that eschews an explicit focus on race—some Black workers do not view this as a deal breaker. The culture exists, but they do not see any relevance to or effect on their daily responsibilities.

Alex is a case in point. Despite being born and raised in New York City, she has a slow, sleepy cadence that I associate more with people I knew growing up in the South. However, I know better than to tell New Yorkers they sound like they're from any place other than New York, so I kept my thoughts to myself and listened carefully as she told me about her experiences navigating various work environments and situations.

Alex turned to work in the gig economy after being laid off from a full-time job. She found gig work basically satisfactory. It allowed her to make ends meet, but she never intended it to be a permanent or long-term position. But while waiting to resume full-time work, she signed up to deliver food through Uber Eats and Postmates. In doing so, she joined the ranks of the 20 percent of Black workers who have worked in the gig economy.[2]

Though Alex signed up to work with both platforms, she didn't identify any real variation in the culture of how they operated. In fact, when I asked her whether she observed any differences in the culture of both places, she seemed a bit confused, suggesting that to her, the answer seemed obvious. "There's no real difference between the two," she told me. "They're pretty much the same. You just get the food and you deliver it." With the basics of the work being pretty straightforward, any cultural differences between the two companies seemed less apparent.

Yet both Uber Eats and Postmates could be considered examples of adhocracy cultures. These organizations exemplify the "move fast and break things" ethos that characterizes many of the start-ups in Silicon Valley. Indeed, by relying on independent contractors like Alex who deliver food to users, these companies have revolutionized previous food delivery service models that relied on individual restaurants to provide what could be a costly and time-consuming service. On these platforms, this work is outsourced to the third-party company that can partner with a variety of different restaurants, giving both consumers and restaurateurs more options for reaching a broader market.

From her position as a driver, Alex seemed satisfied, if rather indifferent, to the company cultures of both organizations. As she noted, some of this was likely due to the fact that the nature of gig work necessarily means some autonomy and distance from the company with whom she is an independent contractor. Unlike Constance, Alex does not work in an environment where the clan culture is belied by her colleagues' obliviousness to the racism she faces. In contrast to Max, there is no race-blind hierarchical culture that makes social support from others in a similar position a necessity. It's pretty straightforward—"You just get the food and you deliver it."

Is Gig Work a Solution to Culture Challenges?

Does this suggest that gig economy jobs, with their link to companies that have an adhocracy organizational culture, are ones where workers are unaffected by racial and gender bias? Can gig work offer a respite from the issues that plague Black workers in more traditional employment models? Alex seems to think so, on the basis of her experience. She is one of the few Black workers I've interviewed who told me that she'd never had the sense that racism or sexism affected her on the job. When I asked about this, Alex told me: "I would say I've been treated fairly. One time a woman tipped me at the door and then gave me a high rating and tipped me again. That was nice and doesn't usually happen. That was probably the best experience I've had with Uber Eats."

I also queried Alex about whether she was satisfied with these gig companies' pay scales and arrangements. She replied affirmatively: "I think the way you are paid is fair for the most part. You actually get paid more with DoorDash than Uber Eats because more people use DoorDash. But they have a system where if they have so many people using DoorDash in a certain area, they won't let you on the platform." This was not a deterrent for Alex, however. She continued: "So I haven't been able to get on to DoorDash even though it would be more money. I might try again at some point." For her, the pay structure seems straightforward enough that even though the algorithms prevent her from accessing a platform that could yield higher returns, she's still content with how she is making her money.

Alex's satisfaction with these platforms is notable considering the pervasiveness of racial and gender disparities in many workplaces in the service sector. The service industries constitute the largest sector of the US economy and include jobs ranging from nursing to consulting to providing manicures.[3] But racial divides exist in this sector as well, with Black workers underrepresented in high-status, high-paying service jobs. For instance, they are only 5 percent of lawyers, but 17 percent of maids and housekeepers, 17 percent of fast-food and counter workers, and 31 percent of transit workers.[4] Disparities also exist within industries in the service sector. In health care, for instance, Blacks are 5 percent of medical doctors, 10 percent of registered nurses, 18 percent of support technicians, and 28 percent of home health-care workers.[5] So although Alex is doing contract work in an industry that, overall, reflects significant racial and gender inequalities, she does not directly observe any racial or gender discrimination in her everyday work routines.

Wage Gaps and Fair Pay in the Gig Economy

Alex also works in a field that, in her view, provides equitable and fair pay to workers across racial and gender groups. This too is important, because racial and gendered wage disparities are rampant across occupations and industries and are particularly acute for Black women. The oft-cited statistic that women earn 79 cents for every dollar men make masks the fact that for Black women, this number is closer to 65 cents, and for Latinas, it is 55 cents.[6] Doubters often dismiss these statistics by suggesting they result from women and men pursuing different career paths or having varied amounts of educational attainment, but pay gaps exist even when those factors are held constant.[7] Additionally, wage disparities persist when Black and white workers hold the same educational levels, have the same number of years of work experience, and are employed in the same positions. In fact, for well-educated Black workers, these racial wage disparities actually increase so that gaining more years of schooling does not necessarily close these pay gaps.[8]

Working in the gig economy, Alex believes she sidesteps these issues. There are no colleagues against whom she can be measured and treated differently, so she does not identify racial or gender discrimination in her work life. In the aggregate, however, the data about gig work present a more complicated picture. For one thing, evaluations of service providers rest on ratings, which can be influenced by users' racial biases.[9] Additionally, gig workers often rely heavily on tips, which also can be subjectively assessed in ways that reflect prejudices and lead to racially unequal outcomes.[10]

Because Alex does not have to interact with any other drivers, she has no way of knowing whether her earnings are in fact the same as theirs. This type of gig work actually puts Alex in a position where, relative to some of the other workers featured in this book, she expresses more satisfaction with and acceptance of the work she is doing. It is not work to which she is especially attached, but she is far less bothered than Constance, Brian, Amalia, and Kevin by the organizational culture because it feels distant from her daily work routine.

What is it about gig work that makes organizational culture seem irrelevant? We know that many platforms for gig work are the product of organizations that have an adhocracy culture of challenging norms, thinking creatively, and upsetting the applecart. Part of encouraging unorthodox approaches means that these companies are not bound by long-standing ideas about employment. Perhaps as a result, companies like Airbnb, Uber, Instacart, and others rely on a model of independent contractors rather than the traditional employer-employee relationships. And there are some merits to this business model for certain workers, as we'll see later in this book.

In particular, the independence that gig work offers may make it easier for Black workers to avoid some of the more direct racist interactions that can occur in traditional work environments. Greater autonomy may correlate with fewer reports of racial workplace discrimination—that is, Black workers in jobs with less oversight, greater independence, and more opportunities to work alone are less likely to report that they experience routine racial prejudice and bias at work, factors that also explain the appeal of remote work for many Black employees.[11] In companies with an adhocracy culture that encourages thinking outside the box, the push toward newer, different business models may reduce interpersonal interactions that can be tense and uncomfortable for Black workers.

But just because workers like Alex are able to avoid direct expressions of racism from users doesn't mean that these biases have disappeared. Even when workers don't directly interact with supervisors or other workers, racial differences remain baked into how these platforms operate and the way they are used. In 2021, researchers from George Washington University discovered that Uber algorithms used to calculate fare pricing in Chicago set rates higher when passengers were going to or coming from neighborhoods with high populations of residents of color.[12] Another study from the National Bureau of Economic Research shows that passengers with names that seem to indicate they are Black men face longer wait times and are more likely to have rides canceled.[13] Studies also show substantial racial discrimination on Airbnb in both the United States and Europe, with Black renters more likely to be denied accommodations, Black hosts less likely to earn the same income for their listings (even after controlling for quality), and homes in predominantly Black neighborhoods netting lower rates.[14] Thus, even when contractors like Alex don't realize it, racism and discrimination persist for those using these platforms. The gig economy has changed how we work, but it hasn't erased or even minimized racial workplace discrimination—just digitized it.

Overall, Alex's accounts of her work give an example of a case where organizational culture does not seem to present implicit challenges or difficulties. This is not because these platforms are created in environments that lack a culture—Silicon Valley firms are notoriously characterized by an ethos that advocates doing things differently and challenging established norms. They are also not known for being race-conscious places. Tech firms have disappointingly low numbers of workers of color and can be disturbingly hostile spaces for Black, Latinx, and Asian American workers, particularly those who are born and/or educated outside of the United States.[15] But the contractors who use these platforms don't have to deal with these issues directly.

Yet other issues remain present. Despite the culture of unorthodoxy and thinking outside the box that animates many tech companies, they still remain unable to anticipate and offset the ways their platforms perpetuate racial discrimination. Though these platforms are reshaping our society and attracting a growing number of contractors, they are doing so in ways that still perpetuate racism and discrimination as bias gets embedded into algorithms. These companies may be characterized by an adhocracy culture that encourages challenging norms, but this innovative thinking does not seem to extend to disrupting racial inequality. For workers like Alex, then, the question of whether the gig economy allows her to avoid workplace racism and sexism becomes a bit more complicated than she reported.

CHAPTER 7

Leveraging Cultural Capital

"I KNOW HOW TO GET ALONG"

Alex was not the only Black worker I spoke with who described being unaffected by organizational climate. Darren, a vice president with a major financial company, made a similar statement. Tall with a trim build and a quick smile, Darren had recently moved into this role after nearly a decade with another financial institution. When we finally managed to connect for a Zoom interview after he requested multiple reschedules, I was reminded that for many people very high up on the corporate ladder, it often feels like their work never stops.

Despite the pace, Darren described fitting comfortably into the organizational culture at his current job. He does so generally by being himself—driven and hardworking, yet amiable and easy to be around. He tries to be the kind of person his colleagues enjoy having as a co-worker. As he told me: "It isn't hard to be personable and approachable at work. It's something that I've tried to do and had some success in."

Although Darren presents this as a pretty straightforward process, it's likely that some of his ability to be a person colleagues like and appreciate working with comes from his background. He grew up in an upper-middle-class environment in the Northeast and then attended an elite private university on the West Coast. Consequently, much of Darren's formative years involved interacting with and becoming comfortable in the kind of circles in which he now finds himself. He has been able to build *cultural capital*—a familiarity with various social aspects that enable one to fit in in a particular environment.[1] In Darren's case, amassing cultural capital that allows him to be friendly and congenial with his colleagues means a certain level of worldliness—a preference for upscale restaurants, an ability to play golf, and political leanings that don't veer too far into the extreme.

Consequently, Darren believes that the current company where he is employed is a natural match for his personality. When we talked, he had been at the job only for a few months, but in that time, the culture had struck him as one in which the emphasis is on collaborative work designed to achieve larger corporate goals. When I asked Darren what he made of the organizational culture thus far, he told me: "The people have been great. I've had opportunities to meet with people at the senior leadership level, in finance. I've had opportunities to fit in and felt very welcomed. The culture is one where people want to win and work together, so there are lots of good aspects."

Given that Darren joined his current company in an extremely high-ranking role, it may be somewhat intuitive that he has been welcomed and treated well. He acknowledged this in our interview, stating: "This job is just a little different because you have more responsibility. There are more interactions with the CEO. Being at that higher level of the organization comes with different feelings, which sometimes are hard to parse." But even in previous jobs where he also held high-ranking roles, there was not necessarily a guarantee that the organizational culture would be a fit. In fact, he described working at several other companies where the organizational culture was more of an obstacle to success for him.

"One company in particular was not a great fit," Darren admitted. "Everyone was serious and *not* friendly. I would come in, say 'Good morning,' and people would look like you were crazy. It just was a really intense culture. Part of it was that it wasn't the industry group I wanted to work in. But some of it was definitely the people who were there. And I've seen some people from that company go on to other places, and it doesn't work for them. Maybe it's that type of behavior they're bringing, from that culture."

Darren went on to compare that culture to the ones that he felt were a better fit for him: "I've worked at other places where it's very, 'Don't even talk to me if you're at a certain level.' But every place isn't like that. At my previous job, it was a consensus-based place. I was there almost seven years, and I probably had to dial back my intensity to fit in. I remember when we worked on one project and I was like, 'Why can't we get it done faster?!'" He laughed at the memory, then continued: "It matters to get things done, but also how you do things. You treat people in a respectful manner. At this company I was in the room with senior people and I could share my ideas. As long as you're thoughtful about it, you can give your opinion and no one looks at you like, 'Why are you in the room talking?' Everyone's opinions matter."

Darren's account highlights two important points. One, his experiences suggest that even within one industry, there can be significant variation between cultures in different organizations. Many—if not most—companies in the financial industry would likely be characterized by a market-based culture. They are places driven by the desire to maximize profits and make money for shareholders; as such, the culture encourages a focus on profitability and results. However, even though this climate may reign in the industry at large, organizations vary in the extent to which they encourage some aspects of cooperation and broad input. Market-driven cultures can create organizations where a social order is rigidly imposed and there are significant, meaningful layers between workers at different levels of the organization. But this does not necessarily have to be the case, and companies that are more welcoming for entry-level and middle-management workers can have favorable effects for Black employees.

This is because strict market-based cultures that discourage collaboration may be particularly hard on workers of color. In a case study of a Wall Street firm, anthropologist Karen Ho found that some organizations took very intentional, explicit steps to ensure that demarcations between groups of workers were strictly enforced. Rules, policies, and everyday norms ensured that entry-level analysts did not talk or interact with senior management. In a particularly memorable anecdote, Ho notes that even the elevator banks were designed to ensure that analysts, as lower-status employees, could not access the floors where senior managers and vice presidents worked. These rigid hierarchies reinforced lower-tier workers' observations that they were disposable, expendable, and not really essential to the corporation—a view that was strengthened by disparaging treatment and frequent layoffs.[2] Market-driven cultures that discourage entry-level workers' feedback, input, and participation may be particularly alienating for Black employees, who are already underrepresented in these jobs and for whom cultural messages may suggest they are not welcome.

Darren's accounts show that there is variation even with certain types of organizational cultures. Market cultures can harden status divisions or they can encourage collaboration and teamwork. These variations presented him with different examples of what work atmospheres could look like, and led to the question of which approaches worked best for him to succeed and thrive. What are his best coping strategies? What does it take to "win" when gray areas affect his work?

Emerging Color Consciousness
in a Market-Driven Culture

One of the most interesting aspects of Darren's work in the financial industry is that he has been able to succeed, even advance, in
an organizational space that is well-documented for its exclusion
of Black workers and women of all races. It's hardly a secret that
the financial industry has a history of being an uncomfortable
place for underrepresented workers. In 2020, Wells Fargo agreed
to a settlement requiring it to pay $7.8 million in response to
claims that it engaged in systematic racial and gender discrimination.[3] This came a decade after the company had settled a previous suit alleging racial discrimination that contributed to the
subprime mortgage crisis of 2008. Written testimony associated
with this case claims that bank officials publicly referred to Black
loan applicants as "mud people" and deliberately steered them to
subprime so-called ghetto loans, even when their credit history
and finances qualified them for better loans with more favorable terms.[4] And Wells Fargo is far from the only place alleged
to foster a racially hostile climate; financial companies including Merrill Lynch, Morgan Stanley, and Bank of America have
all settled lawsuits related to racial and gender discrimination.
Companies in the banking and financial industries in fact have
paid more than $530 million to settle employment discrimination
claims, with most of these centering on racial and gender disparities. (When it comes to these payouts, banking and finance are
tied with retail, which also paid approximately $530 million, but
far outpace other fields like food and beverage [$252 million] or
pharmaceuticals [$209 million].)[5]

Given these widespread, well-known accounts of racism in the
financial industry, it would seem that Darren might face challenges
as a Black man in a highly visible leadership role. And Darren acknowledged to me that "Wall Street isn't a place where you really
talk about race. You kind of keep your head down and get your

work done." But it may be that this strategy of keeping his head down and avoiding discussions and conversations about race has helped Darren acclimate to the firm culture. Explaining how he is able to get along with co-workers, supervisors, and subordinates so easily, he shared: "I probably know how to blend in; I know how to get along. It would just be very rare that I would have a discussion of race at work."

This approach may help Darren manage the colorblind organizational culture that exists in many, if not most, of the companies where he has worked. Darren suspects that acceding to these expectations has, for the most part, helped his career. Even though he is a Black worker in a predominantly white environment, he doesn't stand out as "that person" who is willing to violate cultural norms by drawing attention to racial issues and dynamics. As Constance engaged in her masquerade, Darren too conceals the ways race affects him professionally.

There are drawbacks to this approach, of course. Knowing how to "get along" by avoiding discussions about or acknowledgment of race and racial issues can help advance a career. It can allow Darren to conform to ambiguous definitions of "fit" that frequently screen out Black workers. Conversely, this framework also means that it becomes difficult to identify and address practices, behaviors, and norms that may adversely impact Black workers.

But Darren's company, like many others today, is also grappling with broader systemic, cultural changes. Consequently, as discussions of systemic racism, diversity, and inequality have taken center stage in media, academia, and other outlets, some organizations are moving away from a completely colorblind orientation. This means that at his current company, some of the cultural norms that encourage racial silence are slowly shifting. Reflecting on these changes, Darren mused that more open discussions of race and equity were no longer quite so taboo. "It's becoming more and more common," he said. "You see this with the discussions around culture and fit, and being inclusive. So there's been a lot more training about that. To some extent, some of these things are happening more. We had inclusiveness training recently at my old company, and people talked about their experiences and where they're from. That was kind of interesting. It was an opportunity for me to talk more about my experiences than ever before."

It's important to reiterate, however, that trainings and seminars alone will not be sufficient for creating more racially equitable workplaces. Recall from the opening to Part I, "Doing Diversity Badly," that mandated diversity trainings generally do not result in large-scale change. What may be more significant here is that Darren's company is finally moving away from its colorblind culture to a place where open discussions of race and racism are becoming more central and culturally acceptable. Responding to the #BlackLivesMatter protests of the summer of 2020, the company now acknowledges that there may be ways to talk more about how and why race matters in the workplace. While the inclusiveness training that his company has implemented is not a cure-all, this cultural change opens up space for Darren to consider how he can help work with other Black (or otherwise underrepresented) workers.

For Darren, succeeding in these environments rests not only on what he brings to the table, but the extent to which companies are structured in ways that can support him. His narrative shows that at least in some contexts, a market-based culture can provide a space where Black workers can do well. But their success is likely facilitated by a willingness to become people who "fit" the organizational culture that demands very structured attention to race and inequality, and aided by having the cultural and social capital to be approachable in these environments.

Can We Change the Culture?

An important takeaway from the narratives here in Part I is that whether we are talking about culturally "feminized" or "masculinized" spaces; adhocracy, hierarchical, clan-based, or market-based cultures; a common theme is that many of these spaces are colorblind in ways that are damaging for Black workers. Hierarchical cultures reinforce high-status workers' authority, but Max's experience shows that without explicit attention to the harsh realities of workplace racism, he's still alienated and unprotected. In clan cultures, the race-blind emphasis on diversity can leave employees like Constance never really feeling as though she fits into her predominantly white workplace. Even companies driven by the unorthodox, rule-breaking adhocracy culture fail to factor race and racism into their products, and the result is that contractors like Alex tout the absence of explicit discrimination all while racial bias becomes coded into the very platforms they use.

Erasing Colorblindness

Whether tacit or explicit, the colorblind approach yields some common outcomes across companies; therefore, it's useful to question whether the organizational culture can yield different outcomes if it is explicitly attentive to and structured around race. In other words, if organizational cultures can be "men's" or "women's" spaces, might they also be "Black," "White," "Asian," or "Latinx" spaces as well? And how would workers of color flourish in these environments?

Some researchers argue that just as organizational cultures can be shaped by gender, they can be shaped by race too. In making the case for how some organizations may be "Black" spaces, sociologists Melissa Wooten and Lucius Couloute point to the Black Panther Party for Self-Defense as one obvious example.[1] The organization ceased functioning in the 1970s, but in the late 1960s it was explicitly structured and established to advance Black communities' interests, safety, and social and economic progress in the United States. The Black Panther Party's health programs focused on improving Black children's wellness and nutrition, its educational programs sought to increase literacy and advance multiculturalism, and its social programs sought to ensure that members of the Black community knew their rights when it came to interacting with a police force that then (as now) often engaged in extralegal measures when it came to Black citizens. These efforts had significant influence on later social programs and for many goals and achievements Black social workers made in later years.[2]

Can Black workers fare differently in an organization where the culture is explicitly attuned to issues of race? Bethany, a principal at a predominantly Black elementary school in Washington, DC, told me she thinks the answer is yes. In her workplace, she said, she strives to promote a "culture of excellence, not the culture of mediocrity that we had before." Part of her ability to do this comes from the fact that her leadership team and staff, mostly Black women, are clear and direct about the challenges Black children will face in life, and they seek to prepare them to navigate and excel in a racially stratified world. Thus, in organizations where the realities of race are acknowledged rather than obscured, it may be that Black workers are more involved, included, and better able to contribute.

Some suggestions for how to achieve this shift in organizational culture can be found in the checklist at the end of this section.

Most organizations today will be more racially diverse than the Black Panther Party or the predominantly Black school that Bethany leads. But multiracial companies can take a page from the way organizations like these created a particular culture that recognizes and affirms Black members' experiences. Far too many companies take an approach where they purport to value diversity, may even hire a few Black employees, but fall short of considering how the organizational culture may be unwelcoming or even hostile. We see this in Constance's experiences in her department and Kevin's encounters in the nonprofit and the bank. Today's large multiracial companies can change their culture by being attuned to the reality that Black workers' experiences will include stereotyping, discrimination, and racial bias and factoring this reality into their norms and expectations. Relatedly, companies can also establish a culture where they support and affirm Black workers rather than marginalizing them. This could mean avoiding appearance codes that ban hairstyles disproportionately worn by Black workers (dreadlocks, braids, twists), facilitating discussions of racial matters when they arise, or establishing concrete sanctions for fellow colleagues or customers who engage in racial mistreatment of Black employees.

Though it should not be Black workers' responsibility to fix the gray areas in organizations where they work, there are also ways to consider how they can make these spaces more bearable and supportive. One strategy can involve forming or joining an affinity group. Now common in many workplaces, affinity groups involve collections of workers with a shared social identity (e.g., gender, race, veteran status, LGBTQ+ identity). The logic behind these groups is that by coming together to share their collective experiences, group members can make work a bit more welcoming and less isolating. Although affinity groups can provide much-needed social support, organizations can often succumb to the tendency of assigning or expecting affinity group members to take responsibility for resolving workplace issues related to social identity.[3] Thus, Black workers may find some personal support in these groups, but they should be careful not to make them the catalyst for the equity work organizations need to do to address their gray areas.

Diversity Management

Diversity managers have an important role to play in changing these cultures as well. Recall that Brian, the Hollywood executive, was quite critical of the diversity manager at Worldwide Studios, believing that she inhibited rather than supported his efforts to create a broad swath of films that reflected the complexity of Black life in the United States and abroad. But it is also important to highlight the challenges that even some of the most well-intentioned diversity managers can face in this role.

For one thing, it's not uncommon for diversity officers to feel as though they are the lone voice speaking out on matters of racial equity. Although this is part of their job, their work is undermined if their commitment to these issues does not seem shared by others in the organizational structure. Lana, a diversity manager based in New York City, told me that because her colleagues often fail to advocate for diversity, this work falls solely to her. Even though her co-workers tell her privately that they agree with and support her, their refusal to say so in public settings means that she feels she shoulders this responsibility alone. Consequently, she told me that "diversity work, yes, it takes a toll. It gets tiring." In companies where the diversity officer feels they are the only person supporting and invested in this work, it can become more difficult to advance goals.

Diversity managers may also find themselves subjected to the varying whims of the political economy in which they are hired. Those hired during 2020, when antiracism protests and the Black

Lives Matter movement were at their peak, likely found a different organizational climate than those hired a couple of years later after anti–critical race theory backlash began to take hold. There's historical precedent for this, as managers hired in the late 1970s after the civil rights movement found a much more welcoming climate to focus on race and racism than those in the more conservative 1980s.[4] In addition to balancing the challenge of being the lone voice speaking out about racial matters, these managers may find that they also have to calibrate their messages and approaches in response to shifting winds.

But there are ways organizations can empower diversity officers to be a meaningful part of changing the culture. These managers occupy a critically important role in modern organizations, and when they have the budget, staff, and support to do so, they can help hold a company's proverbial feet to the fire. Doing so successfully, however, requires that all leaders in an organization—not just the diversity manager—share a commitment, not to diversity in the abstract, but to racial equity specifically. This means collecting data to measure and reduce racial disparities, supporting affinity groups, and advancing other approaches designed to support workers of color at all levels of an organization, from leadership on down. Organizations also have to provide resources by making sure that diversity officers have the access to the top executives, funding, and authority that allows them to be effective.[5] It's a major effort, but diversity officers with the proper support are well-poised to help facilitate the change toward a color-conscious culture, whether the organization is clan-based, hierarchical, an adhocracy, or market-driven.

In Part I, we've addressed the ways that organizational culture constitutes one of the gray areas through which work perpetuates racial inequality. But the issues Black workers face do not begin once they move into a job. Rather, the process of getting hired (or not getting hired) is another gray area of work. The processes through which we learn about available jobs and get hired are murky, undefined, and thus ripe for reproducing inequalities.

KEY TAKEAWAYS

- Organizational culture shapes the norms, values, and everyday interactions in a company

- Organizational cultures can take different forms: market, hierarchy, clan, or adhocracy

- Across all types of cultures, companies often promote values of meritocracy and colorblindness

- These cultures and principles ignore Black workers' experiences

- Companies thus become ill-prepared to acknowledge and address the ways organizational culture can be inhospitable for Black workers

CHECKLIST: WHAT YOU CAN DO

For the DEI Practitioner

O Avoid mandatory diversity training

O Establish and support race-based affinity groups

O Work with executives and senior leaders to set diversity targets

For the Executive or Senior Manager

O Adopt a race-conscious culture by explicitly identifying racial diversity as a company goal

O Hire and provide resources to diversity managers

O Commit to reaching diversity targets by a set date

O Make targets, goals, and data about diversity publicly available

O Anticipate that Black workers will face racial bias internally and externally

O Ensure that targets, expectations, and employee goals reflect Black workers' realities

For the HR Director

○ Enact consequences for customers, clients, or colleagues who engage in racially discriminatory behavior at work

○ Collect data to measure Black employees' perceptions of inclusion, satisfaction, and ability to be themselves in the organization

○ Track data over time to see when and where changes need to be made

○ Avoid dress and appearance codes that forbid hairstyles predominantly worn by Black workers

For the Colleague

○ Support attempts to shift organizational culture

○ Speak out against expressions of racial bias and support others who do so

○ Recognize that an organizational culture that reflects and includes Black workers maximizes human capital and benefits everyone

PART II

SOCIAL

Getting the Job

Back in 2014 a colleague of mine, whom I'll call Jessica, emailed me to ask if I'd heard anything about the new sociology department launching at Washington University in St. Louis. Jessica and I knew each other because of our similar research interests, and she'd written a letter supporting my tenure and promotion case a few years earlier. She'd heard that Washington University needed to hire a group of faculty members to restart its department, and she planned to apply. In doing so, she was thinking of other sociologists she knew who she thought might make good colleagues, and I came to mind. I applied for the job and followed the standard procedure for academic positions—sent in writing samples, a curriculum vitae listing my research and teaching experience, teaching evaluations, and letters of recommendations from colleagues.

Because my father is a retired college professor, I typically ask him whether he knows anyone in, or anything about, the universities where I might be applying for a position. Academia is a relatively small world, so he usually does. In this case, he recalled that a colleague he'd once worked with was now employed at Wash U. When I told him that I was really interested in the position, he contacted this colleague to let him know that we were related and to ask if there was any useful information about the university that he could share with me. I found out later that this colleague passed my name and CV along to the search committee chair and recommended that they take a close look at my application. In addition to this, my father also offered a lot of advice during the process based on his experience in academia. (Some of this advice was unsolicited, but that's parents for you.) Ultimately, the end result worked out in my favor. The search committee invited me for a campus visit, and about a month later, they offered me a job.

My pathway into this job underscores how much the process of getting hired and acclimated into a job represents another gray area that perpetuates racial inequality. My route to a job offer was eased tremendously by several factors, including being a second-generation academic and having a well-connected father, that are generally less available to Black workers. I believe my academic record—and of course my immense personal charm—certainly was key to getting hired. But I also had relationships and connections that undoubtedly helped me get a foot in the door from the outset. Many Black workers are locked out of these networks. Thus, when these relationships become central to how people get jobs, hiring turns into a gray area where racial inequality can flourish.

Managerial Screening

Before the advent of the internet when virtually all aspects of life shifted online, it wasn't hard to find jobs through the want ads in newspapers or even by seeking out businesses that displayed "Help Wanted" signs. But today, these hiring methods are largely obsolete. In a society that has grown only more populous, complex, and busy, getting a job today hinges more than ever not on what you know, but who you know. It's much more common to find out about jobs through connections or referrals, just like I did when Jessica contacted me about Wash U. And these connections don't just matter in *finding out* about jobs; they also matter in the process of *secur-*

ing those jobs. Hiring managers today frequently receive thousands of applications for open positions. These can include a cover letter and résumé, which means these managers receive more paperwork than they could possibly read thoroughly. As a consequence, they may spend as little as three minutes reviewing each application. Hiring managers thus have to use other means to make sense of the volume of information they receive when deciding whether to advance one candidate over another. There are several ways this happens.

Creating a Narrative

One process involves creating a story or narrative about potential workers. When managers receive applications, in the absence of time to gain detailed information, they turn to questions that allow them to fit the limited data they do have into a coherent framework. Does anything about this person indicate that they are likely to be a reliable, consistent employee? Are there warning signs that suggest they will be a problem if hired? What explains why a worker has spent time unemployed? What accounts for the years they spent working for a temp agency instead of full time for a company in their chosen field?

This ambiguity can lead hiring managers to fill in gaps with stories that both draw from and reinforce racial stereotypes. For instance, Black men are routinely perceived to lack soft skills such as congeniality, amiability, and affability and suffer an extensive amount of employment discrimination as a result. Consequently, managers may not be surprised when job candidates who are Black men have long periods of unemployment because "it's expected of African Americans to be more unemployed more often."[1] Relatedly, Black men with work histories at temp agencies may fare better than other groups because of the perception that temp agencies go through rigorous screening and will ferret out problem employees.

These stories do not necessarily reflect Black men's work abilities, commitment to jobs, or potential for succeeding in a given career. What they do reflect are the pervasiveness of racial and gendered stereotypes and the ease with which these presumptions shape how Black men fare in the hiring process.[2]

For Black women, similar processes are often in place. Hiring managers do not necessarily have the same low expectations for social skills that they assume of Black men, but Black women encounter stereotypes that present difficulties in the hiring stage and create discriminatory outcomes as well. For instance, managers often assume they will have extensive childcare responsibilities that will prompt frequent absenteeism. In some cases, this is linked to the belief that hiring Black women means dealing with "that single mother element"—the expectation that Black women will be unmarried mothers who lack childcare and cannot fully devote themselves to the needs of their jobs.[3]

How Hiring Discrimination Happens

The stories hiring managers tell to make sense of Black workers' applications may be driven by what economists describe as *statistical discrimination*. According to this theory, when individuals in positions of power make judgments—and then act—on the basis of factors that are generally true of a group, discrimination may result. Thus, hiring managers may be aware that Black women have higher rates of single motherhood than women of other racial groups and use this information to draw adverse conclusions about the Black women in their applicant pools. But when they do so, Black women as a group become penalized by these assumptions, leading employers to miss out on opportunities to hire otherwise qualified, skilled candidates. And employers probably overlook the fact that Black fathers are actually more likely than men of other races to spend time with their children. This fact belies the stereotypes about absent Black fathers, suggesting that even if more Black women are single mothers, that doesn't necessarily mean that they lack support in raising their children.[4]

In other cases, managers may engage in *preferential discrimination* when evaluating Black job candidates. Unlike statistical discrimination, preference-based discrimination is largely a function of decision-makers' personal tastes, biases, and adverse beliefs about the group in question. Adherents of this theory suggest that even with access to information about specific workers that challenges broad stereotypes, managers will still discriminate on the basis of their personal prejudices. This discrimination could explain a manager's refusal to hire Black men on the basis of the belief that they lack social skills, since there are no data to suggest that Black men are less friendly, approachable, or team-oriented than other workers. Thus, when employers use these perceptions to create narratives that justify overlooking Black men in the hiring process, they are drawing more from their own preferences than from specific data relevant to particular applicants. And they are doing so in ways that help contribute to the disadvantages that Black workers face when looking for employment.

Whether statistical or preferential, discriminatory practices have substantial impact. In 2017, after assessing data from multiple studies conducted over the preceding three decades, a team of researchers found that hiring discrimination toward Black Americans had not declined over that time period.[5] Furthermore, sociologist David Pedulla estimates that hiring discrimination accounts for significant variation in employment outcomes between Black and white workers.[6] In other words, Black workers in 2017 faced the same levels of discrimination that were present in 1989—when we still used cordless phones and Ataris. It's amazing to think that as a society, we've made major advances in science, technology, health care, and other areas but have made no progress when it comes to reducing the discrimination Black people face when looking for work.

The Social Network

What else can draw a hiring manager's attention? Narratives are not the only way these professionals decide who makes it through to an interview and potentially employment with a company. In a more complicated, technologically driven society characterized by a declining number of jobs that provide economic security, benefits, and stability, there have to be other ways that potential applicants can stand out from the pack and catch a manager's eye.

With more applications than they can read, and a barrage of ways to find out information about people, managers today rely heavily on connections and existing relationships—what sociologists refer to as *social networks*. These networks serve to unite people into diffuse social webs. And when one person makes a referral, puts in a good word, or suggests to a hiring manager that they give particular consideration to a job candidate, that can make the difference between that candidate getting an interview or being passed over. In some cases, it can cement who is hired, and who continues to look for work.

In a classic research study, sociologist Mark Granovetter noted not only that these networks mattered, but distinguished between "strong and weak ties" in determining advancement. *Strong ties* are the close relationships we have—with friends, family members, and others in our immediate circle. *Weak ties* are the connections that are a bit more distant—the friend of a friend, the neighbor's sorority sister, the brother-in-law's college roommate. Granovetter suggested, perhaps counterintuitively, that weak ties were more likely to provide opportunities for advancement and mobility than stronger ones. This is because weak ties offer a more expansive, broad network of connections, whereas strong ties are likely to replicate the information and opportunities already available.[7]

In my case, I activated both my strong and weak ties in getting the job at Washington University. Jessica, my father, and the faculty members I knew at other institutions who wrote letters of recommendation vouching for me constituted strong ties; my father's former colleague is an example of a weak tie. But collectively, all formed part of the network of people who steered me toward the job, helped me get an interview, and assisted in my getting more information about the position. Had I not been plugged into this existing web of relationships with people who were willing to support this career move, it's hard to imagine that I even would have known about the position, much less been seen as a strong candidate.

But the reliance on social networks in hiring has unintended consequences. For one thing, our networks are often very racially homogeneous. Job seekers are likely to rely on friends, neighbors, casual acquaintances, or classmates for leads on work, but often these circles themselves are racially segregated. A 2014 study from the Public Religion Research Institute reported that approximately 75 percent of whites have no people of color in their close friend networks.[8] This imbalance evokes comedian Chris Rock's joke in a 2009 stand-up routine that "all my Black friends have a bunch of white friends . . . and all my white friends have one Black friend." Data suggest that his experience isn't unique.

Furthermore, in spite of laws that prohibit overt racial discrimination in schools, neighborhoods, and other settings, many whites make daily choices, behaviors, and decisions that serve to maintain racial segregation in these very same settings.[9] Consequently, many white workers aren't just lacking Black friends; they also have no Black neighbors, peers, or family members in their lives. When whites lean on social networks to advance potential job applicants, they are, by default, connecting and elevating other white workers.

Another problem is that even when networks are nominally integrated, Black members are still likely to get the short end of the stick. Racial stereotypes and perceptions about who belongs in what kinds of jobs still factor into who gets referred for what. In practice this means that even if Black workers have friends, neighbors, or colleagues who are white and can share information about jobs, those workers may be less likely to benefit from such largesse.

This can be especially pronounced if the job in question is one in which Black workers are underrepresented, leaving white peers less likely to think of or reference Black associates as strong candidates for the position.

In this context, it's not hard to see how using social networks as a core part of the hiring process can be a mechanism for perpetuating racial inequality at work. When managers rely on networks, referrals, and tips from employees, current friends, or colleagues to determine who makes it through the hiring process, it is all too likely that they will be drawing from largely homogeneous circles. In a society that has yet to become truly fully integrated, using existing relationships and connections as a core part of the hiring process necessarily means that many Black workers are going to be left out and excluded.

Studies of how hiring discrimination occurs indicate that this is in fact the case in practice. In one study of Black and white students interested in finding skilled vocational work, sociologist Deirdre Royster found that white teachers acted as gatekeepers. They were more likely to refer white students to prospective employers than Black ones. This preferential treatment showed up even when Black students had the same skills, interests, and wage expectations as their white counterparts. Other research has shown that not only are whites more likely to refer other whites for jobs, but that even when they refer Black candidates for positions, those Black applicants are less likely to get a callback.[10]

These findings help explain why measures such as the vaunted "Rooney Rule" do not work. Named after the late Dan Rooney, former owner of the Pittsburgh Steelers, the rule was adopted by the National Football League (NFL) in 2003 as an effort to rectify the league's dismal record of hiring Black coaches. Per its adoption, teams are required to interview at least one person of color for head coaching and other senior leadership roles. The logic behind this mandate was that owners just needed to be exposed to qualified

Black candidates, and once they were, changes would result. Advocates of the Rooney Rule touted its potential for reducing these disparities, and companies in corporate America even took note.

What we've since learned, however, is that the Rooney Rule has failed to create measurable, sustained improvement in the numbers of Black candidates hired for head coaching jobs. A 2022 *Washington Post* report found that over the previous four seasons, the NFL had only three black coaches. Furthermore, in the nearly twenty years since the Rooney Rule was implemented, thirteen of the thirty-two teams in the NFL—nearly half—have never had a Black coach in a full-time role.[11] Some of this has to do with the fact that there were no consequences for teams that committed violations. Attorney Cyrus Mehri, one of the rule's originators, lamented on National Public Radio that "in 2017, [the NFL] didn't enforce the rule. What we know from our work—and this is advising companies, litigating against companies, all different arenas—that accountability matters for equal opportunity to succeed."[12]

But perhaps more important, we also know that if hiring managers are predisposed to candidates they already know or are connected to through their networks, forcing those managers to interview a lone candidate of color won't change their minds. Instead, those applicants get brought in for interviews designed to show compliance with the rule rather than being seriously considered for the position—resulting in allegations of "sham interviews" that have led to bitterness, disillusionment, and eventually legal action.[13] A 2022 *Washington Post* profile of influential Dallas Cowboys owner Jerry Jones observes that the first head coach he hired was his former college roommate; the second, a friend with no experience coaching professional football. Both were white men who were already in Jones's social circle.[14] If team owners—or hiring directors—are already inclined to choose candidates from preexisting, exclusively white networks, then implementing the Rooney Rule doesn't do much more than waste a lot of people's time. The policy may mean Black candidates land more interviews now than they did in the past, but that hasn't translated into parity when it comes to job offers.

Whether we are discussing head coaches or administrative assistants, how we find work is a gray area where racial inequalities are reproduced. Today, racial discrimination in which managers and companies overtly and explicitly profess their refusal to hire Black workers rarely occurs. But getting hired is still a process that creates disparities for Black workers and job candidates. As we'll see, Alex, Darren, Brian, Constance, Kevin, Max, and Amalia all encounter and attempt to navigate this gray area in various ways.

CHAPTER 8

Going It Alone

"WHO IN THIS ROOM WANTS TO HAVE DINNER WITH ME?"

Constance's struggle with the gray areas of her field started early in her career. She has always excelled academically, and throughout high school she was often the only Black student in her advanced placement classes. After graduation, she sought out a different experience by attending North Carolina A&T State University, a historically Black college, where she no longer stood out as one of the handful of Black kids taking advanced science and math classes. At A&T, Constance was in the majority for the first time in her life, surrounded by other Black peers and teachers who shared her love for and interest in chemistry and engineering.

College years at HBCUs can be transformative for Black students, and this was certainly the case for Constance. Despite the fact that these institutions enroll a relatively small number of Black students (compared with larger and often more well-resourced predominantly white institutions), graduates of HBCUs are more likely to matriculate successfully and to go on to pursue graduate education.[1] This aptly reflects Constance's experience. At A&T, she enjoyed a college matriculation period where, for a change, she was a part of the majority, expected to succeed and thrive, and free from the biases and inherent assumptions that often characterize the challenges Black students find on predominantly white campuses.

Graduate school, however, was a different story. Constance enrolled at the University of Minnesota, which houses one of the top programs in her desired field. Though she did not realize it at the time, this was one of the first ways that networks began to matter in her professional career. When we spoke, she told me that upon applying to graduate school, she had a successful interview with the professor who agreed to admit her into his research group. But that interview wasn't what really put her over the top. Rather, "There was another woman I knew from my time doing research, and she knew my advisor. When he saw that I'd done summer research at that place, he called her and asked her about me. She's at a different university now. But he called her and she vouched for me. There were all these connections that I hadn't nurtured, but they impacted how I ended up."

Getting references from colleagues is not necessarily unusual in this process. At minimum, faculty members will read interested students' letters of recommendation and may do this kind of informal check-in if they know someone with whom the potential student is affiliated. But it is important to note that Constance actually came to her advisor with a value-add that would not necessarily have been present for other students in the department. In many graduate programs, students are funded by the program, which means that professors are incentivized to admit only those they consider most promising, since they pay (whether through their own funding or the department's) for these students to join. But in Constance's case, "I had my own money and that was for five years. I had a five-year fellowship, and I was competent, so he didn't have anything to lose." Essentially, her advisor was in a position where he could benefit from Constance's free labor for a five-year period. But he still needed personal confirmation from someone who could vouch for her. Her networks still mattered in ways that may have been less critical for her white peers.

Graduate programs, particularly in STEM fields like chemistry, biology, physics, or engineering, are organized on a hierarchical basis. It is typical for students to do the bulk of their advisor's research and even for faculty members to refer to students as their "eyes and ears" or "their hands" or to commodify their labor in other ways.[2] The importance of this working relationship can mean that faculty rely heavily on students whom they admit to their research groups, so it is in their best interest to be sure that these students can pull their weight.

For Black students, however, these arrangements can mean that faculty place additional weight on subjective factors to ensure that these students will be a good fit for the lab. Long-standing racial stereotypes of Blacks as less intelligent, competent, skilled, and capable can mean that there is still additional vetting, even for students like Constance who, for the most part, come at no cost to a professor. In fact, she described meetings with other professors in the program who initially appeared to doubt her skills and abilities, including one who grilled her about her GRE scores and expressed doubts about her performance on the test. Thus, even with Constance's qualifications and the fact that she was willing, per the expectations of these programs, to serve as free labor for her advisor, her networks were still what put her over the top and led to her admission to her mentor's group.

Relying on a Mentor's Networks

Once accepted to the University of Minnesota's chemical engineering program, Constance was back to being the lone Black student. But this is where she also began to learn, in retrospect, just how much networks and connections matter in academia. With a sigh, she told me: "The whole networking issue is my biggest weakness. I was never very savvy or intentional about that. You hear the young kids talk today about 'my brand' and Twitter—we didn't even have those things, but the idea of my network and getting a job was not how I thought about things. It was all about the traditional stuff. I had to get publications and present at conferences—[that's] how I thought about it. I wasn't intentional about meeting with people. I tell students now to look up the top people in the field and meet with them at conferences and talk with them, but I didn't do any of that. I saw people sometimes, but I was never brave enough to talk to them. I didn't start doing that till I was a faculty member, and then I wasn't very successful."

At the same time, however, Constance acknowledged that although she had not actively sought to build a network early on, she was automatically integrated into one by working with her doctoral advisor, a reputable known chemical engineer in the field: "I started to see that because he was well-positioned, I was well-positioned, or better so than others because I was his student. So I went to people and would tell them my advisor was Professor Smith, and that means something. Many of my conference experiences and publications were because his name was the last on the article. It has been disconcerting to realize it's that lineage and who you work with that determines your career."

Note that in her early years of graduate school, Constance focused primarily on what sociologists would refer to as the *manifest functions* of a doctoral program—the formal, overt expectations associated with attaining a PhD in chemical engineering. In this context, her attention to publishing, presenting at conferences, and doing the work of learning about and researching nanoparticles was front and center. But the *latent aspects* of graduate study—the more hidden, covert parts of the program that included making connections, getting to know the big names in her field—initially eluded her.[3]

Constance's connection to a famous doctoral advisor, however, paid dividends. For one thing, her advisor encouraged her to aim for jobs she otherwise would not have pursued. In many PhD programs, tenure-track positions at the most highly research-intensive

(R1) universities are considered the optimal jobs to attain after completing the degree. Some programs outright discourage students from pursuing positions in industry or at small liberal arts colleges that do not offer graduate degrees. But Constance's experiences in grad school left her uncertain about whether she was cut out for the work at an R1 university, given the research demands and expectations at such institutions that faculty continually develop new ideas, seek out funding, and publish regularly. It was her famous advisor, in fact, who persuaded her to apply for these jobs.

"When I was finishing, I talked to my advisor because I was nervous about getting an R1 position," Constance said. "I thought maybe I [should] work at a teaching institution, or go to a journal and be an editor. Maybe I should go to an HBCU or teach and help the community that way, but all of that came from a fear of doing the research part. My advisor said, 'Look, I understand what you're saying, and it would be great to go to an HBCU, but try an R1 first. If you don't like it, you should go to an HBCU, but you should do this first.'"

Constance's experience of self-doubt and worry that she might not succeed in the competitive, daunting environment of an R1 university is common among graduate students of color. I felt this aspect of her experience was completely relatable to my own—I didn't pursue R1 jobs coming out of graduate school because I felt it was a foregone conclusion that I did not have the research acumen to be tenured in those departments (a view that wasn't exactly discouraged by some of the mentors I had at the time). This is one reason initiatives like the Mellon Mays Undergraduate Fellowship, a program designed to increase the number of students of color interested in academic jobs, focuses so heavily on providing support, resources, and encouragement to show students that they have what it takes for academic careers. All too often, Black and Latinx graduate students in particular receive the opposite message and are sometimes openly dissuaded from pursuing this path.[4] In Constance's case, she was fortunate to have the opposite experience in that her advisor pushed her to pursue the challenge of an R1 job. But it is worth noting that without that relationship, and without having that advisor as part of her professional circle, her career path could have taken a wholly different direction.

Not only are networks very influential in the hiring process, but they matter significantly even in fields that rely heavily on supposedly detached, methodical approaches. Despite Constance's early view that her research, presentations, and competence should and would speak for themselves, she came to see that the connections that she had mattered more. When she finally had this realization, it became a major source of regret and frustration.

Building Networks on Her Own

Constance's relationships with her advisor and previous employers helped her land what many academics would consider a dream job. Upon finishing her PhD, she was hired as an assistant professor in a tenure-track position at one of the top research universities in the country. The position came with a very comfortable salary, a research budget, a low teaching load, and the status of being employed at a university that routinely ranks among the nation's best. But these perks were not enough to offset the persistent challenges that the reliance on networking can bring for Black faculty.

"Networks are the bane of my career," Constance told me with a deep sigh. "That's the whole problem. When I started here, I unintentionally changed fields," referring here to her decision to pursue a different area of specialization within chemical engineering. "So all the credit I had for being Professor Smith's student, I lost. I went into a new field, no one knew my advisor, the fact that I came out of his group didn't mean anything for them. I was starting over from scratch with no one to vouch for me. That has been my challenge ever since."

Constance's experiences during her first few years in her faculty position reveal a harsh truth. Networks got her in the door, and they helped to reassure potential academic employers that in a field where less than 5 percent of professors are Black women, she could handle the rigors and demands of a faculty position.[5] But when it came to building those networks on her own, without her advisor's assistance, reach, or involvement, it was a different story. This is the point where being a Black woman in a white male–dominated field that relies heavily on relationships and connections became challenging.

Furthermore, this is where Constance's ongoing struggle—determining whether her issues are ones she can change, like shyness, or whether they are because of gray areas—really begins to take root. With a mix of frustration and resignation, she explained: "Going to meetings, trying to meet people, get in the 'in-crowd'—'cause I'm introverted anyway, on top of being a Black woman—while not being known, it has been terrible. I hate it. I suppose I could have tried to put myself out more. Because if it was just based on merit, if the networks didn't matter so much, I'd be much better positioned. But the networks are what's missing, so I miss out on all kinds of things—awards, nominations, proposals. I know that's what gets said at [funding agency] meetings—'I don't know her, why is she doing this?' I'm not good at networking. It's a weight. It's just not what I want to do. I want to think and write a paper and have it evaluated on its merits."

Constance is able to pinpoint the moment she realized that failing to tend to "the social aspect," as she referred to it, was damaging her career: "I was at a conference and there was a guy presenting there, and he talked about how research collaborations depend on personal relationships with people. You ask yourself, 'Would I spend time with this person? Is this someone you want to sit down and have dinner with?' When he said that, I was just devastated. Because who in this room wants to have dinner with me? And this

is why I haven't had any collaborations with anybody since graduate school, because I haven't done this."

With this realization, Constance began to try to make changes.
But as someone whose scientific approach differed from that of her
more mainstream colleagues in chemical engineering, and in an
environment where she was back to being the only Black woman,
her attempts to make connections with older, usually white, nearly
always male colleagues frequently fell flat. "There were some old
professors who invited me one time to lunch," she said. "When I
first got there [to the university], I was bringing my lunch, and they
asked once. I said no because I had a schedule. I was an assistant
professor, I wasn't tenured, I wanted to make sure I didn't fall behind on research. I didn't know that would be the only time they
would ever ask me.

"Then there were some young guys who gave me a standing
invitation to join any time on their Wednesday lunch. But then
there was a scandal with the department chair that hired me, and
they were going in with the gossip and the rumors, and it put me
off, 'cause I was like, 'I can't trust them. They're not going to have
my back.' It made me feel vulnerable, like I couldn't trust them. So
I excluded myself from that. So I've just been rolling by myself."

But when the ongoing exclusion from key networks continued
to damage her career, Constance attempted again to correct the
issue. Though it went against what felt comfortable, she made an
effort to connect with various colleagues and to be proactive about
integrating herself into the key networks in her department. These
efforts were no more successful: "I've approached people and it was
really depressing. I met with this woman once. She is the vice dean
at my university and is a geologist, and I met with her before I went
up for full [professor]. I was telling her about all the challenges I
had, and she said, 'You need an advocate. Every opportunity I had
was because my former advisor was an advocate. That's what you
need.' So I went to the senior faculty member who seemed cool and
supportive, and he gave me feedback on a paper. I asked, 'Would

you be my advocate?' He stared like a deer in headlights. He didn't say yes and didn't answer. He just stared."

Without her advisor, Constance's attempts to build networks on her own have been largely unsuccessful. And these failed attempts again evoke Constance's dilemma of determining how she can change her circumstances, and how much they are shaped by gray areas outside of her control. By her own admission, she is an introverted person, somewhat slow to warm to people, and rarely comfortable being outgoing or building a "brand." And these are dynamics that, in the modern workplace, have become essential. Today, many companies expect workers to be entrepreneurial, to think of themselves as independent contractors leveraging work opportunities and be willing to move from company to company in search of the right fit. Businesses now value workers who are nimble, welcome change, and find jobs through their existing connections and relationships. So to a point, Constance's discomfort with this process puts her out of step with the way many of today's workplaces have shifted to prioritize workers who are more comfortable and savvy leveraging their networks as a central part of the employment process.[6]

Race and Gender in STEM

The increased emphasis on networking can prove challenging for anyone who considers themselves introverted. But it's essential to place Constance's experiences in the context of the types of challenges that typically befall Black women workers in professions dominated by white men, such as the STEM fields. Research routinely shows that Black women struggle to get into these environments, and that if they are eventually hired, it can be even more difficult for them to thrive. In many cases, these difficulties have nothing to do with their skill sets, competence, or preparedness for the work at hand. In the medical industry, for instance, Black women doctors frequently find their expertise dismissed and suffer from stereotypes that present them as lacking the intelligence and comportment necessary to be successful physicians. Black women attorneys also describe being excluded from key work groups and projects that are essential for laying the foundation for the partnership track. Black women working in corporate America share similar accounts.[7]

These dynamics are specifically shaped by both race and gender. In workplaces composed mostly of white men, white women certainly face challenges too. They struggle to break into old-boys' networks, to be taken seriously, and to leverage the relationships that are essential for getting hired and progressing in the field. But white women are able to capitalize on the benefits of being white in these spaces in ways that elude women of color. For instance, when white women remind white male colleagues and supervisors of their daughters, or present themselves as people who need men's protection or support, they benefit from racial assumptions that work to their advantage even as they are hindered by gendered dynamics in these same spaces. In her classic study of tokenism, sociologist Rosabeth Moss Kanter found that some (white) women workers characterize themselves as the office "pet" as a strategy for fitting in in environments where they are underrepresented. These women can break into networks and develop the necessary relationships with white men in positions of power that allow mobility, even if that advancement may not give way to leadership roles for which they are well-qualified. When women are perceived as the "pet," men want to help them succeed, even as they are infantilized. Black women, in contrast, are more likely to encounter what psychologist Kecia Thomas describes as the "pet to threat" phenomenon, where they initially start off with managers' support and encouragement, but eventually see that support evaporate or even turn to hostility when they begin to advance and exert authority.[8] Roles like these provide some limited opportunities for white women to advance— though it's also worth noting that this token role still constrains them. After all, pets are cute, but nobody thinks Garfield would make a good CEO. Yet to the extent that this role can provide some mobility, it also rests on characterizations of white femininity that are unavailable to Black women and other women of color.[9]

Trying to Rebuild

Constance's struggle to break into these networks highlights issues that Black women face in contemporary workplaces. In many companies today, these networks can make or break an applicant's candidacy, and Constance was no different. Networks got her into Professor Smith's group in the first place (even though she was free labor, and admitting her as a student worked to his advantage), and having Professor Smith as an advisor meant that he pushed her toward her current career path and helped her to secure employment. Constance's experiences thus show that it is not impossible for Black workers to leverage these networks and to benefit from the connections that they bring. Yet for every Constance who has a famous, powerful, and influential advisor, it's worth asking how many Black students slip through the cracks.

From the outside looking in, Constance's career trajectory certainly looks admirable. She has been promoted twice and is now a tenured, senior faculty member in her department. But from Constance's perspective, these accomplishments are bittersweet because they are incomplete. She is always haunted by the knowledge that she could do more. And it's not that she doesn't fully grasp the science behind her work, or that she lacks the drive or the willingness to work hard. It's that the gray areas of work hold her back.

CHAPTER 9

Black Women Opening Doors

"I'VE NEVER HAD A WHITE PERSON HELP"

In Kevin's case, the gray areas of work have nudged him toward a career supporting Black people, particularly those who are lower income. As we have already learned, Kevin knew early on that he didn't want to pursue the cutthroat, competitive world of high finance. As he memorably put it: "The culture of the area was very banally corporate. It was like an episode of *The Office* except it wasn't funny. There was no joke, no punch line. It was so dry." With no guarantee of a Kelly Kapoor, Pam Beesly, or Dwight Schrute to alleviate the drudgery of the office routine, Kevin knew that he would not want to use his MBA to seek out a career on Wall Street, in investments, or in other lucrative, high-profile areas. Instead, he wanted to do something for others, stating, "I don't see myself being in a space where I am not directly supporting Black people, especially poor Black people."

It's not unusual for professionals of color to be motivated by the prospect of giving back to their communities. In many cases, this shapes the choice of career field, employment decisions, or even the ways these workers structure the jobs that they do. For instance, Latina teachers describe focusing heavily on using their position as educators to inspire and create opportunities for young Latinx children. Some Black doctors and nurses intentionally seek out work in the lower-paying public sector (rather than more financially lucrative private-sector employment) so that they can provide health care to low-income people of color, who are frequently uninsured and underserved.[1] Having seen firsthand the ways inequities in schools, health care, and other settings can affect communities of color, many Black professionals view their occupational achievements as a means to creating small-scale racial change where they can.

For Kevin, this meant finding a way to use his business degree to serve others. After a few years of soul-searching, he decided to apply his business background to the educational system. In many ways, his hometown of New Orleans seemed a perfect city in which to do that. As a result of a series of decisions by former governor Bobby Jindal, no public schools remain open in New Orleans. Instead, students in the city attend parochial, charter, or private schools. And in this context, many such schools are open to partnering with businesses or incorporating market-based ideas about success, advancement, and achievement into their missions and curricula. Kevin's idea to bring his business background into the educational arena seemed reasonable enough, and doing so in the city where he grew up, went to school himself, and still maintained roots meant that he could honor his commitment to improving opportunities for Black kids.

Black Networks, White Networks

Things didn't quite work out that way, however. One of the things Kevin learned early on was that access to school systems relied heavily on access to the city's education gatekeepers. In New Orleans, as in many other cities and states, K-12 education is a predominantly white, female profession. As a Black man, this put

Kevin in an awkward position when it came to creating the relationships he needed to get into this field. Sighing, he told me, "It's all about who you know in a small city like New Orleans." But unlike Constance, Kevin is not introverted. He's quite comfortable approaching people, meeting up at happy hours, and being part of the New Orleans social scene. As a Crescent City native he wouldn't hang out in the French Quarter—too touristy—but I can easily envision him networking over brunch at a trendy restaurant on Magazine Street. Kevin has been active and involved with various groups throughout his education and professional life but still hasn't ended up with networks that take him very far.

The challenge for Kevin is that the networks he has built have all been in predominantly Black spaces. Florida A&M University, where he received his undergraduate education, is a historically Black college. The Urban League, where he was active during business school at Emory, has historically been a Black organization focused on racial justice. He has connections, but they are limited mainly to the city's Black middle class, business leaders, and community activists.

Kevin's experiences show how networks can be racially segregated in ways that have implications for how people access jobs. As he tells it, it wasn't so much that he was lacking relationships or connections. He was linked to people in New Orleans who could point him toward potential opportunities. The challenge was that the highly racialized character of most social networks (his included) meant that his access to jobs relied on Black workers in his field who could get him in the door. These links can certainly be of some help, and predominantly Black social relationships are better than nothing. But they have limits, because often, these workers are less likely to be integrated into key leadership positions. When Black workers are less likely to be plugged into these "decision-making roles," networks like Kevin's, which are largely based on historically Black organizations, aren't able to offer the same occupational rewards.[2]

It might seem that earning an advanced degree would change things for Kevin. Part of the often-unspoken appeal of such credentials is that they put recipients in a position where they become connected to similar others who can provide resources, support, and information. Sociologist Shamus Khan's study of an exclusive boarding school in the Northeast indicates that a major part of why parents send their children to a school that bills upwards of $50,000 per year in tuition is the expectation that it will pay dividends both in the present and down the line. Parents believe that this school will offer a direct line of admission to Ivy League and other highly selective universities. They also fully expect that their children will rub shoulders with those from other elite families.[3]

In theory, then, Kevin's MBA from Emory, itself a selective institution, should have expanded and developed his networks further. Yet even with this degree, and a work history that has included employment in many predominantly white spaces, Kevin's networks have not changed substantially. He noted with more than a little frustration: "I have a decent network that again, is more based on FAMU [Florida A&M University] and high school and people I've known in my social circle than people I've known in a professional capacity. No one from Emory or from any other professional setting has—well, let me put it like this: I've never had a white person help me out getting a job. Not ever."

Black Women, White Women, and Who Helps Whom

Kevin's assessment of his network is pretty bleak and fairly critical. But the fact is, he *is* employed, and has been consistently for some time. Thus, it might seem that there is a disjuncture between Kevin's account of a network that has its limitations and his career history as someone who has been able to find work and remain employed in the area of his choosing. This is particularly noteworthy in an era when unemployment continues to be disproportionately high for Black Americans and when he is employed in a field where Black men like himself are very much underrepresented.

So what explains this apparent disconnection? Who has helped Kevin find work? And why? It has been clear from his accounts that white colleagues, peers, and associates in his networks have not been pivotal to his finding employment. And he has noted that he does have a network of members of the Black middle class in both New Orleans and Atlanta who have been very useful in pointing him toward opportunities. What explains how and why that particular network has emerged to be at least partially useful?

For Kevin, this is an easily answered question: "At one school, a Black woman friend recommended me. When I was trying to get the consultant gig, a Black woman I knew said she could help, and she did. At my jobs in Atlanta, a Black woman who I knew worked at the organization. She ushered me through that process, and there was a Black guy in HR who helped me through. At [my] last job, a Black woman handled the entire process."

Black women have been integral to helping Kevin find work. Not only are his networks predominantly composed of Black people in all of the cities where he has studied and worked, but it has been Black women who have taken the lead and been decisive partners in steering tips, opportunities, and information about open positions his way. In many cases, these are also older Black women who have spent more time in these professional environments and see Kevin as someone who could contribute meaningfully to the organizations.

The role that Black women have played in navigating and steering Black workers in their social networks toward key jobs has been largely understudied. But a wealth of information indicates that Black women have, for many years, been the backbone of Black communities, playing critical and necessary roles in many organizations and various causes and initiatives. As far back as the 1890s, Black women formed clubs designed to focus on issues related to health and education, and perhaps most important, to organize for racial uplift and an end to lynching. (Many of these were started by legendary journalist Ida B. Wells-Barnett, who was heavily involved in suffrage and racial justice movements as well.)[4]

In the twentieth century, Black women continued to do this important work. While not as widely known as some of their counterparts in the civil rights movement who were men, Black women like Unita Blackwell, Jo Ann Robinson, and Gloria Richardson were integral in organizing efforts to register Black voters, particularly in areas of the country where overt voter intimidation and harassment were regular, legal, and supported by the political establishment. Though these efforts put these women at risk of unemployment, censure, and even death in some cases, their work laid the necessary foundation for changing centuries of voter disenfranchisement in large swaths of the United States.[5]

Today, many are just beginning to acknowledge and understand the significance of Black women's efforts to achieve particular social, economic, and political outcomes. In 2017, Black women made news as a decisive voting bloc that swung the outcome of close elections in Alabama, Virginia, and New Jersey. In 2020, organizers like Stacey Abrams helped flip Georgia from a reliably Republican state to one that voted for Democrat Joe Biden in the presidential election, supporting a Democratic presidential candidate for the first time since 1992 and electing two Democrats to the Senate. (This is a fact that, as a fellow Spelman College alumna, I never get tired of pointing out to anyone who will listen.) Thus, it is not wholly surprising that Kevin would describe Black women as a group that has been key in steering him toward occupational opportunities and attractive job openings. Black women have been doing this type of work for quite some time.[6]

Crucially, Kevin is quick to point out that the attention and support he receives from Black women does not transcend racial lines. In other words, he does not get the same support from white women, who occupy many of the leadership and gatekeeping roles in the K-12 educational system. Comparing the reactions he gets from Black and white women, Kevin told me: "I notice that there's a bit of maternalism with the way Black women have been able to help me in my career. White women cannot and do not look at me in that way. I will not get the benefit of the doubt, certain levels of grace, love, and care . . . I have to work harder to break down those barriers." Recounting a particular experience at one educational nonprofit, Kevin said: "The executive director was a white woman, and she had a very specific idea of where people are and where they should be placed. It became, 'I don't see Kevin doing this; I see him doing that.' That ends up limiting where I could go."

While the role Black women have played in advancing political causes and movements is just now becoming more widely known, the friction between Black men and white women is far from a secret, and is nothing new. The weight of history has long shaped how race, gender, and sexuality influence interactions between Black men and white women. In the years between 1877 and 1950, more than four thousand Black people were lynched in the United States.[7] These horrific crimes included the murders of Black women and children as well as Black men. But it is well-known that during this time, intimations of relationships of any kind between Black men and white women could be sufficient impetus for white vigilantes to initiate a lynching. The year 1955 saw one of the most famous cases of this form of racial terrorism when twenty-one-year-old Carolyn Bryant accused fourteen-year-old Emmett Till of making an unwanted sexual advance toward her. Bryant's husband, Roy, and his half brother, J. W. Milam, brutally murdered Till in response. Years later, Bryant admitted that she lied about the encounter.[8]

In the shadow of this history, interactions between Black men and white women can remain fraught to this day. Although public, interracial relationships between these two groups are now more common, whites are still the racial group least likely to have exogamous relationships, and when they do, white-Latinx relationships are the most common.[9] And Black-white relationships in the public sphere can still be controversial. As recently as 2013, a Cheerios commercial featuring a Black father, white mother, and biracial daughter generated so much racist outcry on YouTube that General Mills eventually disabled users' ability to post comments. Furthermore, the specter of Black men being perceived as threatening to white women has in no way disappeared. In spring 2020, white executive Amy Cooper made a 911 call to assert that an "African American man" was "threatening [her] and [her] dog," despite video footage that refuted her claim.[10]

Today, Black men continue to tread carefully around white women co-workers for fear of evoking white colleagues' discomfort and fears. Mark, an Atlanta-based engineer, told me that in an environment where he was the only Black employee, "I'm *very* careful with how I interact with female students or female colleagues so that things cannot be interpreted the wrong way." Nick, a nurse from Philadelphia, echoed this sentiment: "I was in a meeting one time, and I said something direct, and this white woman felt threatened. You just have to be very cautious."[11]

The different responses Kevin receives from Black women and white women, then, are tied to both historical and structural factors. White women have not been supportive of his career, whereas Black women, older Black women in particular, view him as someone who can make important contributions to the educational ecosystem in New Orleans and recognize his leadership potential. They refer Kevin to jobs and guide him past the initial screening stages to help him land employment.

Yet by virtue of their own limited power, for the most part, Black women can get Kevin only in the door. Working in the predominantly white female field of K-12 education-based nonprofits means that once he is hired, white women often direct the course of his career from that point. And as he notes, they rarely offer the same level or depth of support and encouragement. Instead, histories of complicated racial and gendered dynamics mean that these interactions are far more cautious and tentative, as white women rarely identify the same leadership potential and skills that seem evident to his Black women counterparts. In navigating gray areas associated with getting hired, Black women have proved to be the people Kevin can trust. But their connections can get him only so far.

CHAPTER 10

Employment in the New Fissured Workplace

"IT'S UP TO YOU"

Constance's and Kevin's experiences show that relationships and connections matter when trying to land employment. Perhaps more important, they highlight the fact that for Black workers, these networks take on nuanced importance. The right early relationships can help land a job, but rebuilding those networks down the line can be particularly challenging for Black employees in predominantly white workplaces. Furthermore, all-Black networks—and the ways Black women in particular deploy them to help Black workers get a foot in the door—can be helpful up to a certain point, but they have their limitations as well.

At the same time, work has shifted to include paradigms that aren't so heavily reliant on networks and connections. Gig employment offers one such example as a growing segment of the new economy, which is characterized by contract work, austerity measures, a shrinking public sector, and the glorification of free markets. In the new economy, many organizations prize workers who are nimble, agile, and entrepreneurial. Companies like Uber, DoorDash, and Instacart utilize independent contractors who have little connection to the company and provide their own equipment in order to do their work. Driving for Grubhub, for instance, contractors assume responsibility for their hours, drive their own cars to pick up orders, and to a degree, determine their own pay by working as much or as little as they like.[1] Grubhub, and other companies that are premised on gig work, thus do not consider their workers employees.[2]

As business models like these have been introduced over the past few decades, direct employer-employee relationships have become increasingly obsolete, leading to what economist David Weil refers to as the "fissured workplace."[3] In a fissured workplace, instead of companies hiring their workers directly, workers are often employed by intermediary companies who then contract out their labor to host companies. As a result, major companies can keep their labor costs down and boost their profits—great for the organization, but what about for the employees?

When it comes to hiring, the new reliance on contract workers changes the role networks play in getting a job. In the gig economy, job seekers can easily find work without having to rely on their connections, networks, and relationships. With a car, smartphone, and internet access, virtually anyone can get a job driving for one of the many food-delivery apps on the market now. If you have transportation and flexibility, TaskRabbit, an app that connects users to workers willing to help them with assorted tasks, is an option. If you own your home, Airbnb allows you to procure additional income by renting it out or rooms within it to guests who are looking for a place to stay. Personal or professional relationships are not a decisive factor for work in the gig economy—your interests and capabilities matter much more. In that way, gig work is very much made for the new economy, as it relies on connecting users with people who can provide services, while relieving companies of the burden that "employees" and their associated labor costs can bring.

Work Without Networks

From this perspective, the gig economy might seem to be a way for Black workers to sidestep some of the issues that vexed Constance and Kevin. Alex, whose job history reflects a combination of gig work and more traditional employment, cites efficiency and flexibility as attractive components of gig work. "The thing I like about these [jobs] is that you set your own hours," she told me. "If you want to work fifteen minutes, you work fifteen minutes. If you want to work five hours, you work five hours. It's up to you." Alex said that in the years before her gig jobs, she worked at a day care for five years, a job she secured through a connection from her prior experience in childcare. Before that, she worked as a cashier in a supermarket, in retail stores like Kmart and Walmart, and in fast food. Some of these jobs she found through connections; others, through ads and straightforward applications.

The job Alex had right before she turned to the gig economy was one she enjoyed and that she secured through her networks. Even entry-level jobs in the service sector can be easier to secure with connections, and Alex's were able to assist her when a friend told her that a company called Perspectives was looking for workers. Perspectives had a contract with the local airport, so employment with the company meant that Alex had access to a variety of positions there. She started in the queue line, which is essentially what it sounds like—she was responsible for directing passengers to the correct lanes they needed to pass through security, monitoring bags to ensure they would pass screening checks, steering passengers to appropriate places in the airport, and otherwise making sure that lines moved swiftly and efficiently. Alex describes herself as a "people person," so the customer interaction suited her fine, but the job came with other unforeseen complications: "I have asthma, and dealing with customers could aggravate it because sometimes they smelled like cigarette smoke or perfume. Plus, you stand on your feet for eight hours a day with only a fifteen-minute break, and that's not really enough when you stand for eight hours."

When the opportunity arose to switch out of the queue line, Alex took it, moving to a position as a wheelchair pusher. Here, she was responsible for assisting wheelchair-bound passengers to and from their gates and ensuring that their needs were met while they were in the terminal. Eventually, however, she transferred out of that position into the equipment room, where she kept stock of inventory and found and provided necessary equipment upon request. It proved to be her favorite of the three jobs she held with Perspectives. Unlike the queue line job, working in the equipment room cut down on interactions with passengers, which meant she was in better health since her asthma was at bay. And in contrast to working as a wheelchair pusher, she didn't have to stand on her feet all day. The equipment room offered a perfect balance.

Unfortunately, that balance lasted only about nine months. As the coronavirus pandemic tore through the United States and multiple businesses shuttered to try to "flatten the curve," the travel industry took a particularly hard hit. Air travel suffered as flyers remained home to try to stay safe, and the airlines sought federal funds to stay afloat. Consequently, Alex wasn't completely surprised by what happened next. Perspectives began laying off workers, and unfortunately, she was one of the employees let go.

Periods of layoffs and downsizing are particularly fraught for Black workers. The old adage "last hired, first fired" has a lot of truth to it. As we've established, rampant employment discrimination means that Black workers face significant obstacles in the hiring process—whether or not they have the social networks that help get them in the door. And when companies lay off workers, which they often do in response to adverse economic conditions, making decisions based on seniority means that Black workers, who have to leap higher hurdles to get hired in the first place, are frequently the newest employees and the first to go.[4]

For Black workers like Alex, who have a history of hourly wage jobs in the service industry, layoffs and economic downturns can be destabilizing. And if they lack the networks to help them move easily into other jobs, then unemployment can present a real challenge—unless another work option is available.

Gig Work to the Rescue?

When Perspectives let Alex go, she didn't fret. She was not happy to be laid off, and being out of work is rarely ideal. But she knew that the gig economy was an option, so she took advantage of it as a temporary solution. At the time, Alex expected that when the economy restarted and people began traveling again, the airline industry would bounce back and she could be rehired easily. It was a logical assumption—she'd been a good worker and was laid off through no fault of her own but because of unforeseeable circumstances beyond her control. Until the economy improved, Uber Eats and Postmates functioned as a stopgap measure that allowed her to set her own hours, count on at least some guaranteed income, and enjoy a fairly predictable routine.

Framed in this way, gig work fills an important gap in the modern economy. It allows workers like Alex to make ends meet when they are in between full-time positions. Economic downturns and layoffs have become increasingly commonplace as companies seek to maximize their profits and invest less and less in labor costs. Given that, gig work becomes an easy option when workers need something to tide them over and cover their basic needs. And as Alex noted, it becomes easy enough to fit into complicated or unpredictable schedules and allows contractors to maximize their wages according to their own needs.

Alex's story paints an optimistic picture of the way Black workers can bypass the modern reliance on networks and relationships, or the gray areas of hiring. This is one of the bright sides of the gig economy. Without using networks, Black workers can still find employment, and that employment has some positive aspects, such as flexibility and ease of access. But Alex's account also reflects some darker aspects of gig work that become clearer once we dig a little deeper.

The Downside of the Gig Economy

Despite its defenders' claims that gig work allows contractors to make as much or as little as they want, the reality is more complicated. Company policies make it hard for many workers to subsist on these earnings alone. For instance, frequent changes to the rules for driver payment rates or service fees can mean that contractors earn less for their work. Additionally, platforms deduct a percentage of contractors' earnings, which can make it difficult for them to earn enough to live on, particularly in cities with a high cost of living. When these dynamics are factored in, it becomes clear that even though gig work provides a means of employment that doesn't rely on extensive social networks, that work is not necessarily very lucrative, and in fact can be exploitative and taxing.[5]

This argument challenges one of the main selling points about the gig economy—that workers can decide how much they want to earn. Indeed, Alex even cited this as one of the advantages that led her to Uber Eats and Postmates. She controls her schedule, the jobs pay her bills, and she can work more (and presumably earn more) if she wants. But studies have shown that the way many companies calculate wages makes it extremely difficult, if not impossible, for many workers to subsist on gig work full time. More commonly, gig workers are "strugglers" who face an uphill battle making ends meet, or "strivers" who do gig work to supplement their incomes and earn extra cash. Thus, when it comes to finding work without relying on networks, Alex is relegated to a sector of the economy that purports to offer more financial security than it actually provides.[6]

Although gig jobs are available without networks, they are also not likely to offer solid benefits. Some companies do provide such perks to workers, but they do so very selectively and to highly skilled employees in jobs that usually require connections to land. Netflix, for instance, offers salaried workers a full year off at full pay after birth or adoption of a child, and Airbnb provides birth mothers twenty-two weeks of paid leave.[7] Given that the United States is the only high-income country not to offer paid parental leave (even significantly poorer countries such as the Democratic Republic of the Congo and Afghanistan offer this very basic benefit), this is a particularly notable provision because companies aren't legally obligated to offer anything, and many provide no paid leave as a result. Consequently, many new mothers return to work within a few weeks of giving birth, despite the health risks, stress, and emotional exhaustion this causes. In most cases, they don't do this because they feel up to it or just love their jobs that much—no one has ever fixed postpartum sleep deprivation by going back to work. They do it because they can't afford not to.

These policies thus generate laudatory responses and no doubt help to attract top job candidates, but they also are far less expansive than may be immediately apparent. These benefits apply to salaried workers who are directly employed by Netflix or Airbnb—their executives, managers, and other high-level earners. In a fissured workplace, policies like this leave out the contractors who take on much of the less glamorous work that allows the two companies to function. Contract work certainly does not provide extensive paid family leave policies—it doesn't guarantee workers' compensation, unemployment insurance, or paid leaves of any kind.

In the predominantly white tech industry, the workers who are directly employed at these companies benefit from the opportunity to balance parenthood and work; bond with children; and for those who have given birth, recover from that arduous physical experience. But Black employees are usually underrepresented among this group, which means they aren't as eligible for these generous benefits. To put it in stark terms, the women (mostly white) who do coding or software design get the paid time off to bond with their children. But Black women who clean their offices or cook the food in the cafeteria?—they get none of these perks. Instead, they figure out how to pay for childcare and go back to work.

This variation in how companies treat certain classes of workers is a major factor driving racial and economic inequality today. A team of economists studying this issue estimated that nearly 66 percent of the explosion in income inequality from 1978 to 2012 is a result of these disparities between firms—the ones that selectively rely on networks and connections to employ workers who get significant pay, perks, and benefits, and the ones that offer none of those things.[8] This is economic inequality today, and given how underrepresented Black workers are in the elite jobs, it has a decidedly racial tinge to it.

Ultimately, Alex's account shows that while social networks are a central mechanism for hiring in today's knowledge-based, tech-driven economy, there are ways that Black workers can subvert this process. Those who forego networks entirely can still find work, but that work tends to be more precarious, uncertain, and lower wage. Black workers like Alex can use the gig economy to sidestep the gray areas associated with hiring, but that path rarely leads them to stable, lucrative employment.

CHAPTER 11

Getting Hired vs.
Doing the Hiring

"I'M KIND OF AN OUTLIER"

When Amalia shared her pathway into journalism with me, it felt very relatable to my own route into higher education, some of which I have already detailed. She also had a father in the same field who exposed her early on to the joys and opportunities of that occupation. She'd always loved writing and found that it was something she was good at and enjoyed. And she briefly considered a career in another field (for her it was dramatic arts; for me it was psychology) before settling back on her initial path and pursuing the same line of work as her father. (I didn't ask her if her dad also regularly provides unsolicited ideas for projects and assignments she could be doing, but I definitely wondered.)

Amalia completed college and graduate school on the East Coast. Midway through earning her master's degree, she applied for an unpaid internship at a major online magazine. At the time, she was also working part time in a restaurant to make ends meet and cover the costs associated with living in an expensive city. That unpaid internship proved to be her foot in the door. Though she initially had to work other jobs simultaneously to pay her bills, she eventually landed a paid internship with the same magazine. That paid internship turned into a part-time position, which eventually became a full-time, salaried job. Thus, in the span of about eighteen months, Amalia went from being an unpaid intern working a restaurant job on the side to a salaried writer for a major online publication.

Getting Hired Without Networks

This meteoric rise is impressive. It's also anomalous. For one, Amalia's ability to thrive even while working an unpaid internship is notable. Such internships have become more common and can enhance a candidate's attractiveness to potential employers, but they also widen racial wealth gaps. The reasons for this are fairly self-evident: expecting people to work for free assumes that they have a level of financial security that can allow them to meet basic needs. But Black families are significantly less likely than their white counterparts to have access to wealth, making these unpaid positions an impossibility. Not only that, Black families that make it into the middle class are often in a more financially precarious position than their white counterparts. They are less likely to be able to draw on generational wealth from parents, grandparents, or great-grandparents and are instead more likely to be in the position where they provide extensive financial support to extended kin networks.[1] Thus, the fact that Amalia was able not only to accept an unpaid internship but to manage to thrive in it enough to leverage it into full-time, salaried work is rather exceptional.

Second, Amalia noted that her pathway into work differed from that of many peers in that the initial hire that set her on the path to her journalistic career was not heavily affected by her networks in the industry. "Connections often do matter," she emphasized. "In my case that's why I say I'm kind of an outlier. Because in my case these weren't connections; I just applied blindly." When it came to the unpaid internship at the online magazine, Amalia was successful in getting her foot in the door even without ties to others there who could vouch for her or direct hiring managers to take her application seriously. However, she observed that this was unusual in journalism, telling me: "Connections are often really important, and that's how I've seen other people in my profession get jobs—having worked with people who move and they move with them, or they hire them away. That happens a lot."

Is Amalia the exception that proves the rule? We know from Constance and Kevin that networks matter significantly in getting a foot in the door, and that Black workers are less likely to be immersed in the ones that direct them toward solid employment. We also know from Alex's account that it is possible to find work without these networks, but the work that is available doesn't provide much economic security. What explains how Amalia landed this entry-level job without the connections or ties that matter so much in our current workplaces?

The Industry

Amalia's account suggests that while social networks can remain a factor, their impact may be mitigated by the field in which Black candidates are looking for work. Changes in employment trends mean that certain occupations have pronounced worker shortages. In some cases, the numbers of workers in these occupations simply dwindle and eventually die out because of technological changes and reduced demand. For instance, the rise in automation allows companies to hire fewer data-entry clerks than a few decades ago. With the rise of the internet, telephone operators have virtually disappeared as an occupational category. And as streaming services proliferate, the ways we access music and movies have transformed to the point where stores like Tower Records and Blockbuster

Video are now just a fond memory of a previous era for Gen X-ers like me.[2]

Labor shortages in other professions, however, worry labor economists, sociologists, and policymakers because they portend a dearth of trained workers who can provide essential services. When these shortages occur not because of technological advancements but because of retirements, a decline in the number of skilled workers, or brain drain, it can mean that large segments of the population run the risk of missing out on necessary training, information, or care. This dynamic is present in health care and public education, both of which are facing a dramatic shortage of providers as many retire, quit outright, or suffer from extreme burnout due to factors including but not limited to the coronavirus pandemic.[3] These labor shortages can potentially create a ripple effect of shifting economic outcomes and diminished human capital.

Journalism doesn't always attract the same sober attention as health care and education, but it is also a field where shifting employment trends may matter in shaping the gray area of hiring. Decreased funding, increased consolidation, and technological advances mean that there are fewer subscribers to and readers of print newspapers in the digital age. Consequently, the number of newsroom employees declined by 57 percent between 2008 and 2020, as many newspapers struggle to stay afloat. My childhood memories of my parents sitting in comfortable chairs, half-hidden behind their copies of the local newspaper, probably sound archaic to anyone who's grown up with Kindles and iPads.

Even as the number of newsroom employees declined during the early 2000s, employment in the digital publishing sector has flourished. The number of employees at online publications (like the one where Amalia started her career) grew by 144 percent during that same time span of 2008 to 2020.[4] Newsrooms may be shuttering and print media may be on the way out, but digital outlets appear to be looking for workers.

Under circumstances like these, social networks and relationships may not be as determinative for hiring. Amalia noted, however, that her connections were a factor for getting hired into subsequent, higher-ranking positions. For instance, when she moved into her second position, she already had a casual professional relationship with one of the higher-ups. When she was recruited to her third position, she'd already worked closely with several other journalists associated with the company, so they had the opportunity to see her work in real-time and to know her as a potential colleague. But her relative ease getting her foot in the door may be explained simply by the reality that in growth industries that desperately need workers, social networks may be less of a deal breaker for Black job candidates.

On the Other Side

As a salaried employee at a prestigious outlet with numerous features under her belt, Amalia has come a long way since the unpaid, entry-level internship that started her career. And in this lofty position, she has an interesting window into how hiring functions as a gray area that disadvantages Black workers. This is because part of her job has involved being the person who helps to bring on freelancers. Consequently, she sees firsthand how this process works—and how it doesn't.

At one of her past jobs, Amalia spent a significant portion of her time trying to publish Black journalists. In that role, this type of recruiting fell well within her purview. It was also consistent with the organization's stated goal of improving diversity and showcasing more voices of color. Recall that Amalia worked at an organization where employees talked openly about racial disparities, and particularly after summer 2020, they wrestled with what they could do to address some of these inequalities in journalism at large. Thus, Amalia was initially excited about using her role to attract more Black voices to the platform.

What she found in practice was that bringing on more Black

writers wasn't quite so easy. This was not because of a lack of qualified candidates, interesting topics, or intense competition from
other outlets. It certainly was not because she lacked the networks
to identify and reach out to Black journalists. Rather, the Black
writers she attempted to hire for freelance opportunities were scrutinized and monitored in a way that made publishing their work
nearly impossible.

Describing this outcome, Amalia told me: "It seems clear to
me—and other Black colleagues—that nonwhite, marginalized
voices were more heavily scrutinized than the white male ones. So,
trying to get pieces greenlit was way more difficult and hindering.
We had certain writers who said, 'I can't work with you because I'm
an expert in this subject and I'm being asked to go through these
unreasonable hoops to prove my argument makes sense.' And these
same concerns were not held up for white voices." Amalia found
this dynamic enormously frustrating. She worked in a newsroom
where conversations about race and equity were legitimized and
allowed, and in a profession that itself was under scrutiny for the
way it had marginalized Black voices. Yet her efforts to provide a
platform for more Black journalists to tell their stories ultimately
was curtailed.

Amalia's perception that Black journalists were subject to
greater monitoring and oversight is supported by the data. Economists Costas Cavounidis, Kevin Lang, and Russell Weinstein
found not only that this is true, but that this selective observation
has significant employment consequences.[5] As managers spend
more time watching Black workers, they are more attuned to potential errors and mistakes that can then become grounds for ter-
mination. When these sanctions are applied early on in a worker's
tenure with a company, they can make it more difficult for that
worker to develop connections and networks with colleagues. Furthermore, incidents that for white workers result in mild penalties
and second (or third and fourth) chances often result in disciplinary
action or dismissal for Black employees.[6] This heightened scrutiny

means that it would not only be more complicated for even a veteran journalist like Amalia to bring in Black writers, but that those who do get hired on a freelance basis are less likely to remain. She was witnessing in real time one of the ways that bias in the hiring process makes it harder for Black workers to secure employment.

Observing this firsthand left Amalia disillusioned and stressed. She remarked, "Feeling stifled, not able to work with the writers I wanted because they were not given the same benefit of the doubt, that was very frustrating." She went on to describe this particular company as "one where Black people were often being doubted, their voices were not being heard. And it was across the board. There was a lot of dissatisfaction and unhappiness." Her successes and accomplishments should have put her in a position where she could open doors for other Black journalists. But the gray areas of work, in particular the ways that greater scrutiny and oversight can be part of the hiring process, undermined her efforts to do so.

CHAPTER 12

When Movements Matter

"A STRANGE THING HAPPENED THAT WEEK"

There's an old saying attributed to Roman philosopher Seneca that "luck is what happens when preparation meets opportunity." This quote emphasizes that for many successful people, their innate skills and talents alone are not what allows them to reach a pinnacle— putting in the work, the preparation, is just as critical. But what about the opportunity? Where and how do opportunities arise for Black workers to get their foot in the door? What do these opportunities look like, and how do workers know when to seize them?

For Brian, the Los Angeles film executive, Seneca's saying is an apt reflection of how he found himself in a high-paying, powerful position in the entertainment industry. Unlike some of his colleagues, Brian did not come from a family with history or connections in the industry. His parents, people he describes as "hustlers and strivers in many respects," were entrepreneurs in the Rust Belt. But their various businesses, running enterprises that ranged from a beauty salon to a cleaning service, allowed him to grow up comfortably middle class in a Detroit suburb, and to entertain dreams of making it in Hollywood.

In other words, his parents' entrepreneurial ventures may have given Brian the foundation he needed to see Hollywood—and the entertainment industry—as a place where he could possibly develop a career. When successful, entrepreneurship has been a reliable method for Black owners to build wealth, even in circumstances where credit is limited and resources are scarce.[1] As far back as the postslavery era, some Blacks engaged in business ownership, though these businesses were usually very small endeavors that offered laundering or other personal services. They also ran such businesses at great risk, because for much of the nineteenth and twentieth centuries, Black entrepreneurs who appeared too successful risked white retribution in the form of vandalism, assault, or lynching. In fact, part of what spurred journalist and activist Ida B. Wells-Barnett's crusade against lynching was the fact that her close friend Thomas Moss had been lynched at least in part because of white resentment at his business success.[2] And it's not a coincidence that thriving Black business districts in Tulsa, Oklahoma, and Rosewood, Florida, were destroyed by white mobs. Entrepreneurship has always represented a path to independence and economic self-sufficiency, and when Black business owners took that path, many whites believed it threatened the racial hierarchy.

For Black women in particular, salon ownership has long been a protected market that enabled them to establish economic stability for themselves and for other Black women. This has been the case up to and including the present day. Many Black women hair salon owners correctly observe that caring for Black women's hair provides an opportunity to fill a gap in the personal care market. Black-owned beauty salons are a place where Black women are made to feel central, important, and pampered, in contrast to how they are often treated in the larger society.[3] Larger chain salons like Supercuts or Hair Cuttery may not provide this same level of service, nor are they equipped to create an environment that centers Black women. They also may not be places where the staff is adequately trained for and familiar with Black women's particular hair-care needs.

Additionally, for some working-class Black women, entrepreneurship in the hair industry offers a path to upward mobility that is unavailable through other lines of work. Opportunities for stable, well-paying employment for non-college-educated workers have declined markedly since the 1970s. And given that Black women consistently face racial and gender discrimination in the labor force, securing jobs that offer the chance for economic advancement often isn't an easy feat. But for those who have the skills to do so, becoming a hair salon owner can enable some Black women to move from working class to middle class. Business equity becomes an asset and a form of wealth and can be a much more lucrative option than working as a data-entry or billing clerk, in fast food, or in janitorial services.[4]

When I was working on my dissertation on Black women entrepreneurs' economic mobility, I interviewed a salon owner my age whose experience reflected this. At the time, Theresa, like me, was twenty-five years old. Unlike me, she hadn't particularly enjoyed school and had no plans to attend college, much less pursue a graduate degree. Theresa tried out a few other jobs before getting a job at a nearby hair salon. When she thrived in the position, the owner encouraged her to move out on her own and open her own shop. At the time of our interview, she casually remarked that the six-figure income she was making from her salon enabled her to buy a new car and was allowing her to invest in opening another shop in a different part of the country. As I walked back to my tiny apartment and reflected on the limits of my graduate student stipend, the contrast between her economic status and mine was definitely enough to prompt some serious thinking about my career choices.

For Brian, seeing his parents model the work ethic, dedication, and drive necessary to build their respective businesses inspired the grit and determination he knew he would need to make and produce his own movies. With that in mind, he told me: "In retrospect, maybe it doesn't seem that crazy, even though I'm a middle-class person from the Midwest, that I decided to pursue a job in the movies. In the independent world where I spent a long time, getting your movie made is like building a business from the ground up—even though most of these fail," he added with a chuckle. Nonetheless, Brian was able to start small, producing an independent film that opened to critical acclaim in 2012, writing for mainstream and trade magazines, and working as an adjunct professor at a local university's drama department to build his dream of creating films.

Brian described his early years working in the industry: "That [first] film was a culmination of maybe over a decade and a half of intense study, desire, and belief in wanting to make such a thing. It was made for a lark, a song, with $25,000. That gets you about an hour of shooting the type of movie I was an executive on when I went to the studio. But yeah, I made indies in New York for a little money; I wrote for magazines mostly about the movies, politics."

For Brian, like for many other creatives, filmmaking and producing felt like a calling. As far back as his childhood, he loved the storytelling aspect of the movies. When I asked him what prompted a kid from Detroit to pursue work in the film industry, he replied: "I grew up watching movies. I thought about who got to tell a story and why. Even back when I was in preschool I wanted to see movies made from the comic books I loved—funny that that's actually happening now. But what drove me to do it was an overarching belief in creating meaning that was valuable in my life and other people's lives."

But as a Black creative, Brian's perspective on telling stories was, and remained, fundamentally shaped by his racial identity. Telling stories attracts him, but he also wants to tell stories that represent the variety and multifaceted experience of Black life, and those of other often overlooked groups as well. As he noted: "African Americans have been historically marginalized, as Donald Bogle suggested, as toms, coons, mulattoes, mammies, or bucks.[5] And why? To what end? These are conversations that I've had in my own head, and have had in public, thinking that the country would be better off if African Americans were better represented. I'm interested in [more than] Black filmmaking, but it is a special interest of mine."

Oscars So White

That commitment, and the preparation that accompanied it, would come in handy when Brian got the opportunity to move from the hardscrabble world of independent filmmaking to the sleeker, more polished life of a studio executive. In 2015, the #OscarsSoWhite campaign rocked Hollywood as critics, activists, and industry insiders noted that no actors of color were nominated for any of the top award categories. When, in 2016, the nominees reflected a similar lack of diversity, pressure grew on the Academy of Motion Picture Arts and Sciences to make changes. Attendees boycotted the awards, some actors spoke out in support of greater diversity in the field, and the academy pledged to include more women of all races and men of color.[6]

It was around this time that Brian got the email that changed his life. He recalled that around the time of Donald Trump's inauguration, "A strange thing happened that week. I was writing and teaching and still trying to make another movie, and I got an email from a guy named Fred Brooks. He's a legendary guy, who, about a year or two before I got this email, had taken over as the head of a major studio, Worldwide Studios. I knew him through my mentor, who had long been a friend and collaborator of his, and I'd written for some websites Fred started, he'd bought my movie, and so forth. And Fred had a subject line that just said, 'Worldwide Studios.' When I read it, it said, 'How would you like to leave academia and journalism and low-budget filmmaking behind and work for Worldwide Studios?' This led to a phone call, and I realized he was serious."

Brian's opportunity came at a time when larger forces were pushing to open more doors for Black creatives in the industry. If luck favors the prepared, Brian benefited from broader cultural changes and social movement activity like #OscarsSoWhite that highlighted the lack of Black voices in the film industry, and the importance of creating opportunities for Black creators to tell the very types of stories to which he was committed—narratives about the vagaries, complications, and breadth of Black life.

That this opportunity emerged for Brian in an era of social protest and action is part of a longer, consistent trend. In her study of Black corporate executives in the 1980s, sociologist Sharon Collins noted that as a result of civil rights–era activism and efforts, many of these workers were able to get a foot in the door of corporate spaces that previously had excluded them. In other words, protests and outcry that specifically focused on the ways Black Americans were being underserved and excluded led corporations to respond by finding, recruiting, and hiring Black executives.[7] Companies thus respond to social pressure if it is sustained, widespread, and visible enough. And for Brian, the push for Hollywood to show changes and more receptivity to diversity helped create a space where senior executives were specifically attuned to the lack of Black workers in their ranks.

Of course, Brian also had access to the relationships that often prove critical to landing a job. His connection to Fred Brooks was essential for getting the notice about the available position in the first place. Once again, social networks can make a key difference for Black workers seeking employment. That Brooks even knew of Brian, and thought of him as a good fit for an executive position with the studio, was due to the connection the two of them had been able to forge working in the industry together on various projects. "The indie film world is entirely relationship based," Brian confirmed. "If you don't have relationships with people who can pay for your film, who are people deeply established who can crew your movie, it won't happen. It's all about relationships. It's not a world where talent speaks for itself." But as Brian's experience shows, these networks help but were also activated by larger social forces of change and protest beyond his control. Those larger forces helped bolster studios' and executives' claims that they were now committed to diversity. But were they really? Did they mean what they said, or was it all just talk?

Demonstrating "Fit"

Getting the call from Brooks was only the first step in Brian's path toward moving into the role of a studio executive. Shortly after the phone conversation, the two of them had a lengthy breakfast and discussed the parameters of the job. They met at a St. Regis hotel where, over breakfast cocktails, eggs, and bacon, they talked about exactly what work at Worldwide Studios would entail. Brian recalls: "Fred described the job as me overseeing a slate of movies, maybe ten or so a year, with an opportunity to make two of those as the executive in charge. And that seemed remarkably appealing to me, to have the power to put on films and filmmakers in that curatorial role, with the largesse of one of the most wealthy and powerful studios on the planet. And working for a man like Fred, with very unusual, subversive tastes, was also attractive. He's probably the only person I can recall working in a studio who supported the Black Lives Matter movement early on. So it seemed like a very unusual moment to have access to those resources, and someone interested in supporting Black filmmakers to show the wealth of our experiences, and a unique opportunity to do that."

But once Brian was hooked on the idea, he still had to go through the standard procedures for getting the job. This meant completing a formal interview for the position, and even with Brooks's support, that process took some time. He told me: "I was up front with Fred that I'm not going to be the type of Black executive that doesn't support Black filmmakers—the type that Black filmmakers complain about. And even saying that openly, I thought it went relatively well, but that interview and job still did not materialize immediately. I didn't do the interview process until September of 2017."

Brian prepared extensively for the interview. He worked closely with Brooks to gauge what sorts of questions might be asked during the hiring tests, he researched the company's principles to ensure he could present himself as someone whose decision making aligned with its stated values, and he studied up on which members of his prospective team he would meet (and need to impress most) in order to land the job. The advance work paid off when he made it through the screening process and was offered the job with World-wide Studios.

The process of having workers interview for jobs is hardly new. But Brian's experience here highlights some of the key ways that, even with the right social networks, interview processes are another area where Black workers can easily face additional disadvantages and hurdles. For one thing, in many interviews, hiring managers are looking for evidence that the prospective candidate is not just capable of doing the job, but is a "fit" with the organization's values and norms. A conservative law firm may blanch at hiring an associate with visible tattoos who operates a grow farm in her spare time, while a nonprofit focused on animal rights might balk at a hire who favors leather and fur and whose hobbies include fishing and hunting. In both cases, hiring managers at these organizations may find such hypothetical candidates to be a bit too dissimilar from the company culture and thus not a good "fit" for employment. When "fit" is a factor, the interview process can be a way that managers screen out candidates who do not seem to identify with the organization's larger values or beliefs.

The trouble with this reliance on "fit" is that it becomes an easy way to exclude Black workers, particularly in predominantly white workspaces. When assessing "fit" is a key part of the interview process, hiring managers may assume (without evidence) that Black candidates are too different and dissimilar from mostly white colleagues to integrate comfortably into the organization.[8] Consequently, Black workers are dismissed not because they lack the skill or proficiency for certain jobs, but because ambiguously defined ideas of "fit" put them at a disadvantage.

For Brian, though, these issues were not a factor. In fact, as he described it, he passed his interview with flying colors. But his success in the interview process underscores just how much broader cultural shifts can matter and change outcomes for Black workers.

Recall that he went into the interview—and approached the job itself—firmly dedicated to using the position as an opportunity to elevate and establish Black filmmakers interested in telling stories about the heterogeneity of Black experiences. At a time when Hollywood professed a commitment to this same ideal, Brian's interests and goals aligned with the studio's. This overlap factored into Brian's hope that the studio, and the industry at large, was finally ready to tell a variety of stories and to include Black voices more fully.

However, the same temporal forces that helped Brian get a foot in the door can change, and this is the downside of corporate hiring practices in the post–civil rights era. While that singular movement pushed companies to seek out and find Black executives who could take on leadership roles in their organizations, those same Black executives also worried about what would happen when the moment faded away. They knew that in many cases, their hiring was a result of external pressure and various companies' efforts to avoid bad press and negative judgments, as well as to maintain compliance with shifting legal structures that for the first time were assessing minority representation. These Black executives feared that when the pressure abated, corporate interest in hiring and advancing Black leaders would wane.

History shows that those fears were well-founded. Although the 1970s saw some growth in the rise of Black executives in the corporate sector, by the 1980s this progress began to be curtailed by shifts in the political economy. Neoconservatism emerged as a political philosophy, and with it came backlash to measures designed to affect racial progress. Affirmative action began to be recast as an example of reverse racism, and companies' efforts to meet the moment changed with the prevailing sentiments.[9]

It's not hard to see the parallels between this era and the events of the past few years. The year 2020 saw the largest protest movements ever in the United States, as record numbers of people of all races took to the streets in support of the Black Lives Matter movement.[10] For a brief moment in time, a majority of Americans expressed their support for this movement and its goals of ending systemic racism. And as we saw in the 1970s, corporations responded to public sentiment. JPMorgan Chase pledged to devote $30 billion to addressing systemic racism in banking, with a particular focus on improving access to homeownership and financing affordable housing.[11] Walmart committed $100 million for a five-year period while also promising to improve its supplier and workforce diversity.[12] As public outcry placed systemic racism at center stage, companies responded with financial commitments and promises for action.

As of this writing, it's too soon to say what has become of these corporate commitments. But the same worrying signs of backlash that emerged after the civil rights movement are certainly present. The rise of legislation against and outcry about critical race theory is mostly focused on educational spaces, but attempts to discourage attention to and discussion of systemic racism parallels the neoconservative backlash to affirmative action that arose in the 1980s. And in states like Florida, efforts to ban any public institutions (schools and workplaces) from engaging in trainings or teachings that focus on creating racial equity mean that companies are far from exempt from these countermeasures. Social pressures might push companies to make changes, but these changes won't necessarily last long.

For Brian, the industry response to #OscarsSoWhite worked to his benefit. It helped set the stage for him to leverage his networks and land the job he thought he wanted. But as we'll see in Part III, it did not necessarily mean Brian's tenure with the company would be all that he hoped.

CHAPTER 13

Successful Networking

"IT WAS A WHOLE DANCE"

The narratives in this part have shown various ways that hiring represents a gray area where racial inequality gets perpetuated in workplaces. We've seen how hiring often occurs through social networks and how Black workers can face significant difficulties integrating into and maintaining networks that can lead them to solid employment. Yet when they secure work without relying on connections, it's usually to access jobs that don't offer a great deal of security or stability. But it is also important to consider Black workers whose patterns don't fall neatly into what I have described above. These workers help us to understand the conditions under which some Black workers are able to leverage networks and move into jobs in their fields of choice. Darren and Max, the corporate executive and the doctor, respectively, offer some intriguing cases of how this happens.

Building Relationships That Work

Born in the Northeast to parents who were educators, Darren was a conscientious student who consistently earned high grades throughout his primary and secondary school years. Those efforts paid off when he was accepted to his first choice for college, a prestigious private university on the West Coast. During his college years, Darren decided to major in finance. He'd always excelled in math and had a head for business, so this course of study felt like a natural fit.

After graduating with a degree in business and finance, Darren attended a job fair and landed his first postcollege job fairly quickly. Many corporations visit elite colleges and universities in search of interns and workers for entry-level positions, and it was through one of these recruitment visits that Darren landed his first job with a major bank.[1] Finance is an elite profession that requires highly specialized technical skills, and while there aren't an overwhelming number of people trained to do corporate banking, it is not a field with the same shortages as health care or education. Darren was able to impress his interviewers and their corporate colleagues enough that he was the only person from his school to get an offer in the prestigious corporate and banking division right after graduating.

From that point on, Darren's career has been a steady rise through the corporate ranks. He worked at his first job for five years before leaving to get an MBA at one of the top-ranked business schools back on the East Coast. From there he went to Wall Street, where he survived the first few rounds of layoffs that followed the 2008 economic recession. However, he too was eventually laid off as companies contracted in the wake of the global financial collapse. After being let go, Darren took some time off before moving to a corporate job outside of the banking industry. He spent a few years there before moving back into banking to work in investor relations. When we spoke for our first interview, he'd recently moved into a vice president role for a major corporation.

The nature of Darren's career field, plus the time frame during which he's been working, means that he has had no choice but to become comfortable and familiar with navigating the hiring process. High-ranking jobs in the financial industry convey significant prestige and high salaries, but it is also a field where layoffs and downsizing are commonplace and job security is quite uncertain.[2] The cyclical nature of work in the financial industry meant that Darren had to learn how to adapt to market changes and to face the inevitable reality that eventual economic downturns would lead to his going through the hiring process again and again. Perhaps more important, he had to figure out how to build the relationships and connections necessary to land jobs that would help him advance, and to assess how to reenter the workforce when downturns and layoffs eventually occurred. Again, this is another aspect of work where Darren has had to discern his best approaches for navigating gray areas, particularly those related to hiring.

There are a few strategies for doing this. Social media, and LinkedIn in particular, offered him some opportunities. Darren recalled that there were times during his career when he was directly solicited by recruiters or companies through his LinkedIn profile. This was particularly the case during a seven-year stretch when he was employed as a vice president for a major financial corporation. He noted these inquiries and responded to the solicitors' messages, realizing that it was useful to cultivate such connections.

But this was not the primary way he maintained the networks he needed for moving into new positions. For Darren, as with most workers in the new economy, connections and social ties were key. "You have to build those relationships," he explained. "That was especially important coming out of business school. The companies would have big events at hotels. They'd have big bankers come in from New York and there would be a cocktail hour, everyone would mingle. Then after that you have to send the emails, 'It was nice meeting you' and blah blah blah. It was a whole dance. Then you would have to come to New York and meet them again. It seemed haphazard, but it was a deliberate process. And it was a competitive process on their side. Multiple places might be recruiting you, so everyone is trying to make their best impressions."

Darren described this process as "a little intense," but it wasn't something he really minded or objected to doing. Schmoozing and getting to know people was a fairly comfortable experience. He described himself as a pretty easygoing person who knows how to get along with people, laughingly stating, "I'm not too socially awkward, so that helps." Thus for Darren, having drinks, engaging in conversations with banking CEOs, and sharing common interests with potential colleagues seemed pretty unremarkable and just another part of the hiring process.

Darren also acknowledged that in addition to his forming relationships with colleagues in the finance industry, it could also be very valuable for him to maintain connections to headhunters and recruiters. He pointed out that prospects who are currently employed are often more attractive than job-seekers who are out of work. It's true: the longer one remains out of the labor force, the bleaker one's chances of finding employment become.[3] In fact, employment data often exclude people who have given up looking for work, which means that many measures of unemployment actually undercount those who are out of the labor force. And given the fact that work in the financial industry comes with a high risk of eventually being laid off because of downsizing or market changes, it is particularly prudent to take steps to avoid being unemployed for too long.

I asked Darren how he developed and maintained these relationships with recruiters. "You just need to stay in touch," he said. "Sometimes they'll call to see if you know anyone for a position, stuff like that. It's good to maintain an active dialogue." Maintaining connections with headhunters was simply, like socializing and forming ties with colleagues, a necessity that his job required.

Why was it so easy for Darren to develop these relationships? What strategies worked? An abundance of research suggests that Black workers like him are often excluded from the kinds of critical networks that are so important in today's workforce. Indeed, the narratives from Constance and Kevin highlight some of the challenges Black workers deal with when trying to form these ties. Why is Darren's experience different?

During one of our interviews, I inquired whether there were any obstacles or impediments that created difficulties for him in the hiring process, whether it came to building relationships or otherwise. He reiterated that making the necessary connections hadn't been that difficult for him, but then added: "I'm not one to focus on race a lot, but you do have to wonder a little. For instance, at one of the previous investment banks where I worked, they hired a lot of Black people for internships, but the offer rate was really low."

Darren trailed off for a moment, thinking, then continued: "It's hard to say if race impacts your career. For the most part I feel like I've been treated fairly. Everything hasn't been perfect, but other people have their ups and downs too. There are things that happen to you that could be because of race, but it's hard to ascribe it to that per se unless it's more blatant. Ultimately it becomes counterproductive to focus on it too much. I just think some people get caught up too much because that can be paralyzing. If someone is going to be racist, you can't—well, there are some remedies you can take, but you can't worry about the things you can't control."

"I Try to Be Easy to Get Along With"

Max, the emergency medicine doctor, shared an account that parallels Darren's. Max was also born and raised in the Northeast, but unlike Darren, Max grew up under much humbler circumstances. His parents were decidedly working class, and he was the first in his family to attain a college degree. Max got a bachelor's of science from Xavier University, a historically Black college known for training future physicians. He then attended Stanford Medical School, one of the top medical schools in the country, and completed his residency at nearby UC Berkeley.

When it came time for Max to seek full-time employment as a physician, he knew that networks mattered for knowing what kinds of opportunities were available. Further, he anticipated that relying on colleagues for their insights and connections would be the approach he would take if he needed to switch jobs as well. Though medicine does not have the same culture of layoffs as finance, doctors can also find themselves subject to market shifts. Their practices may be bought out, hospitals may downsize certain wards, or, as happened during the coronavirus pandemic, they may simply be laid off if circumstances call for trimming certain specialty areas to focus on other priorities.

If that happens, Max told me, "I can reach out to people that I've worked with before and say, 'Hey, do you know of any good jobs out there?'" Maintaining the relationships he needed to rely on for employment and hiring was fairly straightforward. "I've never had a job where I didn't like the people that I worked with," he said. "I'm pretty easygoing. If you don't do anything to piss me off, then we're probably going to be cool on a day-to-day basis." Max did acknowledge that he took a few steps to make sure that he could maintain these connections—he learned to play golf, for instance—but much like Darren, forming contacts he needed was not a particularly challenging process. Given that navigating these gray areas was relatively easy for him, developing these networks helped make looking for work less stressful.

But while networks and connections were important, Max argued that in a field like medicine, technical skills were just as important. Given the extensive education and training (not to mention debt) that doctors accrue, he felt that being a competent physician mattered just as much for getting a foot in the door. "It's about who you know to find out about opportunities," he told me, "but I feel like then my credentials support me getting a new job that's out there. Everybody gets a job out of residency. I don't know anybody that left residency and didn't have a job. It's just about whether it's the job you really want."

One of the Guys

The ease Darren and Max describe in forming ties and relationships underscores some important gender dynamics. In contrast to much of the research on microaggressions and workplace racism—and in some cases, counter to their own expectations—Black men, in particular, sometimes find that they can actually have a relatively easy time forming relationships with the colleagues and supervisors who will be integral to their professional advancement. Ricky, a Black engineering professor in San Diego, told me that he took advantage of his daily workouts in the campus fitness center to chat up the dean of the college, who also usually worked out around the same time. This relationship paid dividends when the two developed a cordial relationship, and Ricky was later able to approach the dean about becoming involved in an important university committee.[4]

However, it is important to put this finding in context. Relative ease developing ties to colleagues appears to be somewhat simpler for Black men than for Black women working in male-dominated professions. In these environments, Black men can play the odds. As they are surrounded by other men, even if some express racial biases or preconceptions, it may be easier to find others who become friends or can be helpful colleagues. As Fred, a structural engineer in Miami told me: "If you're male and African American, you don't have the double bias [that women face]. You're a minority, but you can befriend the other male colleagues. And maybe they won't like you, but there are enough senior male colleagues that one of them will like you, and you can get the information you need."[5]

In fact, Black men may benefit to some degree from the unspoken gendered expectations in these professions. As work has become more precarious and workers' control and autonomy have receded because of right-to-work laws, downsizing, unpredictability, and layoffs, companies have begun to demand more from their workers: more time, more availability, and more productivity. In fields like engineering, IT, and medicine, eight-hour workdays are a rarity. Instead, employees are increasingly expected to be available to handle and respond to demands and requests at all hours. And given that jobs have become more tenuous and uncertain in the new economy, workers are often unwilling to complain or object to these encroaching demands lest they lose their jobs.[6]

The growth of these "greedy professions" does not impact all workers equally, however. Managers typically expect that the extensive time demands that they impose on workers will leave women necessarily unable to meet the expectations and demands required to move into management positions and leadership roles. Company leaders assume that women will inevitably face a choice between work and family, and given those options, they will decide to prioritize their responsibility to kids. Even childless women are not exempt from these dynamics, because managers often preemptively decide that they will at some point choose to put family first.[7] Thus while Black men in male-dominated professions may be able to form connections more easily and benefit from managers' assumptions that they will be unencumbered by childcare and family responsibilities, Black women may find that developing ties and subverting managers' expectations remain as challenging as ever.

In this context where workers feel they have few options and women are expected to tap out, the long hours and extensive demands associated with some jobs can become characterized as a badge of honor. This may be particularly prevalent in occupations where women are an increasing segment of the workforce but have not yet reached parity or become the majority. In a study of (ultimately unsuccessful) attempts in several hospitals to put surgeons on rotations where they worked shorter hours, sociologist Katherine Kellogg found that some doctors clung to eighteen- to twenty-four-hour workdays because they associated such demands with the "manly" expectations required for a successful surgeon.[8]

Other studies of engineers in the tech industry have found that men in this field were willing to commit to long hours as a way of contrasting themselves with their women co-workers.[9]

Finance is different from engineering and medicine in many ways, but it shares some similarities in that workers frequently face layoffs and downturns, and the majority of workers in the field are men. In this context, then, it may be easier for Darren and Max to be a bit more sanguine about their ability to develop relationships with others in the industry. Since they both work in an environment that is not characterized by consistent, overt racial mistreatment from colleagues, it is not that difficult for Max and Darren to be "one of the guys" and to form the connections they need just by being their affable, easygoing selves. This can become a strategy that, for these Black men, offsets some of the disadvantages gray areas present in hiring.

What we should take away from this is that while Max and Darren report some relative ease making the connections that led them to the jobs they have, this is likely shaped by being Black men in industries where men are in the majority. It may be a bit easier for them to develop the networks and connections they need in fields where most of their co-workers are other men. By contrast, for Black women in STEM or corporate America, forming networks may be more complicated, especially given that the social events that facilitate this tend to involve amounts of alcohol consumption that may presage harassment, center around team sports, or occur at times that conflict with family responsibilities.[10] Certainly Constance's difficulties forming connections in chemical engineering provide a marked counterpoint. In other words, although Max and Darren attribute their ability to form networks to being affable and easygoing, it's likely that being "one of the guys" is easier if you are, in fact, a guy.

These accounts do not refute the premise that the heavy reliance on social networks in hiring can perpetuate racial inequalities. Note that even though Darren has been able to use these relationships to find work relatively easily when he needed to, he also has observed disparities in the industry. Some banks will do better offering summer internships to Black workers but fail to make them offers of full-time employment at the same rate as they do to whites. And Black students are underrepresented at the universities that many top companies in the financial industry rely on to staff their entry-level jobs.[11] Similarly, Max pointed out that Black doctors still face higher expectations and have to work harder to prove themselves once they get hired. But Max's and Darren's stories, even with their successes, show that when the conditions are right, Black men can sometimes successfully leverage the networks they do have in ways that work to their benefit.

Getting Past the Networking Hurdle

As we've seen from the narratives from Constance, Kevin, Alex, Brian, Amalia, Max, and Darren, the hiring process constitutes a gray area of work where racial inequalities persist. This is largely because of the outsize impact of social networks on who learns about jobs, who gets interviewed, and who gets hired. When networks steer who gets into a job and who doesn't, it means that nonprofit employees like Kevin, whose networks are composed mostly of older Black women, don't have the "right" connections for the industry in which he works. It means that film executives like Brian have a better chance activating those networks if there's outside pressure on their industry to make changes. And it means that workers like Alex, who eschewed using networks altogether when her financial situation called for it, are tracked into jobs that don't offer much by way of high pay or benefits.

So how can organizations change so that these dynamics aren't an issue for Black workers? In our tech-driven, fast-paced world, it's not quite so easy or realistic just to suggest that companies throw out their use of networks altogether. The problem is not merely that managers rely on connections and relationships, but that those ties are embedded in existing structures (friendships, neighborhoods, civic institutions) that are themselves heavily shaped by race and gender. Instead of suggesting that hiring managers disregard their networks, what if we encouraged them to tap into networks they may not be using?

Here's an example. It's fairly common for companies to recruit entry-level workers by forming partnerships with and making visits to certain college campuses. (Remember, this is how Darren found his first job in the financial industry.) Yet especially for large companies with a certain level of visibility, the colleges they tend to visit, often in the Ivy League, are a small slice of academia.[1] The logic behind this is that students from these colleges are presumably the "best of the best," and if companies hire their students, those students can learn the technical skills on the job. Managers go with the schools that are already in their orbit and draw students who are thus in their broader network.

But this approach is necessarily going to leave Black students and potential employees underrepresented. In 2017, Black students were a mere 8 percent of undergraduates at Ivy League universities.[2] At elite schools ranked just below the Ivies—Northwestern, Stanford, Duke, or MIT—representation is generally not much higher. Focusing primarily on these institutions of higher education yields students who have the associated reputational prestige, but it also means that managers are drawing from a pool with a dearth of Black applicants. Yet if we consider HBCUs, not only do we find academic spaces that house a much larger number of Black students, but we also find institutions that produce students who disproportionately earn advanced degrees and rise to the top of their respective fields.[3] As much as I love to rep my alma mater, I'll resist the urge to rattle off my long list of Spelman alumna who are leaders in business, law, academia, and politics; the point is that HBCUs are fertile ground for producing Black students who are highly qualified and capable of succeeding across industries. The challenge is to get organizations to realize this and act accordingly.

Hard data suggest that programs like this are effective. Sociologists Frank Dobbin and Alexandra Kalev found that among companies that diversify their hiring processes by tapping into networks they've otherwise ignored, there is a measurable improvement in the representation of Black workers in entry-level jobs. Specifically, "five years after a company implements a college recruitment program targeting female employees, the share of White women, Black women, Hispanic women, and Asian American women in its management rises by about 10%, on average. A program focused on minority recruitment increases the proportion of Black male managers by 8% and Black female managers by 9%."[4]

Companies should also reconsider hiring tests, like those Brian had to complete to get into his management role at Worldwide Studios. It's fairly common for organizations to build performance-based tests into their hiring processes, with the idea that these tests highlight whether employees are capable of doing the job for which they are interviewing. In Silicon Valley, potential engineers go through a process where they must show they can solve problems and work with a team in real time. On the face of it, this seems to standardize the hiring process and protect against hiring discrimination—after all, if candidates can prove they have the skills for the job, they should have a decent chance at getting hired, right?

It turns out it's not quite that simple, however. As Brian's experience showed, candidates are also evaluated on whether they "fit" into the corporate culture of a company, with foreign-born, Black, and Latinx workers often less likely to meet this ambiguous test.[5] Additionally, hiring managers assign more weight to the outcomes of these tests when Black workers fail them than when white workers do. Specifically, when skills tests are part of the hiring process, evaluators are more likely to emphasize technical skills when Black or women candidates make mistakes in those areas. Yet these same evaluators downplay technical skills if white applicants make errors on that front.[6] Finally, managers may resent having to use strategies that limit their discretion and authority in hiring. Thus, although attempts to test candidates' abilities seek to create a more even playing field, they are another way that the ambiguities associated with how we work can and do maintain racial inequality.[7]

The data indicate that tapping into new networks, avoiding hiring tests, and rejecting the principle of looking for "fit" can be successful strategies if and when organizations commit to them and do so effectively. It's not enough to set up a program. It's not even enough just to get Black workers in the door. Once hired, they have to encounter an organizational culture that takes their experiences, needs, and realities into account, and they need to work for a company that is designed to facilitate, rather than stymie, their opportunities to move up the career ladder. We'll see in Part III how advancement becomes a third gray area where racial inequality persists, and where Black workers often chart their own paths to success.

KEY TAKEAWAYS

- Hiring is heavily affected by preexisting relationships, connections, and social ties

- Yet these social networks are themselves shaped by race

- Black workers are often excluded from networks that would position them for access to high-status jobs

- Breaking into predominantly white networks can be isolating and alienating

- Jobs that are available without networks are not very lucrative

CHECKLIST: WHAT YOU CAN DO

For the DEI Practitioner

○ Work with executive search firms to ensure hiring slates for senior positions include Black candidates

○ Partner with HR to expand hiring outreach to include HBCUs

For the Executive or Senior Manager

○ Place less weight on "fit"

○ Participate in HBCU recruitment programs

For the HR Director

○ Avoid hiring tests

○ Formalize, advertise, and incentivize referral programs

For the Colleague

○ Refer Black workers for employment

○ Support efforts to increase the numbers of Black workers, especially in fields where they are underrepresented

○ Consistently include Black colleagues in networking and social events

PART III

RELATIONAL
Who's Got Your Back?

What does it take to advance to a leadership role in a company? Hard work certainly matters. Outperforming your peers doesn't hurt, either. And in many settings, showing that you can bring in more money than your colleagues will boost you over the top.

But *soft skills*, or intangible qualities separate from pure performance, are a factor as well. Having "strong leadership skills" is an asset for anyone wishing to advance in their company, as is being a "good team player" and generally being affable and an easy colleague with whom to work. Arguably, soft skills have become even more important than technical skills in some sectors, with companies betting that while they can teach new hires the basics of how to do the job, the ability to work well with others is innate.[1] The importance of these intangibles underscores that it isn't always just objective measures that shape advancement—subjective factors matter too.

For many, this mix of factors creates a deceptively straightforward pathway to advancement in today's companies. In many Western democracies, there is the popular sentiment that with hard work, leadership skills, and perhaps a little luck, anyone can reach the top. If organizations are construed as fair places that simply respond to the free market, where the only color that matters is green, then anyone who contributes the most to a company's bottom line should be able to advance to a leadership role and take on a position of authority.

Alas, the data indicate otherwise. In industry after industry, the available demographic data reveal that those who fill leadership positions are disproportionately white men. Let's take a look at the corporate and financial sectors. As of November 2022, the Fortune 500 companies had only six black CEOs—a record, at barely 1 percent.[2] With the hiring of Thasunda Brown Duckett, TIAA became the first and only Fortune 500 company in history to have consecutive Black CEOs.[3] And Duckett herself is part of a tiny sorority—one of four Black women (along with Ursula Burns at Xerox, Rosalind Brewer at Walgreens, and Mary Winston, who served in an interim capacity at Bed Bath & Beyond) ever to head Fortune 500 companies.[4] No Black woman has ever run a Wall Street bank, and as of 2022 there were no Black CEOs at major US banks. In 2020, Bloomberg reported that "only one of the more than 80 people included among the elite executive teams atop the six largest US banks is Black."[5] And this is a problem that extends to other nations as well: as of 2022, there were no Black chairs, chief executives, or chief financial officers in Britain's largest one hundred companies, either.[6]

Contrast this with white representation in these industries. Historically, leadership of these firms has been all white, with Clifton Wharton Jr. first breaking the color line in 1987 when he became the CEO of TIAA-CREF. So for many companies, particularly big banks that date their founding back to the 1700s and 1800s, leadership has literally been exclusively white and male not for decades, but for centuries. This pattern continues well past the passage of civil rights legislation intended to expand opportunities for Black Americans and white women. In 2018 *Harvard Business Review* reported that 5.3 percent of large companies had CEOs named John, with 4.5 percent run by men named David.[7] That means there are more large companies run by white men named John and David than there are ones run by Black CEOs of any gender or name.

Companies often explain these disparities by pointing to leaks in the pipeline or an inability to find qualified candidates to assume top roles. But there are problems with both of these explanations. For one thing, Stanford Business School researchers found that Black workers are rarely put in charge of divisions likely to yield a profit and loss, though these are often training grounds for how managers end up on the track to become CEOs.[8] If Black managers are steered away from these divisions, it can be more difficult for them to end up on a path to leadership, thus creating an internal environment with additional barriers to advancement. In these cases, it is not that there simply aren't qualified Black workers, but that Black workers are directed away from the areas that would build their qualifications and round out their work experience.

Second, data indicate that even among the most elite, pedigreed classes of workers, Black candidates remain overlooked. As of 2018, Black Harvard MBAs were still less likely to find their way into corporate leadership roles than their white counterparts.[9] Black students are also a growing number of those attaining bachelor's and master's degrees, and in 2019, a higher percentage of Black master's students were earning degrees in business management and marketing than their white peers.[10] The presence of these workers—and their ongoing underrepresentation in corporate leadership—makes it hard to argue convincingly that the absence of Black workers in leadership is simply because qualified candidates don't exist.

And lest we lay all the blame on the shoulders of one sector, this isn't just a corporate problem. A quick look at the top ranks of virtually all influential sectors of US society—tech, government, academia—indicates that these patterns persist across multiple industries. Many tech companies do not share their employment data, but major tech companies like Amazon, Apple, Google, Twitter, and Facebook have few Black executives. The US Congress is disproportionately whiter, older, and more male than the US populace that it purports to represent.[11] In 2017, *Inside Higher Ed* reported that only a fifth of college presidents were people of color, and that that number was artificially inflated by the leaders of HBCUs. Black Americans specifically were 8 percent of all college and university presidents in 2016.[12]

The takeaway here is that, with a few exceptions, leadership in many industries remains the bastion of predominantly white men. This isn't due to a lack of ambition, interest, or existence of qualified Black workers. Black workers are present and are capable of and interested in upward mobility and taking on leadership positions. Thus, it strains credulity to suggest that with growing numbers of Black workers pursuing higher education, joining the workforce, and looking for leadership positions, somehow by and large they disproportionately remain less competent and suitable for advancement than their white counterparts.

The problem does not lie with these workers; it lies with how advancement is structured in contemporary organizations. Often, procedures for upward mobility are opaque. Organizations rarely identify exactly what motivated employees need to do to position themselves for leadership roles. In some fields, by the time positions are announced, companies have already identified candidates for the role, making it difficult for workers who are not in the loop to receive consideration. With the lack of transparency and clarity, many Black workers stall out at middle-management levels rather than moving ahead.

Mentorship vs. Sponsorship

One of the biggest obstacles Black workers face in their attempts to move into leadership positions may be the lack of mentors and sponsors working to advance them into high-ranking roles. Gaining access to the C-suite, university administration, or firm partnership can often hinge heavily on whether those already in leadership enable this mobility. One of the primary ways those at the top of an organization bring others into leadership roles involves the relationships they have with others whom they see as "management material"—and the exclusion of those who do not seem to fit this ambiguous criterion.

Mentorship and sponsorship are key parts of how many workers are groomed for advancement. Both processes involve someone in a higher-up position becoming available to someone lower in the organizational structure in order to provide guidance, leadership, and advice. But it's crucial to distinguish between the two, because they can yield radically different outcomes. A mentor provides feedback and support on any number of workplace issues. A sponsor, however, serves a different function. A sponsor is highly placed in an organization and will advocate for and champion particular workers for plum projects, key opportunities, and, of course, leadership roles. For instance, your mentor might provide advice about firm culture, achieving work–life balance, or navigating office politics. But your sponsor will recommend you to lead an emerging project that is important to the company's development, knowing that this will likely put you on the CEO's radar and lead to additional opportunities for you to shine. Mentors help workers to perform satisfactorily, but sponsors put them on the path to advancement.

Gaps in mentorship and sponsorship are not always driven by intentional efforts to exclude or marginalize Black workers. Sometimes they are just a consequence of unfamiliarity and an unwillingness to step out of a comfort zone. In a study of Black women attorneys, one lawyer lamenting her difficulties finding either a mentor or a sponsor in her firm noted resignedly: "You know, most white [men] don't know any Black women other than their housekeeper or their secretary, like not a single one. It's just coming from a completely different place; they don't socialize with them, they don't see them at the sports bar, they don't play pickup basketball with them at the gym. Most white men have no context for interacting with a Black woman."[13] As noted earlier, given how segregated most schools, neighborhoods, and religious institutions are, many whites have no context for or experience with interacting with Black people, particularly on an equal-status basis. In companies where Black workers are already underrepresented, it may just seem easier for managers and executives to work with people with whom they have some cultural familiarity.[14]

Other times, Black workers don't seem to fit the unspoken image of someone who belongs in a leadership role. This is another area where issues of "fit" can be a disadvantage, with many Black workers recounting examples of times colleagues and supervisors expressed doubts that clients would feel comfortable with Black leaders in visible, public-facing roles.[15] Ironically, this issue of perception can be a double-edged sword. Walker, a Black lawyer in Dallas, told me that partners in his firm did not assign him to key projects because of the expectation that it would be an issue for clients. Yet when the firm wanted to express its commitment to diversity, they sent him to job fairs and outings where they expected clients would want to see Black attorneys. As he put it: "I had to spend time doing that on top of trying to make my billable hours. That's an extra job. Nobody's saying, 'Okay, by the way, for being our token Black attorney this year, you get an extra $20,000.' That ain't going to happen. In fact, I can do all of that, and if I don't make my billable hours, I'm not getting anything. I'm getting demoted."[16] Firm partners did not see Walker as someone to whom they wanted to assign multimillion dollar accounts, but they were fully comfortable putting him front and center for projects that would buttress their claims of supporting racial diversity, even as these actions inhibited Walker's ability to advance.

Advancement, then, is not quite the cut-and-dried case of the person with the most skill and ambition making it to the top. Hard work and talent certainly matter in today's organizations, but intangibles like congeniality, affability, and the ability to get along well with others are major factors as well. Additionally, in today's companies where the paths to leadership are frequently murky and unclear, having a mentor and a sponsor (who may not necessarily be the same person) is a critical factor in getting ahead. For Amalia, Constance, Kevin, Alex, Darren, Brian, and Max, this dynamic has meant an uneven track to upward mobility where some of them managed to advance, others stalled, and still others found alternative paths forward.

CHAPTER 14

Searching for an Advocate

"SOMEONE TO VOUCH FOR YOU"

It's safe to characterize Constance as a fairly ambitious person. She proceeded through college and graduate school at a swift pace and then began her tenure-track faculty position with the intention of advancing through the ranks and taking on a leadership role in her department and her discipline. Constance spent the standard six years as an assistant professor before going up for tenure and promotion to associate professor. That process happened relatively uneventfully. She inquired about going up for promotion to full professor a few years later, but her department refused to support her. Constance was annoyed about this, particularly since she did not receive feedback or explanation for her senior colleagues' lack of support. But she bided her time, waiting patiently for a few more years, and then was successfully promoted. Constance is now the youngest full professor in her department, and the first Black woman in the department who has risen through the ranks to reach this goal.

But Constance's promotion took longer than it should have. A lack of clarity around expectations and requirements contributed to the delay. She told me with a mix of frustration and irritation: "I asked about [promotion] multiple times, but all they would say is that I wasn't ready yet. I did go to my department chair, and he used some sports analogy to the effect of, 'If you're not the star player, you have to work harder.' But no one was checking for me. No one would meet with me on a regular basis to say, 'If you do this, you'll be ready.' And when I went to ask, there was no feedback." Universities, like many other organizations, often obfuscate the criteria for advancement, relying instead on vague and subjectively defined "excellence" in research, teaching, and service. For Constance, it turned out that winning multiple awards, having strong teaching evaluations, and landing major research grants still did not meet her colleagues' imprecise expectations. She still doesn't know exactly what changed—just that she had to wait until they felt she was "ready" before the promotion finally happened.

Black women chemical engineers are a relative rarity, but ambitious Black women like Constance are not. Black women are actually more likely than their women counterparts of other races to express an interest in powerful jobs. A 2015 report from the Center for Talent Innovation (now Coqual) reported that 22 percent of Black professional women openly expressed a desire to advance to a high-ranking, influential position, compared with only 8 percent of white women. Forty-three percent of Black women expressed confidence in their ability to succeed in these jobs (as opposed to 30 percent of white women), and 81 percent of Black women (but only 54 percent of white women) in the sample acknowledged that high salaries are important to their careers.[1]

The study doesn't speculate about why these racial differences exist, but they may be a function of broader factors related to race, gender, and economic status. Black women are more likely to be breadwinners or sole earners in their families, which can make high salaries and the economic stability that they confer more important.[2] For white women, who are more likely to be married to white men (who themselves usually out-earn other racial and gender groups), high salaries and occupational advancement may not take on the same level of importance.

Additionally, Black girls and young women are often socialized early on to pursue work opportunities that will provide financial security and allow them to be self-sufficient. In some cases, part of Black parents' process of socializing their daughters involves challenging dominant messages about racial and gender inferiority by encouraging girls to see themselves as capable, competent, and ambitious.[3] In this context, Black adult women's interest in high-ranking jobs that offer power and command high salaries may be the result of both striving for economic security and fully believing in their abilities to do these jobs well, despite counternarratives that Black women are lazy, unintelligent, and lack a strong work ethic. In my own home growing up, my parents' constant messages to be ambitious and aim high helped both my sister and me believe in our own aspirations even when others did not.

Given this background, what happens to driven women like Constance who believe they can succeed and want to advance, yet are still underrepresented among the top ranks of virtually all professions? What explains their absence from boardrooms, C-suites, and other rarified spaces? They clearly have the hunger and the skill, so why don't we see Black women proportionally represented in these influential, decision-making roles?

Sometimes, Black workers are held to unreasonably high standards that do not seem to apply to others in their fields. Other times, white managers simply fail to recognize and reward excellent work when it comes from Black employees. In their study of Black middle-class life, sociologists Joe Feagin and Melvin Sikes quote at length from one interviewee whose supervisor, after detailing her stellar accomplishments for the year, initially gave her a performance rating of "good" rather than "very good" or "outstanding." Importantly, the respondent noted that this supervisor also publicly expressed his low expectations and doubts that women or Black men could succeed in their profession. Upon hearing that the supervisor gave her a performance rating of good, the respondent refused to sign off on her evaluation, recalling: "I was able to show [my supervisor] that I had . . . exceeded all of [my list of objectives for the year]. I also had my sales performance [documented]: the dollar amount, the products, both in total dollar sales and also in product mix. I sold every product in the line we offered our customers. I had exceeded all of my sales objectives . . . Fifteen minutes later he called me back in and said, 'I've thought about what you said, and you're right, you do have an O [for outstanding]." In this respondent's telling, even objective measures of exceptional performance did not necessarily mean that, as a Black woman, she would be recognized and evaluated as a top performer.[4]

Barry, a Black lawyer in Chicago, expressed a similar sentiment, telling me: "I thought about this six or seven years ago, when I was at my first big firm. And every Black man that was at that firm had either graduated from a top twenty law school, had a law review with a moot court, or had clerked for a federal judge. There were only six or seven of us. We were all elite, so to speak. But we were surrounded by average white guys. I had to be—every brother in that firm had to be—a rock star. He had to be the best of the best. But I could sit next door to this guy who had graduated middle of the pack from a less selective university. Or I could go to lunch with another white guy who had graduated middle of the pack. And I would always wonder, 'Well, how can I be average?' Or 'Why do I always have to be the best of the best?'"[5]

Outsize, often unreasonable expectations, or an unwillingness to reward Black workers for exemplary performance, can curtail advancement. Constance certainly believed that was a factor in why she was initially turned down for promotion. But other workplace dynamics can also operate to Black workers' detriment. Specifically, Black women are less likely than workers of other racial groups to have routine access to managers and supervisors. In the 2015 Center for Talent Innovation study, 26 percent of Black women (compared with 17 percent of white women) also believed that managers overlooked their skills and talents.[6]

This distance between managers and Black women workers is

critical to understanding some of the impediments Black women face trying to advance in today's organizations. Without relationships with higher-ups who can make a case for their ability to succeed, many Black women are at an institutional disadvantage when it comes to upward mobility. This does not necessarily have to be a result of overt bias or intentional neglect. Managers may not harbor any ill will toward Black women who are their direct reports. They may have pleasant interactions with them and may find their work satisfactory or even exceptional. But when Black women are more likely to be at a distance from their supervisors, they miss out on opportunities for these managers to serve as mentors—or even more optimally, sponsors—who can position them for advancement.

Constance certainly found this to be true of her own experiences trying to advance. When we talked about her efforts to move into a leadership role in her department, she stressed that many of the challenges she faced came from the years she spent without anyone who would go to bat for her. Her ongoing challenge of breaking into the networks she needed thus had long-term consequences. As she told me: "You need someone to vouch for you. No one is going to look at you and your accomplishments objectively and say, 'That's good!'" Without someone to vouch for her, doing it all on her own made the process that much harder. And without colleagues who recognized the ways that her experience as a Black woman differed from theirs, it became even more challenging to find supporters who could contextualize her challenges and provide useful guidance with that in mind.

The Advocate

Today, Constance's situation is a little different. Despite the setback with her second promotion, she ultimately did advance. And she only recently has found someone to serve in the role of a sponsor, though she refers to him as "her advocate." She told me: "I've found someone who vouches for me, and now I've got all these new opportunities. And it came about because he was interested in the science I had to offer!" Constance's advocate suggested they apply a technique she developed to some models he'd been working on, and it turned out to be a success. On the basis of their collaboration, this colleague, a world leader in his area, began recommending Constance for other opportunities in their field. The relief in her voice was palpable as she told me, "Through my entire career, feeling like I do not have an advocate—now I have an advocate."

Given that this was the first time since finishing her doctorate that Constance felt she had someone who would serve in this role, I was curious how this unfolded in a different fashion from her previous efforts to find an advocate. It turned out the relationship developed through a combination of initiative and happenstance. In trying to find the balance of where she could effect change and how much the gray areas of work inhibited her, she finally got a lucky break when she reached out to this particular co-worker, Professor Jones. Professor Jones came to the university after several years in industry and ended up working with Constance on a committee to establish a research center that would be affiliated with their respective departments. A naturally shy person, Constance screwed up her courage to invite him to a lunch where she sought to learn more about the science behind the projects he was leading. Once he saw the parallels between their research, Professor Jones suggested they work together, and that began the first collaborative project Constance had had since graduate school.

Prior to this, Constance had been desperate to find some kind of leadership role that would allow her to learn and grow. She jumped at the opportunity to head her department's undergraduate program when no one else would, and even though that did not give her the responsibility, budget, or visibility she sought, it seemed like an opening. Helping to launch the research center was also part of her effort to advance. It would be housed outside of her department, raise her university's profile, and present an opportunity for her to move into a notable role that connected her to multiple schools and departments across the campus.

Constance's experience thus shows how much an advocate matters, even for high-performing Black women. Doors that were previously closed to her are now open because Professor Jones saw merit in her work and recommended her for key opportunities. It was clear she felt an enormous amount of gratitude for and appreciated his willingness to support her. "I'm so thankful to him for this," she told me, "but it's almost like he doesn't want me to thank him." As Constance sees it, however, Professor Jones's advocacy has made an important difference in further developing her research program and heightening her visibility in chemical engineering.

Constance has finally been able to break into closed networks and form the relationships she's been striving for all these years, but it's also important to take stock of the limitations to Professor Jones's influence. Although he has been able to put forth Constance's name for key opportunities to do work in chemical engineering at large, her department prospects are a different story. Though she is interested in doing administrative work and taking a leadership role in her department, it has remained difficult for her to secure a foothold in that area, particularly on key and influential internal committees that carry a lot of weight. Theoretically, her department chair would be the person who would serve as a mentor and/or a sponsor, thus allowing her to gain valuable leadership experience and develop that area of her skill set. So far, that hasn't happened.

"This department, man, it is the Wild West," Constance sighed, shaking her head. "You do whatever you want. We have no bylaws. There are no rules. People would be on committees and do whatever they want. On one committee, the lead person had been in charge since I've been here, so that's over a decade. The person who leads another committee is dysfunctional and everybody knew it. So I kept waiting for it to be my turn to get a chance leading that committee, because it would have been good experience for me. But the person who had it wanted it and never wanted to give it up."

Even when the department decided to change the leadership of various internal committees, Constance still reported regularly being passed over despite openly stating her interest in moving into those administrative roles. Several years ago, her department finally decided to update committee leadership by proposing a new slate of candidates. Constance, yet again, was excluded. But this time the university's vice provost for diversity noticed that her name was missing and inquired why.

She described what happened next, with visible irritation: "The chair called me to his office to say, 'Will you lead this committee?' And I was like, 'Yes, I've been waiting for fifteen years for you all to ask me to do it.' He never followed up. So this summer when they released the roster of people who would be in leadership, once again, my name was not on it. This time, he calls me back thirty minutes later to say, 'Will you be on the advisory committee?' and he makes this stupid offhand comment about how 'I thought about asking you, but you're so busy with the undergraduate student work that I felt bad.' Yeah, but I expressed to you that I was interested in leadership, and you asked me to do the other committee and never followed up."

At this point in her career, Constance has an advocate who supports her and opportunities to take on some of the leadership work she has been seeking. But this all exists outside her department. In the research center with her advocate, colleagues take her advice and opinions seriously. But in her department, where she is a tenured, senior faculty member, she's still "very isolated and alone."

Constance's account confirms that when criteria for advancement and leadership are not clearly defined, it is all too easy for Black workers to be left out. Not only that, given that her chair does not act as an advocate for her, her interest in departmental leadership frequently goes nowhere. This omission, coupled with the absence of clear policies that ensure that everyone who is interested has access to leadership, means that talented workers like Constance easily slip through the cracks.

Her experiences also highlight some of the shortcomings of conventional wisdom about how women can advance in the workplace. Advice to women to speak up for themselves, seek out opportunities, and be proactive about their careers proliferates in many spaces and, on its face, seems to provide useful suggestions for how women can take charge of their futures by charting their own paths. But Constance followed this approach, often to no avail. She told her chair on more than one occasion that she wanted opportunities to gain leadership experience. She led the department's undergraduate program when no one else would. She attempted to foster a connection with senior colleagues that she hoped, in vain, would lead to a mentoring relationship. None of this worked, until she accidentally happened upon a colleague who listened. And even then, his ability to help her navigate the gray areas was limited.

For all too many Black women like Constance, the advice that women take matters into their own hands rings extremely hollow. As former First Lady Michelle Obama bluntly stated in 2018, "It's not always enough to 'lean in,' because that shit doesn't work all the time."[7] Recommendations that women simply become more assertive obscure the structural barriers such as the lack of mentoring programs, consistent policies, and clear expectations for promotion that block women's paths to leadership roles. Not only that, encouragement to be more forthright ignores the fact that for Black women, such an approach can backfire. When Black women try to present themselves as ambitious go-getters, they must also walk a fine line of making sure they do not trigger gendered and racial stereotypes that they are too domineering and controlling.[8] The suggestion that women can help advance their positions just by speaking up and asking for what they want falls particularly flat for Black women like Constance, whose challenges getting into leadership roles aren't for want of asking for them. They are for want of being answered.

CHAPTER 15

When White Women
Are Roadblocks

"THE SAME FIREWALL"

In my discussions with Kevin, the main themes that emerged in his work life were about trust and belonging: how Black women constituted a critical part of his network when it came to getting jobs, and how the performative cultures around race and inclusion in both the business and nonprofit worlds felt alienating. Now I wanted to know how he went about trying to climb the ladder at work. When it came to the gray areas associated with advancement, who was an ally? Who was a liability? He had clearly put some thought into this topic, as his answer was clear and direct: "When it comes to advancement, I have been frustrated, I've been blocked. I feel hampered by white women in terms of where I've gone and what they think I should do. In a nutshell, I would say that has been my consistent problem."

I asked Kevin to tell me more. Reflecting on his work history, he again compared his time in the corporate world with his experience in nonprofits and thought about how his colleagues in both environments moved ahead. In corporate settings, he told me,

"The way white boys operate is they make quantum leaps." By this he meant that his colleagues who were white men found opportunities to develop and nurture informal networks and connections that allowed them to climb and even skip rungs on the career ladder. Initially, Kevin assumed that hard work would net him the same results, but he quickly realized that advancement required more than just doing his job well. "Drink the beers, watch SEC football, set up time to have a conversation with Mike about what I gotta do," he said. "That's the things I didn't realize I needed to do. And for a lot of Black guys, you don't realize till it's too late."

In the bank, advancement required connecting with white men and fitting into a particular culture. But moving ahead in nonprofit spaces was a very different process—and this is where the dynamics of who Kevin could trust and who he couldn't again emerged in sharp relief. "It's the same every time I'm managed by a white woman," he told me. "They're initially nice and friendly, yet we have no rapport. So then when I need feedback, it's obtuse, given with a side eye, we have this impasse, and then I feel like it's, 'I need to leave because I feel like I'm going to be fired.' If I work with a Black woman, I succeed, get feedback, do well. At another job I was managed by a Black man and a white man. That was always good, fine. But in the nonprofit space, it is a world of mostly white women. I [believe] I'm speaking the story of many other Black men in nonprofits or education who have to hide or disfigure themselves or they would be kicked out the door."

White Women and Black Men: Allies or Obstacles?

Kevin's account of the challenges he's faced advancing in nonprofit spaces presents an interesting twist to thinking about gender, race, and leadership at work. In particular, his point that white women have consistently posed challenges for him contrasts the way racial dynamics at work are often characterized. White men are overwhelmingly represented in leadership roles, but women of all races—including white women—face difficulties moving into top positions. But what happens when women, particularly white women, advance to leadership roles? Do they then use that standing to open doors for other underrepresented groups?

The research here is somewhat inconclusive, and much of it focuses on whether and how women help other women. Some studies find that women in leadership positions exhibit what is commonly referred to as a Queen Bee syndrome. In this example, women in positions of power do not necessarily create opportunities or welcome other women into spaces where they are underrepresented.[1] With the Queen Bee syndrome, when one woman advances into a leadership role, she makes it harder for other women to follow behind her rather than dismantling the structures that impeded her own (and their) progress. In this paradigm, some women respond to gender bias in the workplace by maintaining and ensuring that it remains present for other women.

It's important to provide full context for this concept, however. In many cases, there are real material costs for women who try to open doors for or enhance opportunities for other women. And this is not because women simply don't want to help each other but is a function of how many organizations operate. In many male-dominated spaces like finance, tech, or energy, only a few women advance into leadership roles. Furthermore, once one woman advances to a top leadership job, the odds that another woman will be appointed to another similarly elite role in that company drop down to 50 percent.[2] Consequently, concluding that women fail to support other women misses the bigger picture—that implicit gender quotas may make some women less likely to embrace or support other women if they are competing for an artificially depreciated number of opportunities.

Other research casts doubt on the Queen Bee syndrome and

suggests that women's leadership has broader consequences than that theory implies. A 2016 study of companies in the Fortune 1000 found that women's presence in influential positions of corporate power—as CEOs, managers, members of boards of directors, and high-ranking executives—helped to reduce gender segregation within firms.[3] That is, when women occupy various leadership roles, they may intentionally or indirectly work to undo some of the dynamics that hinder other women from advancement. A 2017 study of German workers found that having greater numbers of women in management roles helped to close gender wage gaps for low-skill (though not high-skill) jobs.[4] In other words, these studies suggest that women in positions of power can have a favorable impact on improving gender equity in organizations at large.

There's some evidence, then, to suggest that women in leadership change the organizations where they are employed. Relative to men in positions of power, women may be less likely to sexually harass women subordinates, assume they lack drive and initiative, or believe that family responsibilities preclude them from moving into key roles—all documented factors that help explain the paucity of women in high-ranking positions in organizations.[5] But their ability to create internal changes and increase opportunities for other women raises the question of whether women in leadership are able or willing to help lower barriers for other underrepresented groups in the workplace. Do they earn the trust of Black workers navigating the gray areas associated with advancement?

As Kevin put it very bluntly, in his experience, the answer is a resounding no. This is particularly the case if we are talking about white women. In his view, the nonprofit spaces where he worked provided few, if any, opportunities for him to work productively and collaboratively with white women who often held leadership roles. Instead, working in these spaces required near-constant self-scrutiny, tone policing, and rigid adherence to unspoken expectations of appropriate behavior as a Black man in a space where most leaders were white women.

Kevin acknowledged that working in spaces with mostly white women in leadership forced him to be aware of the privilege men hold in those spaces. He realized that in a workplace where women were in most of the positions of authority, he couldn't come into meetings mansplaining, interrupting, and trying to dominate the discussions. Though that might be an option for white men in the field, he believed that as a Black man, he would not have the leverage to engage in that kind of behavior. Rather, "It's a whole balancing act where I'm trying to modulate my voice, my behavior. And it's hard because I want to be an ally, but if I'm a normal Black guy who doesn't read up on those things—that you always have to be nonthreatening, that you have to use a certain voice—then I'm not going to succeed, because I'm not going to advance."

Some of the challenges Kevin described here are fairly common for many Black workers. For instance, the "balancing act" is a widely reported issue. Many learn early in their careers that if they want to move up in their place of employment, it is imperative that they alter their voices, behaviors, and dress to preempt and offset negative racial stereotypes their colleagues may hold.[6] The 2018 film *Sorry to Bother You* satirized some of this experience with its depiction of a Black telemarketer who uses his "white voice" at work to achieve success. Many Black workers in predominantly white spaces even self-scrutinize their emotional comportment to ensure that they show no signs of feelings like irritation or annoyance that could be misread through the lens of the "angry Black person."[7] In fact, Kevin's description here reminds me of watching Barack Obama's two terms in the presidency, when his carefully modulated emotional expression seemed to work to his advantage as he avoided ever getting publicly upset or angry, even when he was heckled during one of his addresses at a joint session of Congress.

Kevin observed that this pressure to engage in constant self-policing also hurt his opportunities for advancement. Similar to his assertions in Part I, he believed his white women colleagues would support him if he had to break up a fight or run interference between leadership and students of color or their families. But when he expressed interest in taking on leadership roles or took the initiative on projects, he faced backlash. He believed this compromised his ability to advance professionally, stating: "It becomes frustrating because you realize: you don't want me to be a leader, you want me to be a scapegoat. You only want leadership that looks just like you. And that's who advances."

Kevin's perception that those in leadership tend to want others who look like them is documented by evidence. In many cases, leaders are notoriously risk-averse and feel most comfortable hiring others who share their similar characteristics.[8] However, since leadership of most companies is disproportionately white and male, that dynamic puts those who are not in a disadvantaged position. Researchers at the University of Colorado, in fact, found that when search committees include only one woman or one person of color among interviewees for a position, it becomes statistically impossible for that candidate to be hired.[9] They speculate that the one candidate, as the only one, stands out so much that leaders are ultimately too uncomfortable to hire them. In the nonprofit world where mostly white women are the employees and leaders, Kevin's visibility as a Black man likely works against him when it comes to moving up the ranks.

Black Men and the Glass Escalator

Some of the other issues Kevin shared, however, reflect challenges that Black men in particular face when trying to advance in occupations dominated by women. This is present in his view that his value to the organization lies more in his ability to defuse physical situations than his intellectual contributions. Men working in education, nursing, and social work report that in these settings, colleagues emphasize their ability to take responsibility for more physical tasks such as lifting patients, stopping altercations, or defusing tense situations.[10] Thus, Kevin's view that the organization values his contributions on those fronts is consistent with many men's experiences in these fields.

But for Black men, having authority in other settings beyond those that require physical strength is a bit more difficult. As Kevin noted, his colleagues and supervisors welcome his lead when a potentially dangerous situation needs to be deescalated. Despite the fact that it falls within his job purview, he finds supervisors less willing to encourage or support his leadership when he wants to weigh in on areas that necessitate intellectual prowess or credentials, such as shaping school policy or improving interactions with students and their families. Unlike white men in female-dominated professions, who assist in physically demanding situations yet are still solicited for leadership opportunities, Black men like Kevin find these expectations constrain and limit them.[11] And unlike the accounts from many white men working in women-dominated professions, Kevin does not find that his female counterparts solicit and encourage his advancement—in fact, the opposite.

Ultimately, when Kevin summed up his efforts to move into leadership, he characterized the process as a routine one of hitting a glass ceiling. "You reach the same firewall where you go against middle-class white women," he said. "And you can't have these open conversations and all the assumptions don't get diagnosed or talked about. But they still get utilized against you. So now you're 'too aggressive,' you 'don't communicate well.' All these metaphors for 'I don't fuck with you' blunt your ability to advance if you go the normal straight-up route."

Kevin's experiences with advancement, and the particular role he attributed to white women in stymieing his efforts, highlight the specific racial difficulties that can persist for Black men in fields where other men seem to advance. In her study of men working in women-dominated fields like education, sociologist Christine Williams found that in contrast to women who are in the minority in male-dominated professions, men in these occupations experience significant upward mobility. While women in fields like finance, law, and engineering hit a "glass ceiling" where they are unable to advance past a certain point, men in social work, nursing, education, and library sciences find themselves on a "glass escalator." On this escalator, various dynamics position them for advancement and leadership roles, so that they actually have to struggle to remain in place.[12]

The glass escalator operates in multiple ways. For starters, men often take pains to differentiate themselves from their women counterparts, sometimes through making disparaging comments grounded in gendered stereotypes, or by distancing themselves from the perceived femininity associated with their profession. Men may do this by emphasizing their masculinity or making derogatory jokes about women. Even when this occurs, colleagues treat men with a certain level of deference. Women welcome them into the profession on the basis of the expectation that more men will help raise the field's profile, status, and prestige. (This is an assumption based in fact, as more women associated with or entering a profession tend to drive down wages and prestige.)[13] And both peers and supervisors assume that these men belong in or will shortly seek out leadership roles, effectively fast-tracking them for positions of authority.

But Black men like Kevin don't describe these kinds of interactions or this general pattern, and his fraught relationships with the women who are in supervisory roles helps to explain why. Even though he does not denigrate his women colleagues or shy away from the "feminine" qualities associated with education, his white women supervisors keep him at a distance more than they treat him with deference. Perhaps more significantly, there are few assumptions that he is seeking or better suited for leadership positions. Ultimately, Black men have the ambition, training, and qualifications to move into leadership roles, just like many of their colleagues, but dicey relationships with white women mean that for them, the "glass escalator" is out of order.

CHAPTER 16

Opportunity Gaps in Gig Work

"THIS IS FINE FOR NOW"

As the gig economy continues to grow, it's worth asking whether it offers opportunities and potential for advancement and career mobility. We've seen that the lack of close relationships with sponsors or supervisors curtailed Constance's and Kevin's ambitions to move into leadership positions in their respective organizations. But as we know, gig work is structured differently, and with more than a third of all American workers doing some form of employment in the gig economy, it represents a significant part of the current labor market.[1] Not only that, projections estimate that these numbers will double by 2027, suggesting that these work arrangements are here to stay.[2] As more organizations turn to this model of relying on independent contractors who freelance for companies but are not formal employees, it's time to consider what this shift in the business model means for gig workers' opportunities for advancement, particularly Black gig workers.

To some degree, these expectations depend on which kind of gig work is in question. In a 2018 report assessing the impact of these kinds of work arrangements, Gallup characterized modern gig employment as a "tale of two gig economies." One part of the gig economy includes independent contract workers who report high levels of job satisfaction. These workers might be travel nurses who cycle through temporary contracts with various hospitals, allowing them to relocate regularly and land where the need is greatest. Or they might be homeowners with full-time jobs who rent out rooms in their house through the internet. These independent gig workers report high levels of work–life balance, autonomy, and satisfaction with their working conditions.[3]

The picture looks a bit different when we turn to the other gig economy. Here, we find temporary and on-call workers, such as substitute teachers who go in when needed or clerical staff who contract through a temp agency to fill in in offices when called. And among these workers, the picture is far less rosy. Temporary workers are less likely than their independent counterparts in the gig economy to report feeling satisfied with their jobs, having a sense of engagement with their work and the organizations where they are employed, and having creative freedom and autonomy.[4]

Given these differences, we might expect opportunities for advancement in gig work to be quite minimal. After all, these work arrangements are structured to provide short-term employment, not to function as a rung on a career ladder. And even among independent contract workers, despite their higher levels of satisfaction with the work they do, the nature of their employment is such that it comes to a predetermined end. Some independent workers may find that completing these contracts positions them well for full-time employment at a company if and when a position becomes available. But for many others in the gig economy, such as those doing online platform work, opportunities to move into leadership roles might seem to be scarce.

Alex's experiences depict some of these difficulties with advancement when someone is doing primarily gig work. Recall that she had no real complaints of discrimination while driving for Uber Eats and Postmates; however, she also added, "I don't feel like it provides any opportunities, either." When I pressed Alex further about what sort of opportunities might be missing from gig work, I suspect that she was flummoxed by my line of questioning because to some degree, the answers seemed self-evident. When the entirety of the job consists of accessing an online platform, picking up food, and delivering it to the customer, it's hard to see the potential for advancement or mobility. Unlike previous models of employment, companies that are premised on gig employment are not designed with the hope or expectation that workers may eventually rise through the ranks to leadership roles. Drivers for Uber Eats and Postmates are not expected to earn degrees in software design or engineering that would then qualify them for leadership positions in the company. Instead, these models hinge on a strict separation between the technical and operations side of the company and the independent workers who are its contractors. The gig economy allows Alex to avoid some of the gray areas of work associated with hiring, but it costs her opportunities for occupational mobility.

This is not to say that Alex had no aspirations for advancement or for other work. When we spoke, she was clear that gig work was simply a stopgap measure until her previous company, Perspectives, reinstated its contract with the local airport and could rehire her. But even that was not the sum of her ambitions. As Alex and I discussed her future plans, she reiterated: "This isn't a long-term goal for me. At all. I'm just doing this till my old company calls me back or I go into something else." When I questioned what that "something else" might be, she confessed: "I really want to own a doughnut shop. I've always been interested in owning my own business. But this is fine for now."

Alex's ambitions here are noteworthy for a few reasons. For one, Black women are the fastest growing group of new entrepreneurs in the United States. In the five-year period between 2014 and 2019, the number of Black women–owned businesses grew by 50 percent.[5] In many cases, these entrepreneurial designs reflect the stifled ambitions and thwarted opportunities in paid employment this book describes—denied promotions, disrespectful treatment from colleagues, and wage inequities that eventually drive these women to seek opportunities elsewhere.[6] Black professional women often cite these challenges as part of their impetus for moving into business ownership. When their credentials, education, and skills cease to yield rewards in the organizations where they are employed, entrepreneurship can seem like a viable alternative.

Alex's employment history has largely not been in professional or managerial spaces, however. As such, her account highlights some of the limitations inherent in gig work, particularly the platform-based kinds. Even though Alex does not observe examples of racial or gender discrimination as part of her regular routine, driving for Uber Eats and Postmates offers minimal opportunities for her to reach her long-term career goals. This temporary work does not pay enough to secure significant seed money to launch a business, which is a major impediment for many new entrepreneurs and a particularly pronounced one for Black would-be business owners.[7] Nor does it offer experience with accounting or bookkeeping, managing employees, or building relationships with suppliers—all factors that would be useful to Alex as she pursues her entrepreneurial goals. Instead, gig work offers a few basics—a steady paycheck, flexible hours, and autonomy—but no way to leverage these into a path toward economic or social mobility.

But other gig workers using online platforms gave different accounts of opportunities for advancement. For instance, Rashida, a choir director at a church who supplemented her part-time income by driving for Lyft, also had long-term aspirations to become a business owner. I met her through a mutual friend and was immediately struck by her warm demeanor and cheerful smile. Thin and petite, she talked a mile a minute, occasionally punctuating her statements with religious references and taking moments to thank God for her blessings.

Rashida turned to gig work when she had to reduce her work hours to care for her terminally ill mother. And like Alex, Rashida observed that driving for Lyft offered a flexible schedule that provided the supplemental income she needed to make ends meet. But also like Alex, her long-term goal was to pursue entrepreneurship. Rashida wanted to become a grief counselor. As she put it: "I want to normalize grief. I want grief to be a coffee table conversation, where people feel like it's okay, it's not avoided, and people don't isolate themselves."

Unlike Alex, however, Rashida felt that her experience driving for Lyft was giving her very good preparation for moving into business ownership. Whereas even without noticeable racial and gender discrimination, Alex noted that gig work did not really provide her with any opportunities, Rashida believed that she was gaining useful skills that would position her well for advancement into entrepreneurship. "Driving Lyft did teach me some things," she told me. "I don't even know if I realized it at the time. I always have an interest in people and their stories, and if people started talking, I just let them talk. You know how people talk about how hairstylists and barbers are low-key therapists? That's sometimes what happens as a driver. Depending on where people are coming from and where they're going, you hear their stories."

Rashida paused to think, and then continued: "It made me more empathetic and realize there's a lot of stuff going on in the world. Sometimes all they need is to hear people say 'I hope the day goes well,' or 'I'll be praying for you,' or 'Have a great day and enjoy the party,' whatever that was. In its own right, it did help me, because it helped me to be more of a people person. There were times that there would be silence and I would push it. I would say, 'Hey, how you doing,' and I could tell if they were going to respond. If they were in a hurry I would just say, 'Have a good day,' but I always made sure I made space for that."

Rashida's circumstances thus differed from Alex's, and they present another side to the ways that gig work can potentially provide important job training for Black women seeking advancement. Though this is not built into the job, Rashida used the opportunity to hone certain soft skills: empathy, relatability, active listening, and effective communication. Importantly, for many Black workers, perceptions that they lack such soft skills become used to justify racial discrimination in hiring and advancement.[8] Thus, Rashida benefits from doing gig work in several ways. It's not just the flexibility and financial security. For her, it also provides a valuable opportunity to gain experience that can help facilitate advancement and mobility, even if that comes incidentally.

Black women like Rashida and Alex aren't usually the face of entrepreneurship. Rather, Black women who work for an hourly wage are usually invisible—economic policy is not made with their experiences in mind, workplaces do not cast them as the model worker. And as gig work becomes an increasingly relevant part of the modern economy, the way in which it is designed misses opportunities to enhance and support these women's potential for bigger things. In some cases, for women like Rashida, driving for Lyft offers soft skills that can possibly be useful down the line, but the platform is not designed to connect her with venture capitalists, provide access to start-up funds, or address other ways Black would-be entrepreneurs often lack advantages. In other cases, women like Alex don't see any real benefit that platforms like DoorDash or Uber Eats can provide. Premised on a model that offers no opportunity for advancement or mobility, the gig economy provides a disproportionate number of Black workers with short-term employment without mining their untapped potential.

CHAPTER 17

The Cost of Advancement

"I DON'T WANT TO GO VIRAL"

Constance, Kevin, and Alex highlight some of the challenges Black workers face with advancement in today's companies. Their accounts indicate that blurry, unclear expectations; difficulties finding mentors or sponsors; and blocked routes to leadership roles all create challenges for Black workers trying to move ahead.

But what about workers who do manage to advance professionally? Though they are underrepresented, and challenges persist in every industry, obviously some Black employees do make it to high-profile, influential leadership roles in their chosen fields. Business leaders like Mellody Hobson, Ursula Burns, and Vernon Jordan are, if not necessarily household names, very familiar to many. Others such as Ruth Simmons, former president of Brown University (and the first Black woman ever to lead an Ivy League institution), and Bozoma St. John, former chief marketing officer at Netflix, are less well-known but are also widely respected in their particular fields.

What does it take for Black workers to move ahead in their careers? Is it as simple as finding a mentor or sponsor who can provide guidance? Does clarity around expectations for promotion make the difference? And maybe most significant, what price, if any, do they pay for advancement? What are the costs of success?

For Amalia, the path to advancement required several steps. The first was relocation. Recall that she got her start at an online magazine, where she developed several stories, some of which focused on issues related to race and racism. This fell within her job purview, and she was able to get such pieces out on a regular basis. With these stories came a rising public profile and more visibility, and after a few years, she was recruited to join a desk at another major publication. This was a clear advancement for her, as the desk she joined was one of the most high-profile ones at that particular outlet. However, this was the job that, as we already learned, gave her few opportunities to bring on and showcase other Black journalists. It also was the outlet in which the hierarchical organizational culture made it harder for her to publish pieces about race. As her frustration built, Amalia became more open to reconsidering her options. And when a third noteworthy news organization approached her, she took a position there in a higher-ranking role.

Amalia's ability to advance in her profession has thus been clearly tied to her willingness to move and change companies. In some ways, this is a marker of the new economy. The days when workers remained with one company for the duration of their careers and could reasonably expect to rise through the ranks and eventually retire from that organization are largely obsolete. Organizations are flatter, with fewer levels of middle management, and leaders fully expect some turnover and mobility.[1]

Amalia believed that following this path was a common strategy for mobility in journalism. "It's often the case that you have to leave and then come back to do what you want," she told me. "That's what I've gotten from a lot of media companies. If you start earlier, you have to leave, find another job, and then reenter at a more experienced level. It's hard to advance within the company." Furthermore, she believed this to be true for journalists across the board, regardless of race: "It's a weird profession because there really is this whole thing where you won't get promoted till you have a job offer somewhere else, regardless of who you are. Often, even if you do get promoted you still may feel like you'd rather leave!" Thus, the fact that advancement required her to hop across various organizations fit the norms of her profession. It meant that new opportunities were open to her, but like most others in her career field, she had to leave to achieve them.

Amalia's route to advancement was also shaped by some informal mentors. She didn't define these as people with whom she had established relationships; rather, these were all more senior women colleagues with whom she worked on developing projects in the short term and whom she could "bounce ideas off of" when she needed to do so. She noted: "Those are the sorts of things where I worked on something with them, and we become close and they're older and I still stay in touch but I'm not necessarily calling them for advice. But sometimes I have if deciding whether to take a job." Amalia also recalled that the current organization where she worked had a formal mentoring program in place, and she benefited from that to make connections with another more senior well-known woman of color in the journalism field.

Amalia wasn't sure whether the absence of a consistent mentor figure (or a sponsor who would consistently advocate for her) had held her back in her career. And as we've seen, she has advanced to a lofty and very influential position. From her vantage point, seeing what other women—especially women of color—can achieve in journalism has in itself been helpful. Even if they were not formal mentors or sponsors, their presence in her professional career has shown her how to think more expansively about her own opportunities. Reflecting on this further, she told me: "If anything, it's helped [me] to see what's possible because these are women who've had distinguished careers. So knowing what's possible, they've taught me how to negotiate and not sell myself short—that has been valuable."

The willingness to pursue new opportunities coupled with informal mentoring relationships with highly placed senior figures in her field thus were key steps in Amalia reaching her current career heights. I suspect these factors are part of the story for many Black workers who've reached the tops of their professions. Rosalind Brewer, current CEO of Walgreens, previously held leadership roles at Starbucks, Sam's Club, and Kimberly-Clark. Rashida Jones, current president of MSNBC, arrived at that role after stints at local news networks and The Weather Channel. And Cynthia Marshall, the first Black woman CEO in the NBA, was recruited to the Dallas Mavericks after working as an executive for AT&T. I don't know details of their biographies, but I would guess that in addition to being willing to move, these women also navigated their pathways to and success in these roles with the help of advisors who provided at least some career guidance.

I asked Amalia to consider how she felt about her career when she looked back over her rise to her current position. Most of what she expressed was positive. "I feel mostly lucky," she replied. "I've obviously worked hard to get where I am. But I think about all the breaks I've had, especially considering how dire my profession is right now, and how I know so many people and have friends who are freelancing not because they want to, but no place will hire them as full-time staff. I don't have that sort of stamina and I admire anyone who is able to keep up with that. The fact that I have been able to land in a full-time job and had these outlets want to hire me, and my salary has only increased since I was twenty-five— all of that makes me feel really fortunate." She concluded, "I feel good about where I am right now and happier than I was in my previous job."

Paid the Cost to Be the Boss

For Amalia, however, advancement came with a hefty price tag. Although she enjoyed the fundamental parts of her job—digging into new ideas, thinking critically about various topics, reporting the news and current events—her commitment to focusing on issues related to race had consequences. Her work brought success and visibility, but it also meant that her status in the public eye caused enormous amounts of stress. Dealing with racist attacks and harassment adversely impacted her mental health and peace of mind, yet the more successful she grew, the more pronounced these issues became.

We have already learned that news organizations acknowledge the fact that journalists will face pushback from the public but that there are specific ways these responses take on racist and sexist dynamics for Black women. Being a successful journalist meant that Amalia had to continue to expose herself to this vitriol and hatred. Thus, even though she has had enviable professional successes and continues to count herself lucky and fortunate to have job security and work in a field she loves, the price of such success is accepting the fact that her rise has come at a cost to her peace of mind.

After the first time one of her pieces attracted major, extensive attention, and the racist responses that came with it, Amalia told me that she "went into a deep depression. A lot of the attention was good, but a lot was negative. I had people emailing me death threats, saying I should be raped, and it made me really retreat, and I was like, I don't ever want to do something like that again. I don't want to go viral."

This concern about mental health is a real and serious one that I've heard echoed from other successful Black workers as well. Laila, an elementary school teacher, told me that she had moved from a district that was 96 percent white with virtually no professional or personal support from parents, colleagues, or supervisors to a predominantly Black school district in Baltimore where she flourished and became an administrator. Describing the circumstances that led to the move, Laila showed the first cracks in her playful exterior. Her ready smile disappeared, and her demeanor turned melancholy. I began to get a hint of what she later told me was a severe depression and acute misery associated with that period of her life. "I was losing my mind," she said bluntly. "We had to leave for my mental health because I was going crazy. I was literally going crazy. Every day I had to deal with things. So yeah, we left. And work was a major reason why. Every day my husband was like, 'I know. I know you're not happy here. I'm going to find something else, I'm going to get us out.'" She was silent for a few minutes, then continued in a low voice: "If I wanted my kids to have a mother who was sane, who could be a parent to them, we had to go. We had to go for my sanity."

Like Amalia, when Laila talks about "dealing with things," she's not referring just to normal disagreements with a colleague or two, or even to impassioned critiques of her work. This wasn't just the second-guessing she regularly faced from parents or her principal, or the repeated requests that she prove her qualifications. Those things were bad enough, but Laila's issues went much further. Neighbors called her a nigger to her face. She was harassed by police. And all the while, almost no one around her cared. Her colleagues didn't support her. She had no close friends in the area. Law enforcement did nothing. Seeing this up close and personal, her husband knew that getting her out of that environment was not just a matter of preference; it was a matter of survival.

Hearing these remarks from Amalia and Laila took me aback momentarily because they reminded me of the more visceral, gut-level consequences of living with racism. They made me feel sad in a way that my own experiences with racist hate email didn't. I brushed off my own encounters with anonymous emailers because I knew they wanted to upset me, and I wasn't going to give them the satisfaction. But when Amalia and Laila described long-term depression, sustained hate campaigns, and prolonged suffering, I felt profoundly saddened and discouraged by how they, and so many other Black workers, experience so much pain just for trying to make a living.

We should never forget that facing sustained, daily, and explicit racism is traumatic. Being regularly reminded that much of the world around you sees you as deficient, unimportant, and fundamentally less human is a shattering experience that leaves few Black people unaffected. And it's not just mental health that's at risk here. Repeated incidents of racial harassment or discrimination can have a cumulative effect on recipients, compromising their physical health as well. Higher rates of self-reported racial discrimination are also connected to obesity, hypertension, lack of sleep, alcohol abuse, and poor heart health. Furthermore, worrying about or anticipating racial discrimination is linked to hypertension, increased body-mass index, and depressive symptoms.[2]

The process by which discrimination compromises health can occur through several pathways. Cultural racism in the form of racial stereotypes can mean that Black workers regularly confront and respond to perceptions of their inferiority and incompetence, leading to heightened stress and higher blood pressure. Workplace incidents where Blacks are misperceived as lower-status workers, denied due process, or treated poorly relative to their white colleagues can also prompt these health conditions. As Amalia rose in her profession, she had to take on an increasingly public presence, which resulted in racist harassment in an organization that was not fully prepared to deal with the tenor and depth of this for Black women journalists. Amalia's hard work got her the lofty career, status, and an enviable position in her profession, but as a Black woman, she is paying for this with her mental health.

CHAPTER 18

Looking Elsewhere for Leadership

"CATCHING THE ZEITGEIST"

When it comes to advancement (and pretty much everything else), Brian doesn't mince words. "I left Worldwide Studios when it was made clear that advancement was not in my near future," he told me. The studio had hired him during a period when it was focused on improving diversity and representation. He joined the company with optimism and excitement about what the opportunity could bring. Yet Brian described many instances when he had to weigh the studio's stated commitments to diversity against the reality of its actions, and he detailed his ongoing journey of trying to determine whether it was serious about making change. He grew increasingly frustrated with a corporate culture that touted its appreciation for innovation, creativity, and loyalty yet failed to support Black filmmakers and executives in ways that would allow them to advance the studio's stated goals. So it was not much of a surprise to me when he told me that a few weeks before our first interview, he'd given his notice.

I was curious, however, about the details of his departure.

When I questioned him about it, he mentioned two factors that he felt were key in his decision to leave. One was financial. World-wide Studios did not want to give him a promotion, and as such, he was essentially being asked to take a pay cut because he would not receive the stock options that accompanied a move to senior management. For Brian, being asked to work for less was an un-tenable situation, as it would be for many employees. The second factor was the opacity surrounding the denied promotion. Brian saw no reason why he was denied promotion that would have en-sured commensurate compensation—in fact, he felt that his work more than justified the move up the corporate ladder. "As the only executive on the team who had advocated for and been part of the acquisitions team on two different Academy Award–nominated movies, and the only executive at this level who had sourced two different movies that had gone into production, I did not know what in my work was not worth promotion."

As it turned out, neither did his managers. Though he repeat-edly sought feedback about how to improve his performance to ensure his supervisors' satisfaction and continue his climb up the career ladder, he faced obfuscation, stonewalling, and undermin-ing. His annual review contained positive written feedback, but he also received notes that other leaders in the firm felt he "needed improvement." When he tried to clarify where, how, and to what extent he needed to improve, no information was forthcoming.

This dearth of feedback is not unusual. One particular chal-lenge many Black workers face in trying to advance is the diffi-culty of getting clear advice, especially when that feedback needs to be constructively critical. This may seem paradoxical, given that other studies have shown that many Black workers are treated more harshly and face greater disciplinary action and punishment than their white counterparts.[1] Yet there is a key difference. Black workers are closely scrutinized, making them more likely to be sanctioned and reprimanded for even small mistakes.[2] At the same time, they are much less likely to receive honest, direct feedback about how they can improve performance in a way that enables them to develop and advance.

Frequently, this tepid feedback is a consequence of white managers' uncertainty about and discomfort with interacting with Black employees. Benedict, a Black partner in a prestigious Seattle law firm, shared with me that many colleagues perceive him as "the asshole" because he is always direct and pointed with junior Black colleagues about areas where they need to improve. He is relentlessly critical of their writing skills, demands perfection in oral arguments, and insists that they do whatever it takes (ethically) to meet his high expectations. But Benedict told me that he operates this way because he sees the differences in how white partners demand excellence and high performance from white associates but fail to convey these expectations to Black ones.

As he saw it: "People can be passive-aggressive—they'll stop working with people rather than giving them feedback; then they'll look at minority lawyers' hours and ask how we can justify keeping them on. That's because they can give candid feedback to whites but not Blacks. My former mentor gave it to me straight. He told me my work was crap, but this helped me to do better. So I try to share that bluntness, but I do it to help. Because I know Black lawyers are getting evaluated on this, even if people won't do it openly or give them the tools to help. I'll be the jerk, the asshole, but it's because it's what you need to improve. But also, this is the way white guys treat other white associates. But they'll tiptoe around the Black guys because they don't know how to talk to them."

Risk Aversion vs. Fear of Missing Out

Up to this point, Brian's story echoes much of what we know about the challenges many Black workers face advancing past a certain point in the organizational structure. The unclear expectations for promotion, the lack of support from sponsors and mentors, the absence of a relationship with managers who could provide clear feedback about expectations—all were present, and all are common phenomena that make it particularly difficult for Black workers to move into leadership and management roles.

But Brian's decision to leave was compounded by other factors as well. Given how frequently and forcefully he advocated for Black filmmakers and projects, I wondered whether he believed that explained some of the lack of support he received from managers. When I asked him this, he immediately answered affirmatively. Brian then elaborated, describing Hollywood as a conformist space ruled by "two different kinds of fear." In his view, this included the fear of getting fired, which was common, and the fear of doing something different and seeing it fail. In this framework, he explained that it was more comfortable for a studio to spend $10 million greenlighting another installment of a successful franchise because of its proven record of success than to take the risk of bankrolling a new and unproven idea that might not recoup its expenses.

"The only way anything interesting happens," he said, "is if a more progressive fear takes hold and you're able to use it. And that's the fear of missing out on that which is unusual and catching the zeitgeist. Everyone knows *Fast and Furious* or whatever franchise here or there is in the marketplace. Everyone also knows there are things no one sees coming that will work—there will be another *Get Out, Sixth Sense, Memento.*"

In some ways, Brian's account reflects the fact that entertainment is a business like any other. Bottom lines and market returns take precedence over inventiveness and originality. Films are creative, artistic endeavors, but at the end of the day, studios want to ensure that the products they create will generate a return on the investment. This certainly explains why franchises like *Jurassic*

Park span multiple decades and why the principal characters keep returning to islands filled with dinosaurs when, in this viewer's humble opinion, they really should know better. The fear of taking risks on new ideas leaves studios, like publishing houses, record companies, and other industries that produce creative products, relatively risk-averse and conservative about what they are willing to support.

Brian's assessment of the general state of the industry indicates how these more conservative norms can present both limitations and opportunities for Black workers seeking to advance. Because most companies are generally risk-averse, managers often are reluctant to support changes that seem too unsettling or far from the norm.[3] Unfortunately, this logic can extend to diversity in leadership, with companies unwilling to support Black candidates for high-ranking positions because it represents such a sea change from their general practices. Thus Brian's assessment of the landscape of the entertainment industry suggests that even though it is a creative field, the reigning business and corporate ethos can still limit the ability for someone to think and act in groundbreaking ways. This appears to be particularly apt when it comes to questions of race and leadership.

However, Brian's discussion of the zeitgeist also highlights where opportunities may lie for Black creatives looking to advance. He emphasized that the second motivating fear in Hollywood is the fear of missing the "next big thing"—the next film that, despite modest financing or low expectations, strikes a nerve with audiences and becomes an unexpected hit. Because of the lack of diversity among leadership and these executives' unfamiliarity with the nuances and experiences of Black culture, Black films may be more likely to be these unexpected sensations. A 2021 McKinsey report found that films with Black off-screen staff (e.g., producers, writers, and directors) received 40 percent less funding than those helmed by their white counterparts. Yet per dollar spent, movies with Black leads yielded 10 percent more in box office returns.[4]

Perhaps as a consequence, there are multiple cases of Black movies that were breakout successes and defied expectations (such as *Girls Trip*, *The Best Man*, and *Moonlight*) at least in part because studio executives did not anticipate that these films would resonate widely with audiences.

As cultural shifts occur that generate more discussion of and attention to issues of diversity and racism in all sectors of US society, it may be that the fear of missing the "next big thing," coupled with the realization that Black films actually can and do generate significant profits, may motivate studio heads and other corporate leaders in this field to consider investing more in Black leadership (in terms of both resources and finances). Films that are lacking in diversity and authentic representation actually take in less at the box office, so a business case can be made for creating more opportunities for Black executives who are interested in financing and supporting diversity among films.[5] Thus, it is possible that one route to advancement may be that the fear of missing out pushes top executives to pursue Black leaders who can identify and support diverse films that would otherwise go unnoticed. Societal and cultural changes may mean that these companies' actions are finally catching up to their rhetoric.

Hollywood Shuffle

For Brian, however, it was too late for Worldwide Studios to take such a route. He'd spent enough time grappling with the question of whether the company's commitment to diversity was real or pretend, and he felt that he had his answer. Though Worldwide Studios did many of the right things, the gray areas of work revealed to him that it was not going to be the place he hoped it could be. Working at a studio where he believed that senior management denied him a promotion he earned was a nonstarter. And his belief that his advancement was derailed at least partially because of his vocal support for Black filmmakers (despite the studio's public advocacy for racial equity) helped persuade him that it was time to take his talents to South Beach, proverbially speaking. When he failed to receive any information about what improvements he needed to make to advance at Worldwide Studios, he took matters into his own hands. "So simultaneously," he told me, "I had been in talks with a friend of mine who happens to be a film director of some repute who had directed a movie that received six Oscars. They reached out to see if I wanted to join a new production company. So that is what I've left, and that is where I'm going."

Despite Worldwide Studios' reputation and clout in the entertainment industry, Brian's move into production is actually a move forward. He shared the news with pride and evident relief, noting that he would now become a fairly visible producer with the ability to support new films that excited him. And he looked forward to drawing on his industry knowledge and experience at Worldwide Studios to expand the landscape further for up-and-coming Black filmmakers.

It's also worth noting that the production company where Brian is headed is helmed by a person of color. After his frustrating experiences with Worldwide Studios, the opportunity to work with a Black producer and to give free rein to his commitment to Black filmmakers was no small part of the appeal of his new job. Brian felt that his professional and personal goals were more likely to be satisfied in a company that already had diverse leadership at the top, rather than in struggling to break barriers and advance through the ranks of a company that seemed unwilling to offer opportunities.

This is a route that may be more available to workers in certain industries or with certain levels of visibility. In fact, Brian's decision to leave Worldwide Studios for a Black-owned production company calls to mind the 2021 controversy and media furor around journalist Nikole Hannah-Jones. Hannah-Jones was initially offered a faculty position at the University of North Carolina–Chapel Hill, but after conservative, white board members complained about her scholarship, the university took the highly unusual step of offering her the position without the protection and job security of tenure. After public outcry, the university reversed its decision, but the damage was done. Hannah-Jones instead took a position at historically Black Howard University, along with fellow MacArthur Foundation "Genius" grant winner Ta-Nehisi Coates. For these visible, high-status figures, pursuing work away from a "white gaze" may be liberating and freeing, particularly when work in predominantly white organizations comes with thwarted opportunities for mobility, public humiliations, and broken promises.

Everyday Black workers may find, however, that moving to predominantly Black organizations can come with some trade-offs. The peace of mind may be tempered by the fact that Black-owned businesses frequently operate with fewer resources and with lower operating budgets than their white counterparts. Often, this is a function of wealth disparities in Black communities and the fact that Black entrepreneurs tend to start businesses with less capital.[6] Even Howard University, one of the top HBCUs in the country and now, with Hannah-Jones and Coates on its faculty, academic home to two of the nation's most well-known Black intellectuals, had an endowment in 2022 of about $700 million. That might sound impressive until you compare it with the endowment of Harvard University, which that same year was $51 *billion*, a figure larger than the gross domestic product of several countries.[7] Similar disparities are replicated across many companies and may make it harder—though not impossible—for Black-owned businesses to secure Black talent.

Ultimately, when the ambiguous and unclear expectations around promotion make it easy for outspoken workers like Brian to face penalties, Black businesses can be an attractive alternative.

But systemic, long-term patterns of discrimination and disinvestment make it hard for these businesses to operate on equal footing. Nevertheless, for Black workers like Brian who have the option to work at the more well-resourced institutions, organizations with Black leadership can provide both routes to leadership and a more equitable work environment.

CHAPTER 19

When Advancement Isn't the Answer

"I WENT BACK ON MY OWN TERMS"

The first time I spoke with Max, the emergency medicine doctor, we were in my office in Atlanta. He had been out of medical school for a few years and also lived in the city, working at a hospital in an affluent part of town. When we talked, he shared with me some of the mixed feelings he had about medicine and health care and described some of his struggles to find happiness with his work given the gray areas that made it difficult. On one hand, he loved the excitement and challenge of medicine. He felt that he'd built a solid reputation as a good doctor and enjoyed his relationships with his co-workers. And unlike many other Black workers, he also was fortunate to have found a supportive supervisor who understood the impediments that Black employees often face.

But when I asked Max whether he also wanted to move into a supervisory role, he told me, "You know, honestly, not really." I was a little surprised to hear this, given his history of lofty achievements. He was the first in his family to finish college, graduated early, attended some of the top schools in the country, and was passionate about medicine and health care. It seemed that moving into a leadership role in his facility would be a natural next step in an already impressive trajectory.

Max's ambivalence about advancement, however, actually made perfect sense once he explained his goals in the field. As he put it: "I don't like the political side of it. I don't want to deal with hospital management and their expectations, and the expectations and ramifications as far as reimbursement and so forth. That's not really why I'm there." Max was there to provide care to patients in emergency situations, and like many Black providers I spoke with, he particularly wanted to ensure that Black patients got the respectful, thorough treatment that they are often denied in the US healthcare system.

Max and I had this conversation in 2011. When I followed up with him a decade later, I was particularly curious to know whether and how his thoughts about advancement had changed. Was he still indifferent or opposed to moving into leadership? Had time in the profession shifted his views about the increasing corporatization of health care and its chilling effect on medical practice?

As it turns out, he did at one point attempt to move into a leadership role, but the circumstances around that process only reinforced his doubts about advancement in the medical field. During his time at the hospital, Max was approached by a private group that wanted to recruit him for a partnership role. He agreed to join this group under the condition that he would become a partner within a few months; he then subsequently quit his old job and started the new position. But before he could finalize his move into the partnership role, his new company was acquired by a larger conglomerate. As happens with these kinds of deals, the new conglomerate had different ideas. It ruled that only existing partners would get any equity in the deal and that those on the partnership track were simply out of luck.

To say that Max was not happy about this arrangement would

be an understatement. The financial hit alone was significant. "I left a job making over $400,000 a year," he said, "and went to a job making around $300,000 with the understanding that I was going to become a partner. With a partnership comes all of the bonuses, comes the equity, comes [the fact that] when there's a sale, you are involved in a part of it. And then that was snatched out from underneath me six months prior to the final sale. And then the buyout offer that we were given was a terrible offer."

Apart from the financial consequences, the sale of the group and his missed chance at partnership solidified for Max many of the things he already had observed (and disliked) about the growing corporatism and commodification of health care. It also soured him on moving into a managerial or leadership role. He liked being a doctor, providing care, and helping others. He particularly liked the aspect of his job that involved being the first Black doctor many of his Black patients, particularly elderly ones, had ever had. It made him feel proud and underscored his trajectory of being a kid from a humble background who had achieved more than he thought possible. But these parts of medicine aren't reflected in a field that has become increasingly focused on the bottom line. Consequently, moving into leadership holds less and less appeal.

Max's thwarted pathway to a leadership role was not directly due to overt or even institutional racism from his employer. The factors that drive the increasing corporatization of medicine are larger, more structural ones. For many years, health care has increasingly become commercialized and treated as a private commodity to be purchased in an open market rather than as a public good that should be widely available to all. In this framework, health care becomes a product to be sold to those who have the means to afford it, rather than a service best distributed to all for the collective societal benefit. This is evident in the declining amounts of resources provided to public care facilities, the ease with which efforts to provide some form of publicly funded health care become inaccurately described as "socialism," and the emphasis in the Affordable Care Act on mandating private insurance and state exchanges through which Americans could purchase insurance that would allow them to access health care.[1] As a consequence, the process in which groups are sold and profit maximization takes center stage has become increasingly common not just in health care, but in many other industries as well. Max was unfortunately caught up in this process in a way that worked to his disadvantage.

But there's another aspect to consider here. Although the increasing commodification of health care can and does affect doctors of all races, this path may have specific implications for Black physicians. Many Black doctors are motivated to go into certain specialty areas, or even to pursue this career path at all, because they want to improve conditions for Black communities. And this drive is present not just among doctors, but among many Black teachers, nurses, attorneys, and others who want to address the racial disparities they see every day in their lines of work.[2] Laila, the special education teacher in Baltimore, taught kids who were primarily Black. She told me: "I feel it is my duty as a woman and a Black woman to protect these kids. I honestly feel in my soul that they should not be here. They should not be in these special education classes. I feel they were done a huge disservice, and I make it my mission to fix it in any capacity, even if it's just giving them life skills." When organizations move to a model in which they prioritize making profits and maximizing returns, they may yield larger gains and satisfy shareholders, but they also run the risk of dissuading motivated Black workers from leadership.

Max's experience suggests that part of the challenge Black workers face moving into leadership positions has to do not just with blocked paths inside organizations, but with structural shifts happening in the economy as well. As he recounted, Max had a supportive supervisor who wanted to see him succeed and, importantly, understood the biases Black doctors encounter in the work-place. He was able to thrive and built a solid enough professional reputation that he was recruited for a leadership position in a top facility. But the push for organizations to build profits, rather than connect with patients, disillusioned Max and made him question what he would have to give up—and what he would ultimately lose—should he advance further in the field. It turned out that mobility wasn't what would make him happy after all.

Taking a Different Path

After the group was sold, leaving Max without the partnership op-tions he had expected, he took a short hiatus from medicine. He was fortunate that his wife, also a doctor, had a stable position at her own facility, so taking a break from work was a feasible option. He spent about three-and-a-half months at home with his young daughters before deciding that it would be a waste of his time, ed-ucation, and experience to throw away his career in medicine com-pletely. So Max decided to work through a staffing company that provides health-care workers on an as-needed basis. Here, he sets the rate he's willing to work for and works when he finds an orga-nization able to meet that rate.

It turns out that what it took for Max to find happiness and contentment in his work was not moving into an administrative role but returning to the initial principles he held at the start of his career. He'd always had qualms about leadership given the health-care system's shift toward an increasingly corporate structure. Yet when an opportunity arose, he followed that path anyway, perhaps seduced by the salary structure and potential profits. When it fell apart, Max went back to where he started—focusing on finding an employment arrangement that would allow him to do what he really loved, which was simply providing medical care to patients in need. He found that he couldn't give up on medicine, but when he went back, it was in a way that finally allowed him to find joy in his work. As he put it, "I went back on my own terms."

A Bright Side of Gig Work

Max's narrative gives us a mixed picture of advancement for Black workers. In his case, it turned out that moving up in the organization and in the profession was not what he really wanted. And certainly it's true that everyone does not, should not, and will not want to move into a leadership role. By his own account, Max has genuinely found happiness by being an independent contractor. He has flexibility in his schedule, he spends valuable time with his family, and he does all this without having to sacrifice the things that bring him joy about medicine—treating patients, caring for people, and under the best circumstances, saving lives. If, as Gallup suggests, the state of gig work today is a tale of two gig economies, Max's path appears to situate him among the happier, more satisfied independent contractors who work when and how they want, and appreciate the autonomy and flexibility that these arrangements can bring.

However, it's important to contextualize the fact that Max did not choose this alternative route in a vacuum. Although he does not describe accounts of explicit or overt bias that derailed his attempt to move into leadership, he nonetheless was discouraged by the pursuit of profit and the way that, in his view, it compromised and distracted from providing medical care. This suggests that organizations that genuinely want to bring Black workers into leadership roles may benefit from taking a more expansive approach that extends beyond the singular focus on expanding margins and increasing returns. Many Black workers, particularly in service industries, are not motivated just by making money for the organization. There is often a broader, more visceral calling grounded in a sense of racial solidarity that pushes Black workers to try, or at least want to try, to open doors for other Black employees. We saw some of this with Brian's commitment to telling stories of Black life on film and Kevin's determination to assist Black children through his nonprofit work. Even when Black employees face fairly unimpeded routes to advancement, some may be motivated to pursue other paths if it seems that moving into leadership precludes opportunities to affect Black constituencies positively.

CHAPTER 20

A Path Forward

"I'LL SEE WHAT ELSE I CAN DO"

What about Black workers who defy the odds to take a more traditional path to leadership? The accounts in this book show that for many Black employees, avenues to top positions are unclear, blocked, or require unappealing compromises. But certainly some Black workers do make it into the uppermost ranks in their organizations. How does this happen? If, generally speaking, the same barriers are in place, then why do some get to this point while others do not?

Darren's experiences offer some helpful insights. As with forming connections and navigating the organizational culture in his workplace, his skill in establishing critical relationships with mentors and sponsors has been a major factor in his ability to advance professionally. Without prompting from me, he revealed during one of our conversations: "Mentorship has actually been a big part of my success over the years, particularly at my previous job. I had several mentors that really supported me."

From Darren's viewpoint, it was not a coincidence that he had had consistent mentorship and sponsorship and that he had advanced to the top of his profession in the corporate world. Rather, he felt that the support he got from others was a critical factor that aided his success. He recalled that at each stage of his career, he had been fortunate to have senior colleagues who took him under their wings, provided guidance, and steered him toward opportunities and resources that otherwise would have gone untapped. Reflecting back to the start of his career, Darren recalled that at his very first job, the boss he reported to told him: "Some people think that an analyst program is two years and that's it. But this is a job that you can really make a career of here. It doesn't have to be just two or three years." Those words of wisdom transformed the way Darren approached that entry-level position and helped him believe that there was a place for him in an organization that had a fairly poor track record in hiring and retaining Black employees.

Darren found that as he pursued his career in various companies, he was able to secure key relationships at each place. These mentors welcomed him and offered valuable feedback and advice. One offered general support; another was more practical, steering him through the process of getting a retention agreement when the company was being sold. In each case, there was at least one colleague from whom Darren learned a great deal about leadership, management, and business.

Ironically, it is perhaps the job Darren had just left that had the most significant impact on his ability to climb the ranks in his field. At this prior company, management had recently established a mentoring program for Black workers. In this program, Black workers were assigned to a senior mentor who would host them for group meetings to form relationships with them and address any concerns or questions they had. The mentor/mentee assignment was originally scheduled to last for a year, but after that, Darren and his mentor remained in regular communication, setting up monthly meetings for Darren to check in and get feedback.

That formal program was critical for broadening Darren's relationships with colleagues who could serve in important mentoring roles. But apart from that program, he had independent relationships with other higher-ups as well. Those relationships were essential for his thriving in that company, but those colleagues also served as references when Darren got the opportunity to take his career to the next level. He noted, "I don't think [anyone at my current job] ever actually called them, but I guess part of it is just hopefully having impressive people who are willing to vouch for you, you know?"

Not Everyone Is Darren: How Organizations Can Help

Darren's experiences highlight how much relationships with senior managers matter for advancement. While he is certainly a skilled, capable, and hard worker, having an array of mentors and sponsors allowed him to weather the uncertainty when one company was sold, gave him impressive colleagues to list as references, and helped him solve problems and think through issues that arose in the daily course of his work. Throughout his career, Darren benefited from being able to form personal, close ties to senior colleagues who could aid his rise up the corporate ladder.

I suspect this part of Darren's experience is familiar for many Black workers who've made it to or near the tops of their professions. I'm reminded of former President Barack Obama's recollection that back when he was just a junior senator from Illinois, Nevada senator and majority leader Harry Reid saw his potential and promise and urged him to run for the presidency. Before she became CEO of Xerox, Ursula Burns benefited from the mentorship and guidance of Paul Allaire, a senior executive at the company. And although I'm certainly not a CEO or a president, even in my own case, several senior administrators and department chairs helped open doors for me in academia. Given the extent to which Black workers are underrepresented at and near the top of most industries, it's likely that many of the most visible and high-profile ones benefited from a similar dynamic where at least one white senior leader championed their careers.

But relying only on idiosyncrasies and quirks to build connections to mentors and sponsors can come with disadvantages. Black workers who are shyer, more socially awkward, or lack the cultural capital to fit into these environments may find it difficult or impossible to develop such links. Like Darren, I grew up comfortably middle class, and my father had already navigated multiple university bureaucracies. I won't comment on my level of social awkwardness, but I will say that cultural capital and class privilege likely made it easier for me to forge relationships with potential mentors and sponsors. But this isn't the case for all or even most Black workers. Thus, it's not enough to conclude that Black workers just need to develop these relationships to ultimately get ahead. It is also important to account for the subtle barriers that may hinder these ties.

This is why the mentoring program that Darren mentioned is so significant. Though Darren is a friendly, engaging person who finds it relatively easy to form connections with people, this will not necessarily be the case for all Black workers in these settings. Particularly for Black workers who are unused to navigating predominantly white spaces, or who lack friends and family members who have been able to instill strategies or pass on knowledge about these environments, the expectations to form social ties on their own can be daunting and intimidating. And this uncertainty goes both ways. As we have established, senior white managers who have very little exposure to and contact with Black workers may be, for a variety of reasons, unwilling to reach out, or uncomfortable doing so, to develop the close ties necessary for those workers' advancement. In some cases, this may stem from a fear of inadvertently saying or doing something racially offensive; in other cases, it may be a consequence of outright bias. But Darren's account highlights how organizational mentoring initiatives can help close some of these gaps and create more exposure and connections between

Black workers and the mostly white senior managers who work above them. When these programs are in place, Black workers don't have to rely only on happenstance to form such connections. Official programs provide an infrastructure that makes developing critical relationships easier.

Formal mentoring programs are particularly useful given the facts that not only are Black workers underrepresented in organizations, but many white managers have little exposure to or understanding of the breadth and diversity of Black communities and how widely experiences may vary within them. Consequently, some whites may be daunted by Black workers who do not seem immediately familiar with the culture of these spaces and may be less likely to take steps to mentor them as a result. Legal scholars Mitu Gulati and Devon Carbado write insightfully about how, even within racial groups, markers of cultural identity can be sources of exclusion and marginalization at work.[1] Referencing the legal field, they imagine two equally qualified Black women associates at a law firm. Both associates have law degrees from the same prestigious institution, comparable work experience, and similar LSAT scores. But one associate served as president of the Black Law Students Association, attended an HBCU for her undergraduate degree, does not chemically straighten her hair, and grew up in a single-parent family in an urban environment. The other associate was active in predominantly white student law organizations, earned her undergraduate degree from a comparably ranked predominantly white institution, straightens her hair, and grew up in a suburban neighborhood in a two-parent family. Despite these two women being equally qualified, Gulati and Carbado posit that the second associate would receive more support and encouragement in a firm.

Though this exercise is hypothetical, it underscores some of the dynamics that make formal mentoring programs valuable in organizational spaces. It is already difficult for Black workers to find mentors and/or sponsors who can guide them through the promotion process. For Black workers who do not come from a background that white senior managers find relatable or familiar, this task can prove to be nearly impossible. Black workers who are women, LGBTQ+, or have other socially disadvantaged statuses may also experience additional difficulties finding mentors. Simply expecting mentoring and sponsoring relationships to develop organically creates an environment where Black workers continue to be excluded and left behind. However, when companies establish programs to ensure that everyone has access to someone who can guide their career, by design, no one is left out.

"Lifting as They Climb": Being a Company Leader

Seeing that organizations were beginning to encourage and support programming that could help Black workers inspired Darren to be part of these efforts. With firms sending the message that they are actively on board with addressing these issues, Darren is beginning to think about ways that he can use his position as a senior Black executive to benefit other Black managers and analysts in the company. Specifically, he expects that he can take an active leadership role in making his company a more hospitable place for Black workers coming up behind him. This shift toward a more racially conscious organizational culture opens the door for senior-level workers like Darren to be part of the solution.

But where does someone like Darren begin? Shortly before his arrival, the company established a Black employee resource group. Employee resource groups, also known as ERGs or affinity groups, are informal clusters for individuals whose identities are underrepresented in the workplace. It's not uncommon for companies to have ERGs for veterans, women, Black workers, single parents, or other groups of employees who might benefit from connecting with similar others and finding social support. Darren wanted to start there. He also planned to meet with the head of the personnel department to see how he could be involved in that department's efforts to support Black employees. And he hoped that this would be just the beginning. "I'll see what else I can do," he told me. "I mean, I think it's just starting to get ingrained. And I haven't heard as much about any kind of a mentoring program, so I think that's something that I will inquire about too."

With organizations talking more openly about becoming spaces where Black workers can thrive, there is now a route for Black leaders like Darren who have made it to the top to help carve out routes to success for other Black workers. This is a laudable outcome, but there is also cause for caution here. Black employees who advance to leadership roles in companies often find that outsize and excessive mentoring expectations are then placed upon them, particularly when it comes to helping other underrepresented groups. Some Black workers relish this opportunity to change internal norms and to "lift as they climb," helping others along the way. But when Black senior managers and leaders do this additional work of their own volition and make themselves especially available to other Black workers in a company, they can find themselves becoming burned out, overstressed, and exhausted.[2]

This may seem like a Catch-22: Black workers advance to the top ranks only to risk more stress by becoming mentors to other Black employees, but if they do not create more opportunities for other Black workers, underrepresentation persists. There are a couple of ways to offset these potential challenges. One is for the work of mentoring to be spread broadly and widely among an organization's leadership, which is something that formal programs can achieve. Another possibility is for organizations to ensure that they have enough Black workers in influential roles so that the work of being a touchstone does not fall to one or two people. Darren hopes to create these avenues for others, so that more Black workers have the opportunities that he had.

Moving On Up

The narratives here in Part III show that advancement represents another gray area where racial inequality persists. Even in companies that do a decent job of getting Black workers in the door, many of those workers stall out at middle-management levels rather than rising to the top of their professions. Thinking of advancement as a gray area helps to explain why this happens, as it shows that many Black employees are not placed on leadership tracks or lack the relationships with supervisors that are essential for getting ahead. Whether the specific challenge is Kevin's issue of white women gatekeepers, Max's disillusionment with a corporate model that prioritizes profits over people, or Alex's contract work that is ill-equipped to feed her entrepreneurial spirit, the consistent theme here is that this ambiguity does not serve Black workers well.

How then to address some of the problems that arise here? Constance, for instance, struggled in her job to find someone who could provide guidance and support in her (ultimately thwarted) attempts to move into leadership. How do we position Black workers so that they avoid this experience and can be matched with an "advocate" earlier on? What steps can companies take to prevent ambitious Black workers from floundering?

We see from Darren's account that formal mentoring programs made the difference in his career, and evidence shows that these initiatives do work.[1] Instead of leaving it up to workers to seek out mentors on their own or opening programs only to selected employees, organizations can establish companywide programs that match all interested employees with senior workers who can provide guidance and support. When these senior leaders, who are disproportionately white men, work in close contact with motivated, eager Black employees, an opportunity is presented both to diminish racial biases and to broaden networks so that they are less racially homogeneous. Senior leaders become more familiar with Black workers' skills, talents, and qualifications and are in a better position both to advise them on their careers and to engage in the important sponsorship work of recommending them for key opportunities. Perhaps most important, these programs actually move the needle, on average nearly tripling the representation of underrepresented workers in management roles.[2]

Formal mentoring programs can change the workplace environment so that chemical engineers like Constance don't have to seek out mentors (or advocates) who respond with blank stares when she asks for support. They can improve opportunities for Black men like Kevin who hit "the firewall" when attempting to advance in occupations where most of the leadership is composed of white women. With more programs in place that provide such support, organizations can do a better job equalizing opportunities for Black employees.

Black workers who ascend to leadership roles can also take a page from Darren's narrative and consider taking steps to implement organizational policies that are shown to maximize diversity. A beneficiary himself of mentoring programs that allowed him to connect with senior leadership, Darren planned to inquire about installing these programs now that he was in an executive role. Many Black workers in a variety of jobs describe the importance of providing fairer, more equitable services to communities of color, whether as doctors, teachers, or counselors. There is often a strong sense of responsibility among Black workers for creating more opportunities for Black populations who are frequently overlooked. One way to do this in the workplace is for Black leaders to champion the policies that have proven rates of success. And companies that support these efforts may find it easier to retain workers like Max, rather than seeing them leave out of disappointment and frustration.

Accountability is also key when trying to improve the access Black workers have to leadership opportunities. Companies can facilitate this by launching internal task forces that investigate and highlight Black workers' paths in the organization. Researchers have found that diversity task forces that are convened by the CEO and include department heads and members of underrepresented groups can be very influential. This is because such task forces include and involve workers from across the company, have the CEO's blessing, and are designed not just to identify problem areas but to offer solutions. They also push workers to be reflexive and aware of actions and areas where bias may be festering—for instance, are managers promoting only white workers, as Kevin noted in the nonprofit where he worked? Are Black workers being excluded from the relationships that engender mobility, as Constance experienced? Data suggest that with these task forces in place, companies on average can expect to see increases of up to 30 percent of underrepresented groups in management roles within five years.[3]

There is room for public policy in these efforts, as well. Legislators can mandate that federal contracts with private-sector companies will go only to those that report employment data and are able to show racial and gender parity at all levels of the organizational structure. They can also ban wage secrecy policies, which preclude workers from asking questions about pay and allow disparities to persist (though women are more likely to violate these policies).[4] Improving funding to the Equal Employment

Opportunity Commission, the federal agency tasked with enforcing antidiscrimination claims—whose staff has been reduced by nearly half since 1980—could help that body more effectively sanction organizations that perpetuate racial discrimination.[5] And of course, consistent enforcement of existing antidiscrimination laws could help to ensure more racial equity in workplaces.[6]

KEY TAKEAWAYS

- Many companies are not designed to offer Black workers the same opportunities for upward mobility as their white counterparts

- Advancement doesn't always reflect just talents and skills. Subjective factors also affect which workers have opportunities for advancement

- Black workers are less likely to have access to sponsors and mentors who can position them for mobility

- If companies aren't attuned to the challenges they face, advancement can take a toll on Black leaders' mental health

- Companies that embrace social responsibility may be more attractive to Black leaders

CHECKLIST: WHAT YOU CAN DO

For the DEI Practitioner

○ Collect internal and benchmarking data

○ Use this data to explain internal patterns to company leaders

○ Partner with managers to provide input when they are making decisions about promotion

○ Establish diversity task forces that can identify the firm's weaknesses and develop solutions for maximizing Black workers' retention and advancement

For the Executive or Senior Manager

O Provide clear guidelines about expectations for promotion

O Serve as a mentor and sponsor to Black employees

O Join a diversity task force

O Lobby legislators and policymakers to support public policies that would reduce racial disparities

O Provide regular, consistent feedback about ongoing projects rather than performance evaluations, which can reflect bias

For the HR Director

O Institute mentoring programs that are available to everyone

O Match mentors and mentees based on shared interests

O Consider matching mentees with teams that could build their networks, rather than just one individual

For the Colleague

O Facilitate connections between Black colleagues and senior leaders

O Offer emotional and social support to Black co-workers

O Lobby company leaders to offer robust corporate social responsibility plans that focus explicitly on racial equity

The Way Out of the Gray

Irene Branch is not a household name. Profiled in historian Michael Honey's book *Black Workers Remember*, she is one of the millions of largely unknown, unfamiliar Black workers who were part of the Great Migration to northern cities in the mid-twentieth century.[1] Many of these workers' stories are lost to history, but collectively, they highlight the extent to which work has long been a vehicle for maintaining oppression and racial inequality. In narrating her life story, Branch describes a work history characterized by significant barriers—overt racism, hard labor, and explicit sexism. Being a Black woman living during that time period meant that most jobs were closed to her, and the ones she could work were specifically designed to be as demeaning, difficult, and low-paying as possible.

Branch was born and raised in Athens, Georgia, but moved to Memphis in 1924. Working in a Southern, segregated city before the civil rights movement, she had to take two jobs to ensure her survival and to feed her family. Like many Black women during that time, she did domestic work—cooking, cleaning, and providing childcare—for a white family. Branch also had a factory job working at a Firestone tire plant, which she began in 1944. Her accounts of work at the Firestone plant illustrate what work looked like for Black women during those years.

"When I first went in," she recounted, "they'd give the hardest jobs they could to the Blacks. They'd give you the jobs a white person wouldn't want and you'd be making less money. It was really tough. You could be working side by side with a white person, and they'd get double the money that you got. You'd get less money, but you were doing the work; they weren't doing the work. But you had to take it, see! You couldn't do nothing else but take it or get going on, go somewhere else and get another job. One place was as bad as the next, there was no use if they didn't have a union. It was just rough.

"Before the union, those supervisors would curse you, call you names, do you any kind of way. They'd call you 'nigger' and everything else, and spit on you. Do *anything* to you. Blacks was really treated bad. And they'd fire you in a minute. I know a lot of men—women too—quit out there. But I didn't quit. I had a hard time, but I stuck on in there."[2]

Stories like Irene Branch's are far less common now than they were in her day. When I talk to Black workers today about their experiences in their current places of employment, they no longer describe workplaces where managers can legally refuse to hire, retain, or promote them expressly because of their race. Black workers less often describe the kinds of explicit workplace oppression that was common a few generations ago, and there are examples of Black workers who have undoubtedly achieved major successes in areas ranging from government and politics to entertainment, business, law, and beyond.

Yet, as in Irene Branch's day, work continues to perpetuate racial inequality. This no longer happens through openly declared intentions and actions; instead, it occurs because of the gray areas associated with work—the cultural, social, and relational parts of employment. The organizational cultures built with white workers in mind, the reliance on networks when making hiring deci-sions, the outsize roles that mentors and sponsors play in advancing careers—these are the mechanisms that drive how we work in the modern economy, but they are also key reasons why we have yet to see racial equity in most workplaces. Gray areas help explain why Black workers remain so underrepresented in many prestigious professions and among the top ranks of many organizations.

The gray areas of work are why these disparities persist de-spite periodic national conversations around race, a multibillion-dollar diversity industry, and organizations that proudly tout their commitment to racial equity. In the aftermath of George Floyd's murder at the hands of police and the Black Lives Matter protests that followed, many corporations took to social media to proclaim their opposition to systemic racism and to profess their commit-ment to racial equity.[3] Yet many of these same companies do not have a history of promoting racial equity; in fact, their ongoing practices reproduce the same racial hierarchies that they took to social media to critique.[4] We now have legislation that prohibits overt racial exclusion and discrimination at work, but that public policy was designed to address how workplace racism manifested in a previous era. For work to be more equitable now, we have to address the gray areas.

Now that we know what does not work, how should we do things differently? Change is possible, but for change to happen, organi-zations need to operate in alternate ways that actively create more equitable opportunities for Black workers, and employees have to support and participate in these efforts. The good news is that re-search documents evidence-based strategies organizations can use to improve racial diversity within their ranks. As I've discussed at the close of each part of this book, we know that measures like instituting targeted recruitment at HBCUs, empowering diversity officers and equipping them to focus on racial equity, creating task forces that can address racial disparities, establishing formal mentoring programs, and developing public policy that enforces rather than stifles antidiscrimination measures can help transform these gray areas from sites that perpetuate racial inequality to those that effectively reduce it.

Case Studies from the Field

Some organizations are already taking steps like these, with varying degrees of success. For instance, Google responded to criticism about the lack of diversity among its employees by establishing a partnership with several HBCUs in an effort to bring in more Black engineers. Google, which like many other companies had a history of recruiting students from what it considered "elite" schools, began a relationship with Howard University, one of the country's foremost historically Black universities. This initiative was designed to tap into predominantly Black talent pools that are frequently overlooked and to increase the numbers of Black workers in the pipeline and employed in the tech industry.

But the Google initiative shows how expanding networks is only a first step. Companies have to see these programs all the way through to hiring, and media reports suggest that did not happen here. A 2021 *Washington Post* report on the program pointed out that although the company offered Black students internships, these did not lead to an uptick in full-time employment for Blacks. The report attributes this gap to internal screeners' low name recognition for the schools that applicants attended, assumptions that students would not easily assimilate into the company culture, and a perception that advocacy for the program from Black women recruiters at Google was too "aggressive." The program was ultimately shuttered in 2020, though the *Post* quotes a Google spokeswoman as saying, "Any suggestion that we have scaled back or cut our diversity efforts is entirely false. Diversity, equity, and inclusion remain a company-wide commitment and our programs are continuing to scale up."[5] Yet Google's own 2021 Diversity Annual Report indicated that despite hiring more Black workers than the company had in previous years, it was still having a difficult time retaining Black women.[6]

Google's results indicate that it's key not just to focus on hiring, but to change the organizational culture so that when Black workers are hired, they join a company that recognizes and responds to their realities. Whether the company has a market-based, adhocracy, hierarchical, or clan-based culture, companies with a colorblind organizational culture are unable to do this. Candice Morgan, director of diversity and inclusion for the venture capital firm GV, offers an example of how managers can take a lead role in engaging these cultural shifts. Morgan advocates four steps toward creating a race-conscious culture at a firm: committing to an internal focus on racial equity; making space for nuanced, ongoing, candid conversations about race and racism; developing a diversity task force that can set goals and ensure accountability; and incorporating this focus into the business's core.[7] These suggestions offer ways not only to make issues of race and racism central to the organization's business, but also to establish a culture where discussions and openness around racial issues become the norm. This approach makes the focus on race and equity an organizational approach, rather than one that is borne by a few individuals who, independently, may not have the clout, time, or bandwidth to change an organization's entire culture.

In a company with this color-conscious culture, Black workers should not have experiences like Kevin's where they are pressured to be silent even when attention to racial issues feels performative rather than genuine. Embracing this culture would help workers like Amalia, employed in an organization that encouraged discussions of race even while hierarchical structures constrained her ability to create change. A color-conscious culture can also encourage attention to ways organizations can use their power and influence to reduce racial disparities. This perspective would appeal to workers like Max, who was disillusioned by the primarily profit-driven nature of the health-care facility where he worked, and the growing chasm between prioritizing patient care and reducing health disparities. It could also benefit gig workers like Alex by creating opportunities for them to realize long-held ambitions. Instead of treating racial considerations as secondary or nonexistent, this method forces organizations to be cognizant of the challenges that Black employees encounter, and to work to alleviate them.

Coca-Cola is an example of a company that has objectively improved its numbers of Black workers in managerial roles over time. After settling a lawsuit in 2000, executives launched mentoring and recruitment programs in which they set target goals for improving representation of underrepresented workers. Leaders from across the company got involved, even some from the very top ranks of the organization. Five years later, 80 percent of all mentees had risen within the organizational structure, and between 2000 and 2006, the numbers of Black workers in professional or middle-management roles went from 12 percent to 15.5 percent. In 2016, the company could boast of having seventeen Black women who hold the rank of vice president or higher—an enviable statistic that not many companies could match.[8] Those numbers have dropped since then as the company tightened budgets and eliminated some jobs, indicating that even among some of the companies that have made the most strides, it's essential to be vigilant to make sure hard-won gains are not lost.[9]

Coca-Cola's success is evidence that institutionalized mentoring programs can work. Notably, the company did not make these programs invitation-only or seek out perceived high-performers for inclusion. Those are common approaches but ones that run a high risk of incorporating implicit biases and excluding motivated, interested Black employees. In fact, with these programs open to all races, Black workers composed 36 percent of those enrolled, reflecting Black employees' general interest in moving up through the corporate ranks. We've seen in this book how employees like Darren benefited from such programs, and the research suggests that certainly workers like Constance and Brian might have as well.

Where We Are Now and What Comes Next

The examples from Google, GV, and Coca-Cola are instructive, offering not just case studies with varying degrees of success, but a representation of the current discourse around diversity and inclusion. Irene Branch worked during a time when companies openly discriminated without pretense or illusion. That isn't the case today. Instead, corporations express their commitment to diversity, loudly proclaim their opposition to systemic racism, and in some cases even earmark large sums of money to go toward redressing racial inequality in their industries or in society at large. This is a welcome and important departure from the days when Branch struggled to get hired at a Firestone plant that openly segregated Black employees and allowed them to endure racial slurs and worse just for trying to work.

But these public statements are not yet cause for celebration. Although it's important and laudable that companies are finally acknowledging these issues and committing to doing their part to resolve them, as a society, we've been here before. This is not the first time the United States has wrestled with a racial reckoning or that public discourse and discussion have focused on how America can resolve its racist past and present. In the 2021 documentary film *Who We Are: A Chronicle of Racism in America*, attorney Jeffery Robinson describes these moments as *tipping points* and identifies two such points from the past. The first was the post–Civil War era, when the United States grappled with how to reconcile itself as a postslavery nation. The second was the post–civil rights period, when the country attempted to figure out how to move forward with legal segregation outlawed. Robinson argues that in both cases, the country failed its test of whether it could be a truly racially equitable place.

Today, we're at another tipping point. Companies are acknowledging the reality of systemic racism, and they have the numbers, influence, and power to take steps to address it. But, just like during the Reconstruction and post–civil rights times, signs of backlash are already visible. In 2020, the Trump Administration issued an executive order that prohibited federal agencies, the military, and organizations receiving government contracts from offering diversity trainings that include "divisive, anti-American propaganda." The order included examples of terms and phrases, such as "systemic racism" and "unconscious bias," that would be considered objectionable and in violation of the order if used in such trainings. In response, many companies and federal agencies canceled their diversity and inclusion programming rather than risk running afoul of vaguely worded directives clearly designed to prohibit broad discussions of race and racism at work.[10]

President Joe Biden revoked this executive order upon taking office the following year, but the fallout continues. In Florida, the Stop Wrongs to Our Kids and Employees Act, or Stop WOKE Act, mandates that no one in schools or workplaces should, because of their race, "feel discomfort, guilt, anguish, or any form of psychological distress." Nor should companies promote the idea that anyone "bears responsibility for, or should be discriminated against or receive adverse treatment" because of past actions by the members of that group.[11] Although this law does not prohibit diversity initiatives specifically, it's expected to have a chilling effect given that legislators are outlawing statements or actions in the workplace that could potentially cause discomfort. It's not hard to see how this bodes poorly for improving racial equity at work.

Again, as a society, we have to decide which path we'll take. Do we pass more Stop WOKE laws that criminalize efforts to recognize and resolve the ways workplaces perpetuate racial inequality through their gray areas because some workers might get their feelings hurt in the process? Or will companies finally reckon with the fact that as we continue to become an increasingly diverse and multiracial society, creating organizations that reflect this demographic reality is imperative for their long-term success? There are not too many models for successful multiracial democracies, but if the United States is going to become one, establishing workplaces that eradicate rather than perpetuate racial inequality is a necessary step. Otherwise, we not only fail once again to pass another tipping point, but we set ourselves on a path where work continues to compromise a growing number of US citizens, undermining both our ability to innovate and all Americans' right to have productive, healthy, gainful employment.

The challenges that Darren, Constance, Max, Brian, Alex, Kevin, and Amalia have faced in their respective workplaces are not ones that they can fix alone through initiative, will, or personal effort. Nor should they have to. It is incumbent upon companies that say they want more racial diversity to take responsibility and accountability for creating environments where Black workers can be hired, thrive, and advance. Eliminating the gray areas that foster racial inequality is a good place to start.

ACKNOWLEDGMENTS

I always thank the same people. This book is no exception, so if you've read any of my other work, you'll know these names. The first shout-out goes to my absolute favorite people in the entire world, Johari and Jada Wingfield, better known as the best girls ever. Mommy loves you always and forever. Thank you for being such kind, considerate, generous, thoughtful people. Thank you for being my daughters. Thank you for being my everything. I hope that by the time you start work the issues I describe here aren't so pervasive, but I know that whatever careers you pick, you will change the world. Thanks also to John; Brandon; my parents, William and Brenda Harvey; my sister and brother-in-law, Amina and Matt Dearmon; my nephew Nolan; and as always, the best ones—Felicia Jackson, Ashley Herndon, and Karmen Davis. Love you all, and thanks for your consistent support in every possible way.

Professionally, I want to thank Katherine Flynn, the best agent I ever could have imagined. I still remember being at the St. Louis Science Center with the kids, checking my email in the food court, and seeing the message from you introducing yourself. I didn't intend to write another book so soon after *Flatlining*, but I am so glad you reached out to me! Thanks also to Daniella Wexler, Gideon Weil, Abby West, and the editorial staff at Amistad and HarperOne for supporting this project; and to Maggie Wood for providing exceptional research assistance. David Pedulla, Victor Ray, and Steve Vallas also read early drafts of this manuscript, and I very much appreciate their time, generosity, and thoughtful feedback. Their insights have made this book much better than it would have been otherwise. I'm very grateful to the seven Black workers who agreed to speak with me for this book. Thank you for sharing your time and experiences with me. I sincerely hope I've done you justice. And finally, this book is dedicated to the memory of Sherida Hare, Lee Stiff, Elijah Sanders, Bernadine Harvey-Walker, Eric Williams, and John Wingfield Sr. I miss you all.

NOTES

Introduction: Getting into the Gray Area

1. Adia Harvey Wingfield, *Flatlining: Race, Work, and Health Care in the New Economy* (Berkeley: Univ. of California Press, 2019).
2. Tsedale Melaku, *"You Don't Look like a Lawyer": Black Women and Systemic Gendered Racism* (Lanham, MD: Rowman & Littlefield, 2019).
3. Louwanda Evans, *Cabin Pressure: African American Pilots, Flight Attendants, and Emotional Labor* (Lanham, MD: Rowman & Littlefield, 2013).
4. Ilana Gershon, *Down and Out in the New Economy* (Chicago: Univ. of Chicago Press, 2016).
5. Derald Wing Sue, *Microaggressions in Everyday Life: Race, Gender, and Sexual Orientation* (New York: Wiley, 2010).
6. Douglas Blackmon, *Slavery by Another Name* (New York: Anchor, 2008); Talitha LeFlouria, *Chained in Silence: A History of Black Women and Convict Labor* (Chapel Hill: Univ. of North Carolina Press, 2016).
7. W. E. B. Du Bois, *The Philadelphia Negro* (Philadelphia: Univ. of Pennsylvania Press, 1899).
8. Marianne Bertrand and Sudhil Mullainathan, "Are Emily and Greg More Employable than Lakisha and Jamal?" *American Economic Review* 94, no. 4 (2004): 991-1013; Vincent Roscigno, *The Face of Discrimination* (Lanham, MD: Rowman & Littlefield, 2007).
9. Enobong Branch and Caroline Hanley, *Work in Black and White: Striving for the American Dream* (New York: Russell Sage Foundation, 2002); Arne Kalleberg, *Good Jobs, Bad Jobs* (New York: Russell Sage Foundation, 2003).
10. Alex Rosenblat, *Uberland: How Algorithms Are Rewriting the Rules of Work* (Berkeley: Univ. of California Press, 2020).
11. A. Nicole Kreisberg, "Nativity Penalty and Legal Status Paradox: The Effects of Nativity and Legal Status Signals in the US Labor Market," *Social Forces* 101, no. 3 (March 2023), https://doi.org/10.1093/sf/soac055.
12. Ryan W. Miller, "46% of Whites Worry Becoming a Majority-Minority Nation Will 'Weaken American Culture,' Survey Says," *USA Today*,

March 21, 2019, https://www.usatoday.com/story/news/nation/2019/03/21/pew-survey-whites-fearful-minority-country-will-weaken-american-culture/3217218002/.

13. Caitlyn Collins, *Making Motherhood Work* (Princeton, NJ: Princeton Univ. Press, 2019); David Weil, *The Fissured Workplace* (Cambridge, MA: Harvard Univ. Press, 2014).

14. Richard Alba, *The Great Demographic Illusion: Majority, Minority, and the Expanding American Mainstream* (Princeton, NJ: Princeton Univ. Press, 2020); American Community Survey, "ACS Demographic and Housing Estimates," 2018, United States Census Bureau, https://data.census.gov/cedsci/table?q=United%20States&g=0100000US&tid=ACSDP1Y2018.DP05&vintage=2017&layer=state&cid=DP05_0001E.

15. Jennifer Miller, "For Younger Job Seekers, Diversity and Inclusion in the Workplace Aren't a Preference. They're a Requirement," *Washington Post*, February 18, 2021, https://www.washingtonpost.com/business/2021/02/18/millennial-genz-workplace-diversity-equity-inclusion/.

Part I: Cultural

1. Pamela Newkirk, "Diversity Has Become a Booming Business. So Where Are the Results?" *TIME*, October 10, 2019, https://time.com/5696943/diversity-business/.

2. Amanda Abrams, "Black Developers Call for Reckoning in Real Estate," *Washington Post*, April 1, 2021, https://www.washingtonpost.com/business/2021/04/01/black-developers-call-reckoning-real-estate/.

3. Andrea Shalal and Jonathan Landay, "Black Cops Say Discrimination, Nepotism Behind U.S. Police Race Gap," Reuters, July 2, 2020, https://www.reuters.com/article/us-minneapolis-police-blackofficers/black-cops-say-discrimination-nepotism-behind-u-s-police-race-gap-idUSKBN2432T8.

4. Newkirk, "Diversity Has Become a Booming Business."

5. John Carreyrou, *Bad Blood: Secrets and Lies in a Silicon Valley Startup* (New York: Knopf, 2018).

6. Kim Cameron and Robert E. Quinn, *Diagnosing and Changing Organizational Culture: Based on the Competing Values Framework* (New York: Wiley, 1999).

7. France Winddance Twine, *Geek Girls* (New York: NYU Press, 2022).

8. Keon Gilbert and Rashawn Ray, "Why Police Kill Black Males with Impunity: Applying Critical Race and Public Health Theory to Address Determinants of Policing Behaviors and the Justifiable Homicides of Black Men," *Journal of Urban Health* 93, no. 1 (2016): 122–140.

9. Scottie Andrew, "Incoming Rep Cori Bush Said She's Buying Her Capitol Hill Wardrobe Secondhand. 'The Squad' Offered Affordable Fashion

Tips," CNN, November 16, 2020, https://www.cnn.com/style/article/cori-bush-thrift-fashion-trnd/index.html.

10. James Jones, "Racing Through the Halls of Congress: The Black Nod as an Adaptive Strategy for Surviving in a Raced Institution," *DuBois Review* 14, no. 1 (2017): 165–187.

11. Eduardo Bonilla-Silva, *Racism Without Racists* (Lanham, MD: Rowman & Littlefield, 2017).

12. Bonilla-Silva, *Racism Without Racists.*

13. Victor Ray and Danielle Purifoy, "The Colorblind Organization," in *Race, Organizations, and the Organizing Process,* ed. Melissa E. Wooten (London: Emerald, 2019), 131–150.

14. Sharon Collins, *Black Corporate Executives* (Philadelphia: Temple Univ. Press, 1987).

15. Lauren Edelman, *Working Law: Courts, Corporations, and Symbolic Civil Rights* (Chicago: Univ. of Chicago Press, 2016).

16. Frank Dobbin and Alexandra Kalev, "Why Diversity Programs Fail," *Harvard Business Review* 94, no. 7 (July–August 2016): 52–60, p. 54.

17. Alexandra Kalev, Frank Dobbin, and Erin Kelley, "Best Practices or Best Guesses?" *American Sociological Review* 71 (2006): 589–617.

18. Ellen Berrey, The Enigma of Diversity (Chicago: Univ. of Chicago Press, 2015).

19. Adia Harvey Wingfield, "Views from the Other Side: Black Professionals' Perceptions of Diversity Management," in *Race, Work, and Leadership: New Perspectives on the Black Experience,* ed. Laura Morgan Roberts, Anthony J. Mayo, and David Thomas (Boston: Harvard Business Review Press, 2019), 173–188.

20. Berrey, *Enigma of Diversity*; Wingfield, "Views from the Other Side."

21. Matthew Goodrid, "Racial Complexities of Outdoor Spaces: An Analysis of African Americans' Lived Experiences in Outdoor Recreation" (master's thesis, University of the Pacific, 2018).

22. Jim Whitehurst, "Meritocracy: The Workplace Culture That Breeds Success," *Wired,* October 2014, https://www.wired.com/insights/2014/10/meritocracy/.

23. Emilio Castilla and Stephen Benard, "The Paradox of Meritocracy in Organizations," *Administrative Science Quarterly* 55, no. 4 (2010): 543–676.

Chapter 1: Race Blindness and the Liberal Paradox

1. Kim Parker, "The Growing Partisan Divide in Views of Higher Education," Pew Research Center, August 19, 2019, https://www.pewsocialtrends.org/essay/the-growing-partisan-divide-in-views-of-higher-education/.

2. Christopher Newfield, *Unmaking the Public University: The Forty-Year Assault on the Middle Class* (Cambridge, MA: Harvard Univ. Press, 2011).

3. Greg Allen, "Koch Foundation Criticized Again for Influencing Florida State," *Morning Edition*, NPR, May 23, 2014, https://www.npr.org/2014/05/23/315080575/koch-foundation-criticized-again-for-influencing-florida-state.

4. Anna Guizerix, "With Dissent: James Thomas Granted Tenure by IHL," *Oxford Eagle*, May 21, 2019, https://www.oxfordeagle.com/2019/05/21/with-dissent-james-thomas-granted-tenure-by-ihl/.

5. John Brooks Slaughter, Yu Tao, and Willie Pearson Jr., eds., *Changing the Face of Engineering: The African American Experience* (Baltimore: Johns Hopkins Univ. Press, 2015).

6. Louis Archer, Jennifer Dewitte, and Jonathan Osbourne, "Is Science for Us? Black Students' and Parents' Views of Science and Science Careers," *Science Education* 99, no. 2 (2015): 199–237.

7. Women of all races encounter similar challenges in STEM fields. See Dana Britton, "Beyond the Chilly Climate: The Salience of Gender in Women's Academic Careers," *Gender & Society* 31, no. 1 (2017): 5–27.

8. Adia Harvey Wingfield, "Are Some Emotions Marked 'Whites Only'? Racialized Feeling Rules in Professional Workplaces," *Social Problems* 57, no. 2 (2010): 251–268.

9. "Being Black in Corporate America: An Intersectional Exploration," Center for Talent Innovation, 2019, https://www.talentinnovation.org/_private/assets/BeingBlack-KeyFindings-CTI.pdf; Devon Carbado and Mitu Gulati, *Acting White?: Rethinking Race in "Post-Racial" America* (New York: Oxford Univ. Press, 2013).

10. Danielle Boykin, "Bias in the Engineering Workplace," *PE Magazine*, National Society of Professional Engineers, May/June 2017, https://www.nspe.org/resources/pe-magazine/may-2017/bias-the-engineering-workplace.

11. Travis Hoppe et al., "Topic Choice Contributes to the Lower Rate of NIH Awards to African American/Black Scientists," *Science Advances* 5, no. 10 (2019): 1–12.

12. Kimberle Crenshaw, "Framing Affirmative Action," *University of Michigan Law Review* 105 (2006): 123–133.

13. Brian Schaffner and Stephen Ansolabehere, "CCES Common Content, 2014," Harvard Dataverse, V5, https://dataverse.harvard.edu/dataset.xhtml?persistentId=doi%3A10.7910/DVN/XFXJVY.

14. Collins, *Black Corporate Executives*.

15. Chris Weller, "Apple's VP of Diversity Says '12 White, Blue Eyed, Blond Men in a Room' Can Be a Diverse Group," *Business Insider*, October 11, 2017, https://www.businessinsider.com/apples-vp-diversity-12-white-men-can-be-diverse-group-2017-10.

16. Joyce Bell and Douglas Hartman, "Diversity in Everyday Discourse: The Cultural Ambiguities and Consequences of 'Happy Talk,'" *American Sociological Review* 72, no. 6 (2007): 895–914; Frank Dobbin, *Inventing Equal Opportunity* (Princeton, NJ: Princeton Univ. Press, 2009).

17. Erin Kelly and Phyllis Moen, *Overwork* (Princeton, NJ: Princeton Univ. Press, 2020).
18. Robin Ely and Irene Padavic, "What's Really Holding Women Back? It's Not What Most People Think," *Harvard Business Review* 98, no. 2 (2020): 58–67.
19. Wingfield, *Flatlining*.

Chapter 2: Gendered Occupations and Organizational Culture

1. Megan Tobias Neely, *Hedged Out* (Berkeley: Univ. of California Press, 2021); Catherine Turco, "Cultural Foundations of Tokenism: Evidence from the Leveraged Buyout Industry," *American Sociological Review* 75, no. 6 (2010): 894–913.
2. Joan Acker, "Hierarchies, Jobs, Bodies: A Theory of Gendered Organizations," *Gender & Society* 4, no. 2 (1990): 139–158.
3. Jim Ainsworth-Darnell and Doug Downey, "Assessing the Oppositional Culture Explanation for Racial/Ethnic Differences in School Performance," *American Sociological Review* 63, no. 4 (1998): 536–553.
4. Karolyn Tyson, *Integration Interrupted* (New York: Oxford Univ. Press, 2003).
5. Karolyn Tyson, William Darity Jr., and Domini Castellino, "It's Not a 'Black Thing': Understanding the Burden of Acting White and Other Dilemmas of Black Achievement," *American Sociological Review* 70, no. 4 (2005): 582–605.
6. Christine Williams, *Still a Man's World* (Berkeley: Univ. of California Press, 1995); Joel Heikes, "When Men Are the Minority: The Case of Men in Nursing," *Sociological Quarterly* 32, no. 3 (1991): 389–401.
7. Adia Harvey Wingfield, "Racializing the Glass Escalator," *Gender & Society* 23, no. 1 (2009): 5–26.

Chapter 3: When Hierarchy Doesn't Help

1. Elisabeth Rosenthal, *An American Sickness: How Health Care Became Big Business and How You Can Take It Back* (New York: Penguin, 2017).
2. Allison K. Hoffman, "Health Care's Market Bureaucracy," *UCLA Law Review* 1926 (2019): 1930–2022, p. 1933.
3. Max Weber, *From Max Weber: Essays in Sociology* (New York: Routledge, 2009).
4. Yanan Fan et al., "Gender and Cultural Bias in Student Evaluations: Why Representation Matters," *PLOS ONE* 14, no. 2 (2019), https://doi.org/10.1371/journal.pone.0209749.
5. Wingfield, *Flatlining*.
6. Dan Ly, "Historical Trends in the Representativeness and Incomes of

Black Physicians," *Journal of General Internal Medicine* (2021): https://www.newswise.com/pdf_docs/161860566877749_LyJGIM_4-19-21.pdf

Chapter 4: Colorblindness and the Market

1. Neil Gross, "Why Is Hollywood So Liberal?" *New York Times*, January 27, 2018, https://www.nytimes.com/2018/01/27/opinion/sunday/hollywood-liberal.html.
2. Maryann Erigha, *The Hollywood Jim Crow* (New York: NYU Press, 2019).
3. Tent-pole films are expensive, major undertakings that are expected to produce significant revenues for studios.
4. "Black Women Aren't Paid Fairly," Lean In, https://leanin.org/data-about-the-gender-pay-gap-for-black-women#!, accessed July 21, 2021.
5. Jasmine Tucker, "The Wage Gap for Black Women: Working Longer and Making Less," National Women's Law Center, August 2019, https://nwlc.org/wp-content/uploads/2019/08/Wage-Gap-for-Black-Women.pdf.
6. Erigha, *Hollywood Jim Crow*, 54.
7. Constance Grady, "Black Authors Are on All the Bestseller Lists Right Now. But Publishing Doesn't Pay Them Enough," Vox, June 17, 2020, https://www.vox.com/culture/2020/6/17/21285316/publishing-paid-me-diversity-black-authors-systemic-bias.
8. Katie Smith, "#PublishingPaidMe Reveals Racial Disparities," Book & Film Globe, June 11, 2020, https://bookandfilmglobe.com/creators/writers/publishingpaidme/.
9. Kathryn Zickuhr and Lee Rainie, "A Snapshot of Reading in America," Pew Research Center, January 16, 2014, https://www.pewresearch.org/internet/2014/01/16/a-snapshot-of-reading-in-america-in-2013/.
10. Khalisa Rae, "Seen, Known, and Heard: Black Readers Find Education and Healing in Book Clubs," NBC News, November 5, 2020, https://www.nbcnews.com/news/nbcblk/seen-known-heard-black-readers-find-education-healing-book-clubs-n1246665.
11. Erin Kelley and Frank Dobbin, "How Affirmative Action Became Diversity Management," *American Behavioral Scientist* 41, no. 7 (1998): 960–984.
12. Adia Harvey Wingfield, Elizabeth Hordge-Freeman, and Lynn Smith-Lovin, "Does the Job Matter? Diversity Officers and Racialized Stress," in *Race, Identity and Work (Research in the Sociology of Work)*, Vol. 32, ed. Ethel L. Mickey and Adia Harvey Wingfield (London: Emerald, 2019), 197–215.
13. Lawrence Otis Graham, *Our Kind of People: Inside America's Black Upper Class* (New York: Harper Perennial, 1999).
14. Patricia Hill Collins, *Black Sexual Politics* (New York: Routledge, 2004).
15. Frank Dobbin and Alexandra Kalev, *Getting to Diversity* (Cambridge, MA: Harvard Univ. Press, 2022).

Chapter 5: Layers and Limitations

1. Kathy Gurchiek, "SHRM Research Finds Need for More Awareness, Understanding of Racial Inequality," SHRM, August 3, 2020, https://www.shrm.org/hr-today/news/hr-news/pages/shrm-research-finds-need-for-more-awareness-understanding-of-racial-inequality.aspx.
2. Nandita Bose, "Roe v Wade Ruling Disproportionately Hurts Black Women, Experts Say," Reuters, June 27, 2022, https://www.reuters.com/world/us/roe-v-wade-ruling-disproportionately-hurts-black-women-experts-say-2022-06-27/.
3. Tressie McMillan Cottom, "'Who Do You Think You Are?': When Marginality Meets Academic Microcelebrity," *ADA: A Journal of Gender, New Media, and Technology* 7 (2015), https://adanewmedia.org/2015/04/issue7-mcmillancottom/.
4. Cottom, "'Who Do You Think You Are?'"
5. Marina Villeneuve, "Justice Department Details Threats of Violence Against Election Workers," PBS NewsHour, August 3, 2022, https://www.pbs.org/newshour/politics/watch-live-election-officials-testify-in-senate-hearing-on-protecting-election-workers.

Chapter 6: The Case of Gig Work

1. Weil, *Fissured Workplace.*
2. Risa Gelles-Watnick and Monica Anderson, "Racial and Ethnic Differences Stand Out in U.S. Gig Workforce," Pew Research Center, December 15, 2021, https://www.pewresearch.org/fact-tank/2021/12/15/racial-and-ethnic-differences-stand-out-in-the-u-s-gig-workforce/.
3. Miliann Kang, *The Managed Hand* (Berkeley: Univ. of California Press, 2003); Adia Harvey Wingfield, "The (Un)Managed Heart," *Annual Review of Sociology* 47 (2021): 197–212.
4. "Labor Force Statistics from the Current Population Survey," U.S. Bureau of Labor Statistics, last modified January 20, 2022, https://www.bls.gov/cps/cpsaat11.htm, accessed July 3, 2021.
5. PHI analysis of the American Community Survey, U.S. Census Bureau (2015), 2014 ACS 1-year PUMS, retrieved from https://www.census.gov/programs-surveys/acs/data.html.
6. Elise Gould and Jessica Scheider, "Black and Hispanic Women Are Paid Substantially Less than White Men," Economic Policy Institute, March 7, 2017, https://www.epi.org/publication/black-and-hispanic-women-are-hit-particularly-hard-by-the-gender-wage-gap/.
7. Amanda Barroso and Anna Brown, "Gender Pay Gap in U.S. Held Steady in 2020," Pew Research Center, May 25, 2021, https://www.pewresearch.org/fact-tank/2021/05/25/gender-pay-gap-facts/.

8. Valerie Wilson and William Rodgers, "Black-White Wage Gaps Expand with Rising Wage Inequality," September 26, 2016, Economic Policy Institute, https://www.epi.org/publication/black-white-wage-gaps-expand-with-rising-wage-inequality/.

9. Alex Rosenblat, Solon Barocas, Karen Levy, and Tim Hwang, "Discriminating Tastes: Customer Ratings as Vehicles for Bias," *Intelligence and Autonomy*, October 2016, https://datasociety.net/pubs/ia/Discriminating_Tastes_Customer_Ratings_as_Vehicles_for_Bias.pdf.

10. Ian Ayres, Frederick Vars, and Nasser Zakariya, "To Insure Prejudice: Racial Disparities in Taxicab Tipping," *Yale Law Journal* 114 (2005): 1613–1674, available at SSRN, https://ssrn.com/abstract=401201 or http://dx.doi.org/10.2139/ssrn.401201.

11. Wingfield, *Flatlining*.

12. Akshat Pandey and Aylin Caliskan, "Disparate Impact of Artificial Intelligence Bias in Ridehailing Economy's Price Discrimination Algorithms," AIES '21, May 19–21, 2021, https://arxiv.org/pdf/2006.04599.pdf.

13. Yanbo Ge, Christopher R. Knittel, Don MacKenzie, and Stephen Zoepf, "Racial and Gender Discrimination in Transportation Network Companies," Working Paper 22776, October 2016, National Bureau of Economic Research, https://www.nber.org/papers/w22776.

14. Juliet B. Schor, *After the Gig: How the Sharing Economy Got Hijacked* (Berkeley: Univ. of California Press, 2020).

15. Sharla Alegria and Anna Branch, "Causes and Consequences of Inequality in STEM: Diversity and Its Discontents," *International Journal of Gender, Science, and Technology* 7, no. 3 (2015): 321–342.

Chapter 7: Leveraging Cultural Capital

1. Pierre Bourdieu, "The Forms of Capital," in *Handbook of Theory of Research for the Sociology of Education*, ed. John G. Richardson (Westport, CT: Greenwood, 1986), 46–58.

2. Karen Ho, *Liquidated: An Ethnography of Wall Street* (Durham, NC: Duke Univ. Press, 2009).

3. Page Smith, "Wells Fargo to Pay $7.8 Million to Settle Hiring Bias Claims," *Bloomberg Law*, August 24, 2020, https://news.bloomberglaw.com/daily-labor-report/wells-fargo-to-pay-7-8-million-to-settle-hiring-bias-claims.

4. Stacy-Marie Ishmael, "Wells Fargo and the 'Mud People,'" *Financial Times*, June 8 2009, https://www.ft.com/content/c56132c2-266f-3549-8c60-693fa7c84024; George Lipsitz, *How Racism Takes Place* (Philadelphia: Temple Univ. Press, 2011).

5. Katie Kuehner-Hebert, "Banks, Retailers Paying Out the Most for Discrimination and Harassment," BenefitsPRO, January 21, 2019, https://

www.benefitspro.com/2019/01/21/banks-retailers-paying-out-the
-most-for-discrimination-and-harassment/?slreturn=20210110021113.

Can We Change the Culture?

1. Melissa E. Wooten and Lucius Couloute, "The Production of Racial Inequality Within and Among Organizations," *Sociology Compass* 11, no. 1
   (2017): e12446, https://doi.org/10.1111/soc4.12446.
2. Joyce Bell, *The Black Power Movement and American Social Work* (New
   York: Columbia Univ. Press, 2014).
3. Dobbin and Kalev, *Getting to Diversity*.
4. Collins, *Black Corporate Executives*.
5. Dobbin and Kalev, *Getting to Diversity*.

Part II: Social

1. David Pedulla, *Making the Cut* (Princeton, NJ: Princeton Univ. Press,
   2020), 107.
2. Philip Moss and Charles Tilly, "'Soft' Skills and Race: An Investigation
   of Black Men's Employment Problems," *Work & Occupations* 23, no. 3
   (1996): 252–276; Pedulla, *Making the Cut*.
3. Ivy Kennelly, "'That Single Mother Element': How White Employers
   Typify Black Women," *Gender & Society* 13, no. 2 (1997): 168–192.
4. Roberta Coles, *The Best Kept Secret: Single Black Fathers* (Lanham, MD:
   Rowman & Littlefield, 2009); Jo Jones and William D. Mosher, "Fathers'
   Involvement with Their Children: United States 2006–2010," *National
   Health Statistics Reports* 71 (2013): 1–21, https://pubmed.ncbi.nlm.nih
   .gov/24467852/.
5. Lincoln Quillian, Devah Pager, Ole Hexel, and Arnfinn H. Midtbøen,
   "Meta-Analysis of Field Experiments Shows No Change in Racial Hiring Discrimination over Time," *Proceedings of the National Academy of Sciences* 114, no. 41 (2017): 10,870–10,875.
6. Pedulla, *Making the Cut*.
7. Mark Granovetter, "The Strength of Weak Ties," *American Journal of
   Sociology* 78, no. 6 (1973): 1360–1380.
8. Christopher Ingraham, "Three Quarters of Whites Don't Have Any
   Nonwhite Friends," *Washington Post*, August 25, 2014, https://www
   .washingtonpost.com/news/wonk/wp/2014/08/25/three-quarters-of
   -whites-dont-have-any-non-white-friends/.
9. Thomas Shapiro, *The Hidden Cost of Being African American* (New York:
   Oxford Univ. Press, 2007).
10. Deirdre Royster, *Race and the Invisible Hand* (Berkeley: Univ. of Califor-
    nia Press, 2003); David Pedulla and Devah Pager, "Race and Networks

in the Job Search Process," *American Sociological Review* 84, no. 6 (2020): 983–1012.

11. "Key Findings from 'Black Out,' the Post's Series on Black NFL Coaches," *Washington Post*, September 21, 2022, https://www.washingtonpost.com /sports/interactive/2022/takeaways-black-out-nfl/.

12. "One of the Architects of the Rooney Rule Reflects on Its History—And Its Future," *All Things Considered*, NPR, February 6, 2022, https://www .npr.org/2022/02/06/1078689590/one-of-the-architects-of-the-rooney -rule-reflects-on-its-history-and-its-future.

13. In 2022, former Miami Dolphins head coach Brian Flores made many of these same allegations in his lawsuit against the NFL for racial discrim- ination. See Sharon Pruitt-Young and Jonathan Franklin, "Ex-Miami Dolphins Coach Brian Flores Accuses NFL of Racial Discrimina- tion in Lawsuit," NPR, updated February 2, 2022, https://www.npr.org /2022/02/01/1077401749/brian-flores-sues-nfl-racial-discrimination.

14. David Maraniss and Sally Jenkins, "Jerry Jones Helped Transform the NFL, Except When It Comes to Race," *Washington Post*, November 23, 2022, https://www.washingtonpost.com/sports/interactive/2022/jerry -jones-black-coaches-nfl/.

Chapter 8: Going It Alone

1. Robert A. Nathenson, Andrés Castro Samayoa, and Marybeth Gasman, "Moving Upward and Onward: Income Mobility at Historically Black Colleges and Universities," Rutgers Center for Minority Serving Insti- tutions, Rutgers Graduate School of Education, September 2019, https:// cmsi.gse.rutgers.edu/sites/default/files/EMreport_R4_0.pdf.

2. Erin Hatton, *Coerced* (Berkeley: Univ. of California Press, 2020).

3. Robert Merton, *Social Theory and Social Structure* (New York: Free Press, 1967).

4. Michelle Harris, Sherrill Sellers, Orly Clergy, and Frederick Gooding Jr., *Stories from the Front of the Room* (Lanham, MD: Rowman & Littlefield, 2017).

5. "Race/Ethnicity of College Faculty," Fast Facts, National Center for Ed- ucation Statistics, https://nces.ed.gov/fastfacts/display.asp?id=61, accessed September 6, 2022.

6. Gershon, *Down and Out*.

7. Ella Bell and Stella Nkomo, *Our Separate Ways* (Cambridge, MA: Har- vard Univ. Press, 2003); Melaku, *"You Don't Look like a Lawyer"*; Wing- field, *Flatlining*.

8. Kevin Donahue, Tina Gilbert, Melinda Halpert, and Portia Robertson Migas, "The Infuriating Journey from Pet to Threat: How Bias Under- mines Black Women at Work," Forbes, June 29, 2021, https://www.forbes .com/sites/forbeseq/2021/06/29/the-infuriating-journey-from-pet-to

-threat-how-bias-undermines-black-women-at-work/?sh=2c23bf6b6490, accessed March 23, 2023.

9. Rosabeth Moss Kanter, *Men and Women of the Corporation* (New York: Basic Books, 1977).

Chapter 9: Black Women Opening Doors

1. Glenda Flores, *Latina Teachers: Creating Careers and Guarding Culture* (New York: NYU Press, 2017).
2. Adia Harvey Wingfield, *No More Invisible Man: Race and Gender in Men's Work* (Philadelphia: Temple Univ. Press, 2013), 87.
3. Shamus Khan, *Privilege* (New York: Oxford Univ. Press, 2007).
4. Lynne Olsen, *Freedom's Daughters: The Unsung Heroines of the Civil Rights Movement from 1830 to 1970* (New York: Scribner, 2001).
5. Olsen, *Freedom's Daughters.*
6. Adia Harvey Wingfield, "'Reclaiming My Time': Black Women, Resistance, and Rising Inequality," *Gender & Society* 33, no. 3 (2019): 345–362.
7. Equal Justice Initiative, "Lynching in America: Confronting the Legacy of Racial Terror," 3rd ed., 2017, https://eji.org/reports/lynching-in-america/.
8. Richard Pérez-Peña, "Woman Linked to 1955 Emmett Till Murder Tells Historian Her Claims Were False," *New York Times*, January 27, 2017, https://www.nytimes.com/2017/01/27/us/emmett-till-lynching-carolyn-bryant-donham.html.
9. Kristen Bialik, "Key Facts About Race and Marriage, 50 Years After Loving v. Virginia," Pew Research Center, June 12, 2017, https://www.pewresearch.org/fact-tank/2017/06/12/key-facts-about-race-and-marriage-50-years-after-loving-v-virginia/.
10. Stuart Elliott, "Vitriol Online for Cheerios Ad with Interracial Family," *New York Times*, May 31, 2013, https://www.nytimes.com/2013/06/01/business/media/cheerios-ad-with-interracial-family-brings-out-internet-hate.html; Sarah Maslin Nir, "White Woman Is Fired After Calling Police on Black Man in Central Park," *New York Times*, May 26, 2020, last updated February 16, 2021, https://www.nytimes.com/2020/05/26/nyregion/amy-cooper-dog-central-park.html.
11. Wingfield, *No More Invisible Man*; Wingfield, "Racializing the Glass Escalator."

Chapter 10: Employment in the New Fissured Workplace

1. Alexandra Ravenelle, *Hustle and Gig* (Berkeley: Univ. of California Press, 2018).
2. In 2020, California voters defeated a proposal to reclassify gig workers as employees, which would have required companies to offer these benefits.

3. Weil, *Fissured Workplace.*
4. Alexandra Kalev, "How You Downsize Is Who You Downsize: Biased Formalization, Accountability, and Managerial Diversity," *American Sociological Review* 79, no. 1 (2014): 109–135; Pedulla, *Making the Cut*; Roscigno, *Face of Discrimination.*
5. Ravenelle, *Hustle and Gig.*
6. Ravenelle, *Hustle and Gig.*
7. Rani Molla, "Netflix Parents Get a Paid Year Off and Amazon Pays for Spouses' Parental Leave," Vox, January 31, 2018, https://www.vox.com/2018/1/31/16944976/new-parents-tech-companies-google-hp-facebook-twitter-netflix.
8. Dustin Avent-Holt and Donald Tomaskovic-Devey, *Relational Inequality* (New York: Oxford Univ. Press, 2019); Jae Song, David J. Price, Fatih Guvenen, Nicholas Bloom, and Till von Wachter, "Firming Up Inequality," Working Paper 21199, National Bureau of Economic Research, revised June 2015, https://www.nber.org/papers/w21199.

Chapter 11: Getting Hired vs. Doing the Hiring

1. Thomas Shapiro, *The Hidden Costs of Being African American* (New York: Oxford Univ. Press, 2004).
2. "Occupational Employment and Wage Statistics," Bureau of Labor Statistics, last modified March 31, 2022, https://www.bls.gov/oes/current/oes432021.htm.
3. "Nursing Shortage," American Association of Colleges of Nursing, last updated October 2022, https://www.aacnnursing.org/news-information/fact-sheets/nursing-shortage, accessed September 6, 2022; Patrick Boyle, "U.S. Physician Shortage Growing," Association of American Medical Colleges, June 26, 2020, https://www.aamc.org/news-insights/us-physician-shortage-growing.
4. Mason Walker, "U.S. Newsroom Employment Has Fallen 26% Since 2008," Pew Research Center, July 13, 2021, https://www.pewresearch.org/fact-tank/2021/07/13/u-s-newsroom-employment-has-fallen-26-since-2008/.
5. Costas Cavounidis, Kevin Lang, and Russell Weinstein, "The Boss Is Watching: How Monitoring Decisions Hurt Black Workers," Working Paper 26319, National Bureau of Economics Research, September 2019, https://www.nber.org/papers/w26319.
6. Roscigno, *Face of Discrimination.*

Chapter 12: When Movements Matter

1. John Sibley Butler, *Entrepreneurship and Self-Help Among Black Americans* (Stony Brook: SUNY Univ. Press, 2005).

2. Paula Giddings, *Ida: A Sword Among Lions* (New York: HarperCollins, 2008).

3. Adia Harvey Wingfield, *Doing Business with Beauty: Black Women, Hair Salons, and the Racial Enclave Economy* (Lanham, MD: Rowman & Littlefield, 2008).

4. Wingfield, *Doing Business*.

5. Here, Brian is referencing Bogle's 1973 book of the same name, which analyzes the representations of Black images in film.

6. "Academy Takes Historic Action to Increase Diversity," *Explore A.Frame*, January 22, 2016, https://www.oscars.org/news/academy-takes-historic -action-increase-diversity.

7. Collins, *Black Corporate Executives*.

8. Lauren A. Rivera, *Pedigree: How Elite Students Get Elite Jobs* (Princeton, NJ: Princeton Univ. Press, 2014).

9. Michael Omi and Howard Winant, *Racial Formation in the United States* (Philadelphia: Temple Univ. Press, 2014).

10. Larry Buchanan, Quoctrung Bui, and Jugal K. Patel, "Black Lives Matter May Be the Largest Movement in U.S. History," *New York Times*, July 3, 2020, https://www.nytimes.com/interactive/2020/07/03/us/george -floyd-protests-crowd-size.html.

11. Ken Sweet and Alexandra Olsen, "JPMorgan Puts $30B Toward Fixing Banking's 'Systemic Racism,'" Associated Press, October 8, 2020, https:// apnews.com/article/race-and-ethnicity-small-business-charlotte-jamie -dimon-racial-injustice-3cf34a097380b3b0813a52994fbce648.

12. Melissa Repko, "Walmart Donates $14 Million as Part of Broader Pledge to Advance Racial Equity," CNBC, February 1, 2021, https://www .cnbc.com/2021/02/01/walmart-donates-14-million-dollars-as-part-of -pledge-to-advance-racial-equity.html.

Chapter 13: Successful Networking

1. Rivera, *Pedigree*.

2. Karen Ho, *Liquidated* (Durham, NC: Duke Univ. Press, 2000).

3. Ofer Sharone, *Flawed Opportunity, Flawed Self* (Chicago: Univ. of Chicago Press, 2017).

4. Wingfield, *No More Invisible Man*.

5. Wingfield, *No More Invisible Man*, 89.

6. Erin Kelley and Phyllis Moen, *Overload* (Princeton, NJ: Princeton Univ. Press, 2020).

7. Sarah Thebaud and Catherine J. Taylor, "The Specter of Motherhood: Culture and the Production of Gendered Career Aspirations in Science and Engineering," *Gender & Society* 35, no. 3 (2021): 395–421; Catherine Turco, "Cultural Foundations of Tokenism: Evidence from the Leveraged Buyout Industry," *American Sociological Review* 75, no. 6 (2010): 894–913.

8. Katherine C. Kellogg, *Challenging Operations* (Chicago: Univ. of Chicago Press, 2013).
9. Marianne Cooper, "Being the 'Go-To Guy': Fatherhood, Masculinity, and the Organization of Work in Silicon Valley," *Qualitative Sociology* 23 (2000): 379–405.
10. Ethel L. Mickey, "The Organization of Networking and Gender Inequality in the New Economy: Evidence from the Tech Industry," *Work and Occupations* 49, no. 4 (2022), https://doi.org/10.1177/07308884221102134.
11. Rivera, *Pedigree*.

Getting Past the Networking Hurdle

1. Rivera, *Pedigree*.
2. Sharron Scott, Jennifer Johnson, Ayanna Hardaway, and Tiffany N. Galloway, "Investigating Ivy: Black Undergraduates at Select Ivy League Institutions," *Journal of Postsecondary Student Success* 1, no. 2 (2021): 72–90.
3. Jake New, "Positive News for HBCUs," *Inside Higher Ed*, October 28, 2015, https://www.insidehighered.com/news/2015/10/28/survey-finds-big-differences-between-black-hbcu-graduates-those-who-attended-other.
4. Dobbin and Kalev, "Why Diversity Programs Fail," 57.
5. Koji Chavez, "Penalized for Personality: A Case Study of Asian-Origin Disadvantage at the Point of Hire," *Sociology of Race and Ethnicity* 7, no. 2 (2020): 1–21, https://doi.org/10.1177/2332649220922270.
6. Lauren Rivera, "Employer Decision Making," *Annual Review of Sociology* 46, no. 1 (2020): 215–232.
7. Dobbin and Kalev, "Why Diversity Programs Fail," 5–6.

Part III: Relational

1. Rivera, *Pedigree*.
2. Bernadette Giacomazzo, "The Fortune 500 List Has a 'Record Number' of Black CEOs—But There's Still Only Six of Them," Yahoo! News, May 30, 2022, https://www.yahoo.com/now/fortune-500-list-record-number-120011014.html.
3. Jena McGregor, "TIAA Is the First Company in Fortune 500 History to Have Two Black CEOs in a Row," *Washington Post*, February 25, 2021, https://www.washingtonpost.com/business/2021/02/25/tiaa-is-first-company-fortune-500-history-have-two-black-ceos-row/.
4. Kathy Gurchiek, "Rosalind Brewer Becomes Third Black Woman to Head a Fortune 500 Company," SHRM, February 1, 2021, https://www.shrm.org/resourcesandtools/hr-topics/behavioral-competencies/global

-and-cultural-effectiveness/pages/rosalind-brewer-becomes-3rd-black
-woman-to-head-a-fortune-500-company.aspx.

5. Michelle F. Davis, "Black and White on Wall Street: The Unwritten Code on Race," Bloomberg, June 29, 2020, https://www.bloomberg.com/news/features/2020-06-29/rules-of-working-on-wall-street-from-black-employees-who-lived-it.

6. Vicky McKeever, "No Black Executives in Top Three Roles of UK's FTSE 100 Firms for the First Time Since 2014, Report Shows," CNBC, February 3, 2021, https://www.cnbc.com/2021/02/03/no-black-executives-in-top-three-roles-of-ftse-100-firms-report-shows.html.

7. John Levesque, "For Large U.S. Companies, CEOs Named John Outnumber Total Number of Women CEOs," *Seattle Business Magazine*, May 2, 2018, https://seattlebusinessmag.com/workplace/large-us-companies-ceos-named-john-outnumber-total-number-woman-ceos/

8. Te-Ping Chen, "Why Are There Still So Few Black CEOs?" *Wall Street Journal*, September 28, 2020, https://www.wsj.com/articles/why-are-there-still-so-few-black-ceos-11601302601.

9. Anthony J. Mayo and Laura Morgan Roberts, "Pathways to Leadership: Black Graduates of Harvard Business School," in *Race, Work, and Leadership: New Perspectives on the Black Experience*, ed. Laura Morgan Roberts, Anthony Mayo, and David Thomas (Cambridge, MA: Harvard Univ. Press, 2019), 41–72.

10. Chen, "Why Are There Still So Few Black CEOs?"

11. German Lopez, "This Is the Most Diverse Congress Ever. But It's Still Pretty White," Vox, February 8, 2019, https://www.vox.com/policy-and-politics/2019/2/8/18217076/congress-racial-diversity-white.

12. Rick Seltzer, "The Slowly Diversifying Presidency," *Inside Higher Ed*, June 20, 2017, https://www.insidehighered.com/news/2017/06/20/college-presidents-diversifying-slowly-and-growing-older-study-finds.

13. Melaku, *"You Don't Look like a Lawyer."*

14. Wingfield, *No More Invisible Man*.

15. Davis, "Black and White on Wall Street."

16. Wingfield, *No More Invisible Man*, 121.

Chapter 14: Searching for an Advocate

1. Jena McGregor, "Among Professional Women, African Americans Are Most Likely to Want Top Executive Jobs, Report Says," *Washington Post*, April 22, 2015, https://www.washingtonpost.com/news/on-leadership/wp/2015/04/22/among-professional-women-african-americans-are-most-likely-to-want-top-executive-jobs-report-says/; Sylvia Ann Hewlett and Tai Green, *Black Women: Ready to Lead* (New York: Coqual, 2015).

2. Sarah Jane Glynn, "Breadwinning Mothers Continue to Be the U.S. Norm," Center for American Progress, May 10, 2019, https://www.americanprogress.org/article/breadwinning-mothers-continue-u-s-norm/.

3. Dawn Dow, *Mothering While Black* (Berkeley: Univ. of California Press, 2019).

4. Joe Feagin and Melvin Sikes, *Living with Racism* (Boston: Beacon, 1995), 146–147.

5. Wingfield, *No More Invisible Man*, 111–112.

6. Wingfield, *No More Invisible Man*.

7. Erin Durkin, "Michelle Obama on 'Leaning In': 'Sometimes That Shit Doesn't Work,'" *The Guardian*, December 3, 2018, https://www.theguardian.com/us-news/2018/dec/03/michelle-obama-lean-in-sheryl-sandberg.

8. Hewlett and Green, *Black Women*; Joan C. Williams, "The 5 Biases Pushing Women Out of STEM," *Harvard Business Review*, March 24, 2015, https://hbr.org/2015/03/the-5-biases-pushing-women-out-of-stem.

Chapter 15: When White Women Are Roadblocks

1. Kanter, *Men and Women*; Phyllis Kitzerow, *Women Attorneys and the Changing Workplace* (New York: First Forum Press, 2014); David Maume, "Meet the New Boss . . . Same as the Old Boss? Female Supervisors and Subordinate Career Prospects," *Social Science Research* 20 (2011): 287–298.

2. Cristian Dezso, David Gaddis Ross, and Jose Uribe, "Is There an Implicit Quota on Women in Top Management? A Large-Sample Statistical Analysis," *Strategic Management Journal* 37, no. 1 (2015): 98–115.

3. Kevin Stainback, Sibyl Kleiner, and Sheryl Skaggs, "Women in Power: Undoing or Redoing the Gendered Organization?" *Gender & Society* 30, no. 1 (2016): 109–135.

4. Anja-Kristin Abendroth, Silvia Melzer, Alexandra Kalev, and Don Tomaskovic-Devey, "Women at Work: Women's Access to Power and the Gendered Earnings Gap," *ILR Review* 70, no. 1 (2017): 190–222.

5. Robin Ely and Irene Padavic, "What's Really Holding Women Back?" *Harvard Business Review* 98, no. 2 (2020): 58–67; Kellogg, *Challenging Operations*; Katrina Zippel, *The Politics of Sexual Harassment* (New York: NYU Press, 2006).

6. Carbado and Gulati, *Acting White?*.

7. Adia Harvey Wingfield, "The Modern Mammy and the Angry Black Man," *Race, Gender, and Class* 14, no. 2 (2007): 196–212.

8. Lauren Rivera, "Hiring as Cultural Matching: The Case of Elite Professional Service Firms," *American Sociological Review* 77, no. 6 (2012): 999–1022.

9. Johnson, Hekman, and Chan, "If There's Only One Woman."

10. Williams, *Still a Man's World*.
11. Williams, *Still a Man's World*.
12. Williams, *Still a Man's World*.
13. Barbara Reskin and Patricia Roos, *Job Queues, Gender Queues* (Philadelphia: Temple Univ. Press, 1990).

Chapter 16: Opportunity Gaps in Gig Work

1. "Gallup Says 36% of U.S. Workers Are Now in the Gig Economy," Small Business Labs, August 21, 2018, https://www.smallbizlabs.com/2018/08/gallup-says-36-of-us-workers-are-in-the-gig-economy.html.
2. Gabrielle Pickard-Whitehead, "The History and Future of the Gig Economy," Small Business Trends, November 12, 2019, last updated February 6, 2022, https://smallbiztrends.com/2019/11/the-history-and-future-of-the-gig-economy.html.
3. "Gallup's Perspective on the Gig Economy and Alternative Work Arrangements," 2018, available at https://www.gallup.com/workplace/240878/gig-economy-paper-2018.aspx.
4. "Gallup's Perspective."
5. "Black Women Are the Fastest Growing Group of Entrepreneurs. But the Job Isn't Easy," J.P.Morgan Wealth Management, https://www.jpmorgan.com/wealth-management/wealth-partners/insights/black-women-are-the-fastest-growing-group-of-entrepreneurs-but-the-job-isnt-easy, accessed September 17, 2022; Wingfield, *Doing Business*.
6. Ella Bell and Stella Nkomo, *Our Separate Ways* (Cambridge, MA: Harvard Univ. Press, 2003); Adia Harvey Wingfield, "Becoming Entrepreneurs: Intersections of Race, Class, and Gender in the Black Beauty Salon," *Gender & Society* 19, no. 6 (2005): 789–881.
7. Steven Gold, *The Store in the Hood: A Century of Ethnic Business and Conflict* (Lanham, MD: Rowman & Littlefield, 2010).
8. Joe Feagin and Eileen O'Brien, *White Men on Race* (Boston: Beacon, 2003); Philip Moss and Chris Tilly, "'Soft' Skills and Race."

Chapter 17: The Cost of Advancement

1. Christine Williams, Chandra Muller, and Kristine Kilanski, "Gendered Organizations in the New Economy," *Gender & Society* 26, no. 4 (2012): 549–573.
2. David Curtis et al., "Highly Public Anti-Black Violence Is Associated with Poor Mental Health Days for Black Americans," *Proceedings of the National Academy of Sciences* 188, no. 17 (2021); David R. Williams, Jourdyn A. Lawrence, and Brigette A. Davis, "Racism and Health: Evidence and Needed Research," *Annual Review of Public Health* 40 (2019): 105–125.

Chapter 18: Looking Elsewhere for Leadership

1. Roscigno, *Face of Discrimination*.
2. Cavounidis, Lang, and Weinstein, "The Boss Is Watching."
3. Johnson, Hekman, and Chan, "If There's Only One Woman."
4. Jonathan Dunn, Sheldon Lyn, Nony Onyeador, and Ammanuel Zegeye, "Black Representation in Film and TV: The Challenges and Impact of Increasing Diversity," McKinsey & Company, March 11, 2021, https://www.mckinsey.com/featured-insights/diversity-and-inclusion/black-representation-in-film-and-tv-the-challenges-and-impact-of-increasing-diversity.
5. Gerald D. Higginbotham, C. Phil Zhanpeng Zheng, and Yalda T. Uhls, "Beyond Checking a Box: A Lack of Authentically Inclusive Representation Has Costs at the Box Office," Center for Scholars and Storytellers, UCLA, https://static1.squarespace.com/static/5c0da585da02bc56793a0b31/t/5f7bca957449dd1d4db316c0/1601948398047/CSS+AIR+Final+Research+Report.pdf, accessed September 6, 2022.
6. Robert W. Fairlie and Alicia M. Robb, *Race and Entrepreneurial Success: Black-, Asian-, and White-Owned Businesses in the United States* (Cambridge: MIT Press, 2008); Zulema Valdez, *The New Entrepreneurs: How Race, Class, and Gender Shape American Enterprise* (Palo Alto, CA: Stanford Univ. Press, 2011).
7. College Raptor, https://www.collegeraptor.com/college-rankings/details/Endowment/State/DC/; Michael T. Nietzel, "Harvard, Other Elite Universities, Saw Endowments Slide in Fiscal Year 2022," Forbes, https://www.forbes.com/sites/michaeltnietzel/2022/10/13/elite-universities-saw-endowments-slide-in-fiscal-year-2022/?sh=4a613e425995, accessed January 29, 2023

Chapter 19: When Advancement Isn't the Answer

1. Neil Krishan Aggarwal, Michael Rowe, and Michael A. Sernyak, "Is Health Care a Right or a Commodity? Implementing Mental Health Care in a Recession," *Psychiatric Services* 61, no. 11 (2010): 1144–1145; Ron Howrigon, *Flatlining: How Health Care Could Kill the U.S. Economy* (New York: Greenbranch, 2016).
2. Feagin and Sikes, *Living with Racism*; Wingfield, *Flatlining*.

Chapter 20: A Path Forward

1. Carbado and Gulati, *Acting White?*
2. Wingfield, *Flatlining*.

Moving On Up

1. Elizabeth H. Gorman and Fiona M. Kay, "Skill Development Practices and Racial-Ethnic Diversity in Elite Professional Firms," in *Professional Work: Knowledge, Power and Social Inequalities*, ed. Elizabeth H. Gorman and Stephen P. Vallas, Research in the Sociology of Work, Vol. 34 (London: Emerald, 2020), 115–145.
2. Dobbin and Kalev, "Why Diversity Programs Fail."
3. Dobbin and Kalev, "Why Diversity Programs Fail."
4. Shengwei Sun, Jake Rosenfeld, and Patrick Denice, "On the Books, Off the Record: Examining the Effectiveness of Pay Secrecy Laws in the U.S.," Institute for Women's Policy Research, Policy Brief #C494, January 2021, https://iwpr.org/wp-content/uploads/2021/01/Pay-Secrecy-Policy-Brief-v4.pdf.
5. Olugbenga Ajilore, "The Persistent Black-White Unemployment Gap Is Built into the Labor Market," Center for American Progress, September 28, 2020, https://www.americanprogress.org/issues/economy/news/2020/09/28/490702/persistent-black-white-unemployment-gap-built-labor-market/.
6. Lauren Edelman, *Working Law: Courts, Corporations, and Symbolic Civil Rights* (Chicago: Univ. of Chicago Press, 2016).

Conclusion: The Way Out of the Gray

1. Michael Honey, *Black Workers Remember* (Berkeley: Univ. of California Press, 1999).
2. Honey, *Black Workers Remember*, 95–96.
3. "How Serious Is Corporate America About Ending Systemic Racism?," CNN Business, https://www.cnn.com/videos/business/2020/07/07/corporate-america-systemic-racism-orig.cnn-business/video/playlists/business-corporate-responsibility/, accessed April 2, 2021.
4. Tracy Jan, Jena McGregor, Renae Merle, and Nitasha Tiku, "As Big Corporations Say 'Black Lives Matter,' Their Track Records Raise Skepticism," *Washington Post*, June 13, 2020, https://www.washingtonpost.com/business/2020/06/13/after-years-marginalizing-black-employees-customers-corporate-america-says-black-lives-matter/.
5. Nitasha Tiku, "Google's Approach to Historically Black Schools Helps Explain Why There Are So Few Black Engineers in Big Tech," *Washington Post*, March 4, 2021, https://www.washingtonpost.com/technology/2021/03/04/google-hbcu-recruiting/.
6. "2021 Diversity Annual Report: We're Listening, Learning, and Taking Action," Google, https://static.googleusercontent.com/media/diversity.google/en//annual-report/static/pdfs/google_2021_diversity_annual_report.pdf.

7.   Candice Morgan, "How to Build a Race-Conscious Equity, Diversity, and Inclusion Strategy," Fast Company, September 2, 2020, https://www.fastcompany.com/90545070/how-to-build-a-race-conscious-equity-diversity-and-inclusion-strategy.

8.   Dobbin and Kalev, "Why Diversity Programs Fail."

9.   Matt Kempner, "Coke's Former Go-To Executive on Race Sees Diversity Gap at Company," Atlanta Journal-Constitution, August 30, 2019, https://www.ajc.com/news/coke-former-executive-race-sees-diversity-gap-company/oU3myIrL4VQTYbIJWiYa2J/

10.   Melissa Block, "Agencies, Contractors Suspend Diversity Training to Avoid Violating Trump Order," Morning Edition, NPR, October 30, 2020, https://www.npr.org/2020/10/30/929165869/agencies-contractors-suspend-diversity-training-to-avoid-violating-trump-order.

11.   Amiah Taylor, "How Florida's Stop WOKE Act Could Impose a Chilling Effect on Diversity Efforts in the Workforce," Fortune, May 3, 2022, https://fortune.com/2022/05/03/florida-governor-desantis-signs-stop-woke-act-for-school-employers-diversity-race-gender/.

INDEX

colorblind ideology
cultural capital and, 99
defined, 24
erasing, 101–4
frames for, 26–27
in health care, 44
in higher education, 36–42
historical roots of, 25
movement away from, 99–100
organizational culture and, 37–42,
73
pervasiveness of, 101
questioning outcomes from, 101–2
systemic racism denied by, 24, 25,
26, 27, 255
color-conscious organizational
culture, 255–56
communities, giving back to, 132–33,
236–37, 247
companies, American
Black-owned, 157, 211–12, 228–30
culture in (See culture,
organizational)
increasing demands of, 48, 172–73
investment in diversity, 21, 28–29,
257
leadership demographics in, 184–85
performativity in, 253
positive case studies, 254–57
regulatory compliance prioritized
by, 28–29, 46, 258
responses to social pressure, 27–28,
160–61, 165, 253, 257
responsibility of, 14–15, 259
unwillingness to confront racism, 87
Constance (chemical engineer)
career advancement, 194–95, 196
on colorblind culture, 36–42
on dropping the mask and speaking
up, 47–50
on failed diversity initiatives, 42–44
hiring process, 44, 126, 129
"masquerading" by, 40–42
obstacles to advancement for, 131,
190–91, 194–97, 198
social networks, 121–22, 123–29,
131, 174, 194, 196

on sponsorship, 128–29, 194–95,
196
contract work. See gig work
Cooper, Amy, 139
coronavirus pandemic, 13, 144
Couloute, Lucius, 102
critical race theory, 165
cultural capital, 94–100
culture, Black, 27, 29–30, 56–57, 242
culture, organizational
adhocracy, 23, 88–89, 91–93
clan, 22–23, 37–39, 52–59
colorblindness and, 37–42, 73
color-conscious, 255–56
defined, 22
development of, 22
diversity programs and, 47, 103
"fit" bias and, 29–30, 163–65, 178,
179, 188
gendered, 48, 51–59, 132, 173–74,
206
as gray area, 21–22, 23, 87, 252–53
hierarchical, 23, 60–67, 81–82,
83–84, 97
improving, 101–7, 179
market-driven (See market culture)
meritocracy paradox in, 30–33
of overwork, 48, 172–73
systemic racism and, 22, 23–24, 103
variation within, 96–97

Darren (finance executive)
career advancement, 167, 168, 238
cultural capital, 95, 99, 100
hiring process, 167–70
on inclusivity improvements,
99–100
on market culture, 94, 95–96, 99
mentoring role, 243–44, 246
mentors and sponsors, 238–40, 246
personal background, 166–67
relationships with colleagues and
executives, 240
social networks, 168–69, 170, 172,
174–75
DEI (diversity, equity, and inclusion).
See diversity programming